CLIFFS

Writing Proficiency Examinations

PREPARATION GUIDE

by

Jerry Bobrow, Ph.D.

Peter Z Orton, M.Ed.

*Consultants and Contributing Authors
from University English Departments,
Learning Centers, and Writing Projects*

Andrea White, Ph.D.
Robert L. Stoneham, M.A.
Thomas P. Wolfe, Ph.D.
Robert Dixon-Kolar, M.A.
Michael E. Carr, M.A.

INCORPORATED

LINCOLN, NEBRASKA   68501

ACKNOWLEDGMENTS

I would like to thank my family—my wife, Susan; my daughter, Jennifer Lynn; and my sons, Adam Michael and Jonathan Matthew—for their support during the time-consuming writing and editing process.

Jerry Bobrow

This author gratefully acknowledges the lifetime of encouragement, support, and good humor received from his mom, Esta Orton.

Peter Orton

We would also like to extend our sincere appreciation to the following authors and publications for permission to use excerpts from their writings:

Intervarsity Press, *Gender and Grace: Love, Work, and Parenting in a Changing World* (1990), "A View from Other Cultures: Must Men Fear Women's Work?" by Mary Steward Van Leeuwen.

New Age Journal, "The Revival of Homeopathy" by Dana Ullman.

Ballantine Books, *Cold Cures* (1987), "Cures for the Common Cold: A Consumer Guide" by Michael Castleman.

New Internationalist, "Domestic Chores Weren't Always Women's Work" by Debbie Taylor.

Little, Brown and Co., *The Aristos* (1970) by John Fowles.

CONTENTS

PART III: GRAMMAR AND USAGE

WHY YOU NEED THIS GUIDE

If you are planning to take a California State Universities

WRITING PROFICIENCY EXAMINATION

and need an easy-to-use, understandable approach to essay writing and grammar review, this book is for YOU!

WHAT THIS GUIDE CONTAINS

Cliffs Writing Proficiency Examinations Preparation Guide provides approaches to writing four basic essay types:

- Descriptive/Narrative
- Analytical/Expository
- Compare/Contrast
- Argument/Persuasion

These four most commonly used types are explained and analyzed with sample topics, essays, and topics for practice.

This guide also carefully discusses the writing process: analyzing the topic, planning to write (brainstorming and organizing), writing, and proofreading.

The second half of this guide contains an extensive review of grammar and usage, focusing on the common multiple-choice, grammar-type questions that appear on many Writing Proficiency Exams. Diagnostic and practice exams containing all of these types are followed by complete explanations.

Part I: Introduction

GRADUATION WRITING ASSESSMENT REQUIREMENT

Since most schools use a test with one or two essays to fulfill their graduation writing requirement, it is *vital* that you know the exact form and length of *your* examination. Some schools allow the use of a dictionary or a thesaurus, while others do not. Some exams also include a set of multiple-choice questions involving grammar, usage, punctuation, spelling, vocabulary, or a combination of these types.

BE SURE TO CHECK WITH YOUR SCHOOL'S TESTING OFFICE, ENGLISH DEPARTMENT, OR WRITING COORDINATOR TO GET THE EXACT INFORMATION ABOUT THE EXAM YOU'LL BE TAKING.

QUESTIONS YOU SHOULD ASK

Many schools give out a brochure or flyer that should answer most of the following questions. Make sure that you get the answers to these questions and any others you may have.

- When is the test given?
- When should I take the test?
- How do I register?
- What type of essay topic(s) should I expect? Can I get a sample topic(s)?
- How many essays will I be required to write?
- How much time will be provided?
- How much space (in which to write) will be provided? How many pages am I expected to write? Are blue books required?
- Will my outline notes be scored?
- Is scratch paper provided?
- May I write on (underline, circle, make notes on) the essay topic?
- May I use a pen or pencil on the test?
- May I use a dictionary and/or a thesaurus?
- What are the criteria on which my essay(s) will be scored?
- How is the exam graded? What is a passing score?
- How and when are students notified of the results?

- Is there a counseling and appeals procedure?
- Can I retake the test?
- Is there a multiple-choice section on my test? Can I get sample questions?
- Is there a penalty for guessing on the multiple-choice section?
- Are all essay questions and multiple-choice questions of equal value?
- What materials should I bring with me on the day of the test?
- Where is the test given?
- What time does the test start and when should I arrive?
- If there is more than one section, is a break given?

ESSAY TESTS

The following chart gives you an indication of some of the requirements and types of essay exams that have been used in the past. After checking with your school about the exam structure, focus more closely on the sections of this book that will be most beneficial to you. We recommend that you read the complete Grammar and Usage Review section *before* focusing on your essay section.

Key

Descriptive/Narrative—D/N   Compare/Contrast—C/C

Analytical/Expository—A/E   Argument/Persuasion—A/P

Campus	Number of Essays	Minutes Allotted	Type	Prompt Length	Multiple Choice
Bakersfield	1	90	D/N or A/E	short	no
Chico	1	90	A/E	medium	no
Dominguez Hills	1	60	D/N or A/E	short	no
Fresno	2	45 each	D/N and A/E	short	yes
Fullerton	1	90	A/E	short	yes
Hayward	1	60	D/N or A/E	short	yes
Humboldt	2	45 each	D/N and C/C	short	no
Long Beach	1	60	D/N or A/E	short	yes
Los Angeles	1	120	A/E	long	no
Northridge	1	60	A/E	short	no
Pomona	1	75	A/E or A/P	medium	no
Sacramento	1	150	D/N	short	no
San Bernardino	1	180	A/E or C/C	long	no
San Diego	1	60	varies	medium	yes
San Francisco	1	60	A/E	short	no
San Jose	1	60	D/N	medium	yes
San Luis Obispo	1	90	A/E or A/P	short	no
Sonoma	1	120	D/N or A/E	short	no
Stanislaus	No test. Classes required.				

Forms may change at any time.

MULTIPLE-CHOICE TESTS

Since some schools' writing exams include a multiple-choice section, it is important to carefully read the Grammar and Usage Review. The following chart shows the types of questions, number of questions, and time allotted for past exams. Since these parameters could change, be sure to

CHECK WITH YOUR SCHOOL TO FIND THE EXACT TYPE
OF MULTIPLE-CHOICE QUESTIONS THAT APPEAR.

This will help you focus on the type of question that you should review. Regardless of the type of multiple-choice question your school uses, reviewing all of the multiple-choice types will be very beneficial.

Key
Vocabulary—V
Punctuation—P
Spelling—S

Campus	Minutes Allotted	Number of Questions	Types of Questions
Fresno	{ 45	106	Types 4 and 5 and V
	{ 20	60	P, S, and V
Fullerton	35	50	Types 1 and 2
Hayward	40	72	Type 3
Long Beach	80	60	Types 6, 7, 8, 9, and 10
San Diego	30	45	Types 1 and 2
San Jose	40	72	Type 3

Types of questions and the schools that use multiple-choice questions are subject to change.

HOW TO USE THIS GUIDE

____ 1. Review the material regarding *your specific* writing exam provided by *your* state university. This information is available free of charge and usually contains a complete description of the exam and a few samples.

____ 2. Set up a consistent study schedule. The time might be one to two hours each day or every other day, but it should be no longer than about two and a half hours at any one study period. This consistent schedule is conducive to quiet, quality study time.

____ 3. Read the Grammar and Usage Review section, starting on page 251.

____ 4. Work through the complete essay writing section, starting on page 11.

____ 5. Note the specific type of essay your exam requires and reread the sections that focus on that particular essay type.

____ 6. Under the proper time constraints, write an essay using one of the sample topics similar to the type you will encounter.

____ 7. Have a friend or English instructor read and evaluate your essay using the Essay Checklist evaluation form on page 38.

____ 8. Repeat steps 6 and 7 five or six times. The more practice essays you write and have evaluated, the more you should improve. You will also become more comfortable with the time constraints.

____ 9. Check to see if your particular exam includes a multiple-choice section. Match this section with the samples given in this guide.

____ 10. Carefully review and practice the multiple-choice questions similar to your type.

____ 11. Review other types of multiple-choice questions, even if they are of a different type than the ones you will encounter. This review should strengthen your grammar and usage skills.

____ 12. A final review of the sections that cover your essay type and multiple-choice question type will be helpful as you approach your exam date.

Part II: The Essay

The Graduation Writing Assessment Requirement (GWAR) may take many forms. Most universities require one or two essays to be written under time constraints. Some exams also include a set of multiple-choice grammar questions.

TYPES OF ESSAY TOPICS

The essays required by Writing Proficiency Examinations vary in length, from as short as 45 minutes each to as long as three hours. Essay topics also vary in type. The four commonly encountered topic types are

- Descriptive/Narrative
- Analytical/Expository
- Compare/Contrast
- Argument/Persuasion

Frequently, the topic types overlap. Also, each of these topic types can be directed or undirected. A directed topic gives the writer a number of specific tasks to complete, while an undirected topic gives the writer greater flexibility.

Let's take a closer look at the basic types:

DESCRIPTIVE/NARRATIVE

This essay topic generally requires the writer to describe a personal experience, acquaintance, situation, etc. The truthfulness of the response has no bearing on how the essay is graded; the reader does not care whether the essay is fact or fiction. Rather, scoring is typically based solely on several elements (to be addressed in detail later): fullness of response, organization, language, development, and legibility. Therefore, the writer need not worry about recalling the exact details of an event which may have occurred many years ago. Instead, the writer may be "creative" in developing supporting examples and in addressing the topic. A well-written descriptive/ narrative essay allows the reader to see what the writer is saying by using precise, descriptive language.

For instance, suppose the topic were to ask for a description of a certain preschool childhood experience. If the writer either did not have such an experience, or has forgotten it, the writer may invent an experience that fits the topic. This fictionalizing, however, should still be logical, reasonable, and supported by the use of specific details.

11

Remember, a descriptive/narrative essay topic may also be *directed* or *undirected*. An undirected topic allows the writer broad latitude in addressing the topic. For example, here is an undirected descriptive/narrative topic:

Topic—Throughout our lives, each of us has encountered people whom we may consider either friends or enemies. Describe one particular friend or enemy who played an especially important role in your life.

Although this topic asks the writer to describe a friend or enemy, it does not restrict how the writer may explore the issue. Thus, any approach the writer may take to address the topic is appropriate, as long as the essay contains the required elements of organization, development, language, etc.

A directed descriptive/narrative essay, however, may require the writer to fulfill certain specifically defined tasks. For example:

Topic—Throughout our lives, each of us has at one time or another taken a risk. Describe one particular risk you may have taken, tell why you took it, and describe its outcome.

This *directed* topic requires the writer to address three distinct parts: (1) a description of one specific personal risk taken, (2) an explanation of the reason(s) for taking that risk, and (3) a description of the results. All three parts must be addressed. Let's take a look at one way to write the essay:

Response—I'll never forget my first semester at Cal Polytechnic University. My classes were hardly memorable, nor were my instructors, but one particular experience will live with me forever. That was when, that first Sunday afternoon of college, I decided to take a remarkably stupid, yet exciting, risk.

Jumping out of a moving airplane at four thousand feet is not something I ever imagined doing, at least not voluntarily. However, on that lazy autumn weekend I allowed my roommate Tom, a gangly, quick-to-smile Kansan, to drag me along with him to the Undergraduate Jumping Society meeting, held in the rugged foothills fifty miles from campus. I had no intention of even putting on a parachute, much less jumping. But when we reached the jump site—a windy, remote, parched piece of terrain inhabited only by jack rabbits and lizards—circumstances conspired to find me sitting with the instructor, a bored-looking ex-hippie named Mr. Lips, and my roommate Tom, as the pilot took us and the tiny, two-prop plane up to our jump altitude. I fingered the worn leather strap on the day-glo pink parachute pack; it was hardly reassuring. Were those blood stains? Why had I been so accommodating and signed that four-page Liability Waiver (in triplicate) if, as they insisted five times, they were so confident I'd land safely? As the wind whistled past the plane's open hatch and mother Earth below quickly became just vague, pastel brush strokes of green and brown, I shuddered involuntarily. Tom jumped and disappeared from view; I was next. I didn't have time to reconsider—we were passing the landing site. I jumped, or perhaps fell out—I'm not sure which—and suddenly it became quiet, a true silence unlike any I had ever experienced. My body felt weightless, more free and relaxed than any body massage could have delivered. I moved slowly, gracefully, and felt absolutely no sensation of speed as I had wrongly surmised. Free fall was a glorious, slow-motion ballet of smooth and delicate turns and spirals, and suddenly I knew why Tom had taken me with him.

The reasons I decided to jump are rather peculiar. . . .

Note that the first paragraph briefly introduces the essay, while the much longer second paragraph explains, using details and specific descriptions, the actual risk undertaken: jumping out of an airplane. The third paragraph is about to explain the reasons that risk was taken, and the final paragraph will no doubt describe the outcome of having jumped. In this way, the essay will have addressed all tasks of the assignment.

ANALYTICAL/EXPOSITORY

This essay type requires the writer to explain and analyze an issue, idea, problem, or statement. The topic may also ask the writer to draw from personal experience, observations, or readings in order to address the issue.

Here, too, topics may be directed or undirected. For example, the following is an undirected analytical/expository essay topic:

> **Topic—"The typical human response to the unknown is fear and aggression."**
>
> **Write an essay commenting on the above statement, supporting your perspective with relevant examples.**

The above topic allows broad leeway in addressing the statement. However, the writer must use examples to illustrate what viewpoint is taken. A more directed analytical/expository topic would be

> **Topic—It has been suggested that corporal punishment can be the cure-all of the American educational system's discipline problems, that students will become more attentive if they know that misbehavior may result in their being spanked. Do you agree or disagree? Explain your position, using two or three personal experiences and/or observations to support your viewpoint.**

Here you are "directed" to address the topic by using two or three of your experiences or observations to support whatever side you choose. The choice of whether or not corporal punishment is effective is up to you; however, you must choose one side and then use two or three observations and/or experiences to support it.

For example, the introduction to this topic may be written this way:

> **Response—**Corporal punishment is hardly an effective way to discipline students. The side effects of being hit or spanked by teachers may do more harm to student attitudes about school than could be offset by any possible constructive results corporal punishment may hope to achieve. Having been spanked consistently in third grade in parochial school, as well as having seen how my sister reacted so negatively after being hit by a teacher when she was in high school, I am convinced that corporal

punishment should be avoided as a means of disciplining students . . . .

_____

This introductory paragraph indicates that the essay will use the third-grade experience of the writer, as well as the observation of how being hit in high school affected the sister, to support the position that corporal punishment is not an effective means of discipline.

COMPARE/CONTRAST

This essay type is sometimes considered a type of analytical/ expository topic. It requires the writer to juxtapose two or more ideas, arguments, or examples and show similarities and/or differences between them. The word *compare* is typically used to elicit similarities between items; the word *contrast* means to discern differences between items. Therefore, a "compare and contrast" essay topic is directing the writer to analyze both similarities and differences. For example:

_____

Topic—Some have maintained that modern intercollegiate football has a strong positive influence on the well-being of a college and its students. Others have suggested that modern intercollegiate football actually hinders a positive college experience, and some schools have even gone so far as to eliminate their intercollegiate football program.

Drawing upon your own observations, compare and contrast the possible experiences of two different students—one who attends a college with an intercollegiate football program and one who attends a school without an intercollegiate football program.

_____

Or consider this topic:

_____

Topic—Within the past few decades, an increasing number of colleges have offered courses on a pass-fail basis. Some argue that this virtual elimination of grades minimizes distractions and helps students learn; others argue that such a pass-fail policy actually decreases student motivation.

Compare and contrast the implications of pass-fail courses with those of the traditional A-F graded course. Use your observations, experience, and reading to support your generalizations.

The writer may begin the essay as follows:

Response—An increasing number of colleges have offered students the option of taking courses on a pass-fail basis. While the implications of this policy create marked differences for some students, other students find little difference between a pass-fail course and a traditional A-F graded class. Unmotivated students, previously content with a "gentleman's C," will be able to get by with less effort in a pass-fail course. Achieving students, motivated solely by the material, won't be affected by a change in the grading system. They will apply themselves no matter what the grading scale because they are interested in learning, not because of a letter grade. An analysis of these two types of student and their reasons for studying illustrates the similarities and differences of the implications of grading systems. . . .

Since the topic requires a "compare and contrast" response, this introductory paragraph states that the essay will explore both the similarities and differences inherent in the two grading systems' implications.

ARGUMENT/PERSUASION

The argument/persuasion essay is an attempt to persuade the reader to a certain point of view. Its goal is to present facts, ideas, or opinions as strongly as possible in order to convince the reader. Again, this topic type can be directed or undirected.

For example, an undirected topic may look like this:

Topic—The death penalty for major crimes has become a controversial contemporary topic. Some people maintain that the death penalty is warranted for murder and other heinous crimes;

others maintain that capital punishment is actually cruel and unusual punishment which should not be used in the American justice system.

Present one side of this controversial issue. From your own experiences, observations, or reading, support your side as persuasively as possible.

Or this topic:

Topic—The university trustees recently voted that a student must maintain grades of "C" or above in order to engage in school-related, extracurricular activities such as sports and drama. Do you agree or disagree? Write a persuasive argument detailing your reasons for choosing your position on this ruling.

The writer's response may begin as follows:

Response—The trustees' decision to require students to maintain a "C" or higher is, in my opinion, correct. While it is true that often the very students who have problems maintaining grades of "C" or above are the ones who need to achieve success in other than academic areas, permitting low grades is not in their best interests in the long run.

A "D" or "F" should serve as a warning to students, teachers, and coaches that the student needs help. "C" means average and is designed to be attainable by any student who comes to class and does the assigned work. Falling below that mark should sound an alarm and alert everyone concerned that something is amiss and needs to be addressed immediately. After all, the student's number-one job—schoolwork—must get the attention it deserves from everyone involved.

Moreover, condoning poor grades does students the disservice of leading them to believe that society will make special exceptions for the talented athlete or actor. Such bias toward athletic coordination and against mental rigor is antithetical to the purpose of college and, at a time when national test scores are falling and the nation's illiteracy is soaring, we should not be encouraging academic mediocrity. Rather, we should be helping students excel in the classroom. Allowing them to fail sends the wrong message. . . .

_____

Notice that this argument/persuasion essay has a firm point of view. It tries to convince the reader of that point of view by presenting strong, logical reasons.

PROMPTS

Some essay topics include brief statements or quotations about which the writer must comment. These often can be quite long, many paragraphs in length. Topics may also require the writer to have read an entire chapter of a book before addressing the essay topic.

These statements, quotations, or text materials are often called *prompts*. Obviously, it is crucial to understand the material before undertaking to write an essay based upon the prompt. A second or third reading of a prompt may sometimes be required.

One helpful technique when faced with a prompt is to read the essay assignment first (the part that follows the prompt), *before* reading the prompt. For example, suppose the prompt is 35 lines long, but the assignment which follows merely states "Do you agree or disagree? Explain your position." Now, as you read the prompt, you can take a side and anticipate your position as you continue reading it.

This prereading of the assignment *before* reading the prompt may eliminate the need to read a lengthy prompt several times.

For example, try this topic:

_____

Prompt—The object of this essay is to assert one very simple principle, as entitled to govern absolutely the dealings of society with the individual in the way of compulsion and control, whether the means used be physical force in the form of legal penalties or the moral coercion of public opinion. That principle is that the sole end for which mankind are warranted, individually or collectively, in interfering with the liberty of action of any of their number is self-protection. That the only purpose for which power can be rightfully exercised over any member of a civilized community against his will, is to prevent harm to others.

His own good, either physical or moral, is not a sufficient warrant. He cannot rightfully be compelled to do or forbear because it will be better for him to do so, because it will make him happier, because, in the opinion of others, to do so would be wise or even right. These are good reasons for remonstrating with him, or reasoning with him, or persuading him, or entreating him, but not for compelling him or visiting him with any evil in case he do otherwise. To justify that, the conduct from which it is desired to deter him must be calculated to produce evil to someone else. The only part of the conduct of anyone for which he is amenable to society is that which concerns others. In the part which merely concerns himself, his independence is, of right, absolute. Over himself, over his own body and mind, the individual is sovereign.—*John Stuart Mill*

Assignment—Do you agree with Mill's idea that the only just cause for interfering with personal freedom is to prevent harm to others? Use specifics from the passage and from your own experience or reading to support your arguments.

ESSAY REQUIREMENTS

Although the time allotted and the type of essay to be written may vary, all well-written essays share the same common elements. A well-written essay will fulfill these criteria:

- **Fullness of response.** A well-written essay fully addresses the topic and completes all required tasks. It focuses only on issues directly relevant to the assignment.
- **Adequate development.** A well-written essay supports its generalizations using specific examples and details.
- **Skillful language.** A well-written essay expresses its ideas clearly, using an appropriate and consistent style, and demonstrates proper grammar, diction, usage, sentence structure, punctuation, and spelling.
- **Sound organization.** A well-written essay uses correct paragraph form, with smooth transitions from one paragraph to the next. Together, the paragraphs form a unified, coherent whole.
- **Legibility.** Although handwriting is not graded, a written essay must, of course, be readable. Handwriting is clear and legible.

FULLNESS OF RESPONSE

The primary responsibility of any essay is to be *on topic*. An essay may be well developed, carefully organized, and skillfully written, but if it does not address the task(s) prescribed by the assignment, it will not pass. If an essay only partially or tangentially addresses the assignment, it will receive, at best, a minimum passing grade. Therefore, the written essay must be precisely and completely focused *on the topic*.

Fullness of response means that the topic has been correctly and completely addressed. While this requirement may sound simple to fulfill, off-topic essays are commonly encountered by essay graders. Among the many reasons for off-topic essays: topics are frequently complex, requiring many tasks to be addressed; candidates, feeling time pressure, may speed through the reading of the topic, thus missing key words or tasks; important directives like "describe," "compare," and "evaluate" are easily confused; important connective

20

words like "or" and "and" may be overlooked; prompts encountered at the beginning of the topic may start the writer's mind racing with ideas so that later directives do not receive the careful attention they deserve.

Read the essay topics which follow. As you read, identify the exact task(s) in each topic to be addressed. With your pencil, *circle or underline the specific tasks* contained in the text of the topic.

Topic—Cities have been criticized for being centers of crime, for overcrowding, for extremes of poverty and wealth. But cities have advantages, too, in employment or in opportunities for personal growth.

Write an essay in which you discuss three other specific advantages or three other specific disadvantages of cities and explain why they are advantages or disadvantages.

This topic is extremely detailed in the tasks it requires you to address. You may have circled or underlined "discuss three other specific advantages or three other specific disadvantages" and ". . . explain why." Notice that a satisfactory response to this topic will contain six separate elements: you, the writer, will discuss exactly three advantages or three disadvantages of cities, but *not both* advantages and disadvantages, and *not* those mentioned in the topic. Your essay will also explain why each of those three chosen are advantages or disadvantages.

Topic—Our lives have high points and low points. Choose one particular high point or low point in your life and describe how that particular time had an impact on your life.

This seemingly straightforward topic can easily result in an off-topic essay. Although the topic requires you, the writer, to first choose a high point *or* low point which occurred in your life, note that the assignment is to describe *not* the high or low point itself, but the *impact* of that particular time on your life. Simply a description of the actual high point or low point would most likely result in an off-topic, and therefore failing, paper. For this reason, circling or underlining "one high point *or* low point" and "describe *how that particular time had an impact on your life*" may have helped you realize that the assignment is to describe the impact or effect that a certain high or low point had on your life. Merely describing the winning of the million-dollar lottery (the high point of your life) would be *off* topic; describing the results—or impact—of that memorable day—for example, it enabled you to quit your boring summer job and instead go on a world cruise and how that experience broadened you—would be *on* topic.

Topic—Americans are a mobile population. It is not unusual for an American to have lived in several communities, even several states, during a lifetime. Some people find this mobility stimulating; others suffer a sense of rootlessness.

Discuss the pros and cons of American mobility. Where do you stand on the issue?

This topic requires you, the writer, to discuss both the good and the bad effects of mobility, either on the individual American, on families, on yourself, or on the nation as a whole. Notice that no specific approach is required, thus allowing you latitude to address the topic in whatever manner you choose. However, you must explore both positive *and* negative elements (you may have circled "Discuss the pros and cons of American mobility" and "Where do you stand?"). An essay addressing just the negative aspects of American mobility would be incomplete. Finally, you must tell how you personally feel about the issue.

ADEQUATE DEVELOPMENT

A well-written essay supports its generalizations using specific examples and details. An essay which presents generalizations but no supporting examples, details, or illustrations is considered undeveloped and will typically fail.

For example, consider this topic:

Topic—Choose a teacher you have had during your academic years who helped to make school an enjoyable place to be.

Describe that teacher's particular quality or attribute which most helped in making your school experience enjoyable.

To be on topic, the writer must select one quality or attribute that a particular teacher had which helped make school enjoyable for the writer. The writer would then illustrate that quality by using specific examples or specific details.

Consider the following response:

Response—Of all the teachers I have had, Mr. Frank Jackson, my eighth-grade history instructor, was the teacher who made school the most enjoyable. Frank Jackson was knowledgeable, intelligent, and patient, but the quality he possessed which made school so enjoyable was his sense of humor.

Mr. Jackson's sense of humor was renowned throughout the school. Just about the entire student body was aware of his sense of humor. The faculty was certainly aware of how funny Frank Jackson could be. The principal, too, who had known Frank Jackson for almost twenty years, was also fully aware that he had a teacher on his staff who could have made it big as a comedian. It was a rare day indeed when Mr. Jackson did not elicit a laugh from his class. He would do the strangest and funniest things—especially if he could get a laugh from his students. Of course, he knew that laughter got our adrenaline flowing, it kept our attention, and it made us want to attend his class. So naturally, he made us laugh whenever he could. . . .

Notice that these paragraphs make broad generalizations about Mr. Jackson's sense of humor but do not use specific examples to support this point. An essay continuing this approach would certainly not receive a passing grade, as it fails to address the topic by using specific details. Note how these supporting sentences are general and unspecific:

"Student body . . . faculty . . . the principal . . . fully aware . . ." But what *specifically* made them so aware? Was it his original one-liners? Was it his funny faces? His clever puns? His whimsical style of dress? His humorous anecdotes about his weekend activities? There are no *specific examples* cited to support this reputation.

"He would do the strangest and funniest things . . ." For instance, *what* things? This sentence should be followed by examples of the strangest and funniest things.

"Naturally, he made us laugh whenever he could . . ." For example, *when* and exactly *how?* The essay should specifically detail when and how.

Now consider this response:

Response—Of all the teachers I have had, Mr. Frank Jackson, my eighth-grade history instructor, was the teacher who made school the most enjoyable. Frank Jackson was knowledgeable, intelligent, and patient, but the quality he possessed which made school so enjoyable was his sense of humor.

As soon as the first bell rang signaling the start of class, Mr. Jackson would turn out all lights except the one at the front of the room. When it became quiet, he'd then commence a five-minute opening monologue. His jokes were like Johnny Carson's: he'd start with a few zingers about the weather or contemporary current events, and perhaps a few humorous asides about the school, but after we settled in, his pointed sense of humor would target whatever subject we were studying for the week. For instance, when we were learning the American Revolution, Mr. Jackson did a routine about George Washington, his wooden false teeth, and his poor cherry tree. When we studied the Civil War, we were hit with Abe Lincoln, Robert E. Lee, and an uncomfortable bar mitzvah they both had the unfortunate occasion to attend. His "monologue" over, Mr. Jackson would leave the room to rousing laughter and applause. Then he'd return, dressed as a character from that same period of history. For example, during the Revolutionary period, he'd wear breeches and a three-cornered hat, and then he'd answer questions from us, the audience. He once even dressed as a gorilla to help us understand Darwin's theories. Though his answers (and costumes) were hilarious, they always gave us insight into the person or the times we were studying. By using his sense of humor in this way, Mr. Jackson showed us that school and learning could be enjoyable . . .

Notice the extensive use of detailed, specific examples to support the generalization that Frank Jackson has a sense of humor. Phrases like "for example" and "for instance" practically force the writer to present examples or instances. This paragraph, while not brilliantly written, comes from an essay which is far more likely to receive a passing grade because it develops its point by using many detailed examples.

Consider this topic:

Topic—**It has been said that Americans are becoming more like spectators, passively watching, rather than doers actively involved in their own lives. Support or refute this idea, and from your observations, illustrations, or experiences, explain your point of view.**

To be on topic, the writer must choose one side of the issue, and present illustrations and examples supporting that side.

Consider the start of this response:

Response—Americans are more and more becoming mere observers, passive spectators in life. This is strikingly reflected by the growth of spectator sports in the United States, the apathy of American voters, and the pervasiveness of this country's visual media.

The spectacular growth of spectator sports is indicative of the increasingly passive role Americans take, even in their leisure pursuits. For example, every major-league sport during the past decade has broken records for ticket sales and attendance figures. Professional football games in most major cites are sold out for entire seasons. In order to get tickets, a football fan must apply to get on the waiting list for season tickets. Multiply the seventy-thousand-plus spectators each game by the sixteen games played by each of the two dozen teams, and you'll find millions of Americans sitting and watching in the stadiums across the nation each Sunday. Add to that the tens of millions of fans sitting at home watching the games on network and cable television, plus the tens of millions who watch college football on Saturdays. These numbers merely touch the surface of the

spectator-sports phenomenon: factor in 162 major-league baseball games (more popular than ever!) each of the twenty-six
teams play (forty years ago there were only sixteen teams), not
to mention the hundreds of minor league teams, plus the growing
popularity of watching basketball, tennis, golf, soccer, ice-
hockey . . .

———————————————

Notice how many specific details are presented to support the
generalization about the growth of American spectator sports. The
use of specific supporting details and examples is essential for
adequate development of any essay.

SKILLFUL LANGUAGE

A well-written essay expresses its ideas clearly, using an appropriate and consistent style, and demonstrates proper grammar, diction,
usage, sentence structure, punctuation, and spelling.

CLARITY

A clearly written essay is easy to understand. Its language is direct,
as are its sentence structure and paragraphing. Clarity is achieved by
precision and economy in word choice. For example, consider these
sentences:

———————————————

Example—He defenses against the practice of undermining
his carefully constructed enterprise by avoiding the harmful and
often deleterious effects in regards to hiring untrained, unskilled
and incompetent workers and, to a certain degree and extent,
instead by choosing already once proven competent professional
workers.

———————————————

Revision—He protects his carefully constructed enterprise by
hiring proven professionals instead of unskilled, incompetent
workers.

———————————————

The first sentence is preposterous. The second, using one-third the
number of words in the first sentence, is clear and readable.

Unnecessary, repetitious, or vague words can obscure meaning. A clumsy phrase or sentence can slow the reader. A clearly written essay does not have such problems.

APPROPRIATE AND CONSISTENT STYLE

The style of a well-written essay is both appropriate and consistent. It avoids slang, substandard English, trite expressions, and jargon. It recognizes its audience as literate and addresses that audience using informal standard written English.

Consider this paragraph:

Example—The burglar, clever like a fox and wishing to strike while the iron was hot, tippy-toed his way without making nary a peep to the front door. When he arrived, he found it locked as tight as a drum. Well, that didn't stymie him one little bit. No way. He took out his handy knife, and born to be bad, zippoed that lock.

Or this paragraph:

Example—The utilization of macro-technological progress, as it regards American industry, is a manifestation of the unregulated and surprisingly lugubrious state of affairs resulting from the past decade's reliance on economic privatism and individual self-assimilation.

Each of the above paragraphs is awkward. Though the first may be easier to understand, it nevertheless suffers from substandard English, trite expressions, and slang. It would be inappropriate as part of a college-level essay.

The second passage suffers from jargon: vague and abstract language. College students sometimes attempt to use large and important-sounding words in order to impress the reader. However, when writing for a general audience, using overly formal or learned-sounding jargon only confuses the reader.

Look at the following sequence of words, each of which means "lack of clarity." They are arranged from very casual to very formal.

Now select one of the words to fit into the sentence which follows.

smokescreen
fuzziness
vagueness
obfuscation
obumbration

Because of the deteriorating status of his business affairs, Lombard's response to pointed questions was often marked by _____ and sarcasm.

The first word, "smokescreen," is too casual, or conversational, and would be inappropriate for the sentence, as well as for most graduate-level essays. But "obumbration" is overly formal and would also be inappropriate. A word from the center of the list would be a better choice.

Write clearly and directly. Avoid cliches or pompous jargon. The appropriate style for a college-level essay is neither overly formal nor casual. It does not distract from the content.

TONE

Together with style, an essay writer uses a certain *tone*. For example, some essay topics may require a straightforward explanation of one or more ideas or particular points of view. This demands that the writer's tone be as objective as possible, or free from bias, so that as each side is presented, it is done in a manner devoid of prejudice or emotion. For example:

Topic—Thomas Edison once said that genius is one percent inspiration and ninety-nine percent perspiration. Do you agree or disagree with this comment? Explain your position.

The topic requires the writer to juxtapose thoughts and ideas (inspiration) with hard work (perspiration) and decide which is the major contributing factor of genius. An on-topic essay would address Edison's viewpoint (that hard work was most important) and either support it or refute it.

Consider this response:

Response—Thomas Edison was considered to be one of America's brilliant minds, and his remarkable insights—inspirations—led to over a thousand inventions, including the phonograph and the incandescent bulb. However, despite his unique vision, his statement about the importance of hard work is correct. For without the perspiration, the genius of Edison's inspirations would have been forever lost to mankind.

No matter how brilliant a mind is, hard work and perseverance eventually bring the fruits of the inspiration to actuality. For example, Edison believed that a thin filament could create the glow to light a bulb. A remarkable inspiration indeed! Yet it took him thousands of failed attempts and many years until he finally invented the actual filament that would eventually light the world. . . .

Notice that the essay is written in almost "textbook style," explaining rather than arguing. The tone is objective, straightforward.

Another topic, however, may ask the writer to write *persuasively* about a certain point of view. Since the goal is to persuade or convince, the writer's tone may now be forceful, and perhaps even emotional, in order to affect the reader. For example:

Topic—Your community must decide whether to spend ten million dollars on a new library or a new swimming pool, neither of which it now has. Your community does not have the funds for both. Choose one side and make a strong persuasive argument for voting one way or the other.

Response—A library is an essential part of any community. A town without one cares little about its citizens' intellectual growth. To reject the library dooms us to the vulgarities of the television tube and embraces a philosophy that the written word is not to be valued. I strongly urge voting for the new library construction.

First, our town must demonstrate to our children that reading is a valued and important part of our lives. Presently, our children spend an enormous part of the day sitting impassively in front of television sets, growing more and more illiterate in the process. They know cartoon characters but are ignorant of classic novels. They can instantly recognize television stars but can barely decipher a newspaper editorial. What kind of enlightened voting populace will we have if our children grow up, as they are now doing, without any stimulus to read? . . .

Notice how more emotional and forceful this persuasive essay is as contrasted with the previous essay.

Yet another type of essay topic may elicit an altogether different mood. It may allow the tone of the essay to be humorous, or sentimental, or solemn, or suspenseful, or any of a number of other qualities depending upon its subject matter. For example:

Topic—**Throughout our lives each of us has no doubt had a particular friend who, because of his or her ability to make us laugh, or lighten our day, or cause us mirth, is unforgettable. Choose one such friend and describe the qualities that made him or her so unforgettable.**

This topic asks the writer to describe the qualities of an individual who made the writer laugh. While it can be written in a straightforward, objective tone, it need not be:

Response—When "Ol' Cut Up," Charley Blocker, filled my backyard pool with lemon-lime Jell-O, little did I suspect a truck would soon deliver two thousand cases of whipped cream to my door. Little did I imagine a busload of Cut Up's fraternity brothers would soon follow, dessert spoons eagerly clutched in their hands. And little did I know all this would occur on the very day I was trying to impress my fiance's stuffy parents, to prove to them that I was a responsible, mature enough adult to marry their daughter. . . .

Note the considerably different tone here. Since the unforgettable character was a "cut up," this essay's introduction takes a light-hearted, humorous tone.

Whatever tone a writer chooses, it should be appropriate and consistent through the entire essay. The tone should not shift from personal to impersonal, or from humorous to solemn, unless the subject matter calls for it; typically, an essay's tone should be constant throughout.

You may wish to assess the stylistic elements of your writing by using the following analysis sheet:

ANALYSIS BREAKDOWN

Clarity
- Is language direct and precise?
- Are sentences clear?
- Are words understandable?
- Are paragraphs easy to follow?

Style
- Is language appropriate to the topic (no slang or jargon)?
- Is language consistent throughout?

Tone
- Is the tone appropriate to the topic?
- Is the tone consistent throughout?

Sentences
- How many sentences contain twelve words or more?
- How many sentences contain six words or less?
- Are sentences appropriate lengths for the topic?

Word Choice
- Are words appropriate—not too formal or too informal?
- Are figures of speech appropriate and effective?

PROPER GRAMMAR

College writing requires following the standards of formal English. Among these standards is grammar, which dictates the proper declensions (forms of pronouns), conjugations and tenses for verbs, and positioning (placement of modifiers). Correct grammar enables the reader to understand the writer's intended relationships among words and phrases.

A Grammar and Usage Review begins on page 251.

PROPER PUNCTUATION

When we speak, pauses and gestures emphasize meaning. Changes in speed mark, or "punctuate," beginnings and ends of thoughts. So, too, we punctuate in writing. Applying the correct rules of punctuation is essential for a well-written college essay.

A good writer knows when and how to use capital letters, periods, commas, semicolons, colons, quotation marks, exclamation points, parentheses, apostrophes, ellipses, dashes, and hyphens.

Remember that punctuation is not a substitute for correct sentence structure. No amount of punctuation can correct an incorrectly structured sentence.

PROPER DICTION / USAGE

Proper diction or usage means the correct and effective choice of words. Knowing the exact meanings of those words you choose to use in your writing is essential. You should also be aware of the many commonly confused words and phrases. Some examples:

accept/except
affect/effect
allusion/illusion
lay/lie
less/fewer
raise/rise
set/sit

More examples of common usage problems may be found in the Grammar and Usage Review on pages 304–312.

SPELLING

As you write, you no doubt think sentences faster than you can write them on paper. You no doubt concentrate on words to come, not necessarily on the correct spelling of a particular word or words. So misspellings may appear in your timed essay. In proofreading your essay after you finish writing, you will usually find such errors and correct them. Even if you don't catch all of them, an occasional misspelling should not dramatically alter your grade.

Nevertheless, you should realize that misspellings affect your reader. If the misspellings are numerous, they will cause the reader to slow, perhaps even stop the flow of reading, especially if the misspelling is unusual. As a writer you don't want anything to distract your reader, and that includes misspellings.

However, being overly concerned with proper spelling can stop the flow of a writer's thinking. Do not interrupt your writing—and your train of thought—in order to consider how a word is spelled. It is more important that you get your thoughts down on paper. You can return *later* to the sentence (during the time you allot for proofreading) to determine the spelling of a particular word.

PROPER SENTENCE STRUCTURE

The elements of a sentence must be in proper grammatical relationship with one another. This is called correct syntax or sentence structure.

The following are some, but not all, of the requirements of proper sentence structure:

- complete sentences: no fragments, run-ons, or comma splices
- subject-verb agreement
- agreement of pronouns with antecedents
- clear pronoun reference
- no mixed constructions or shift in tense
- no misplaced or squinting modifiers
- no split infinitives
- no dangling participles, gerunds, infinitives, or clauses
- correct parallelism
- no redundancies

A discussion of the standards of sentence structure may be found in the Grammar and Usage Review on pages 251–321.

SOUND ORGANIZATION

A well-written essay uses correct paragraph form, with smooth transitions from one paragraph to the next. Together, the paragraphs form a unified, coherent whole.

A well-written essay has a clear beginning, middle, and end. The beginning serves as a springboard into your subject. The middle is its development. And an effective ending brings your paper to a logical conclusion.

There are as many different ways to write beginnings, middles, and ends as there are writers. But all good writers use paragraphs, their number depending upon the length of the essay. One paragraph may sometimes suffice for the beginning and one for the end. The middle, or development, may use two, three, or many more paragraphs, depending upon the number and extent of points to be developed. How many paragraphs is usually not important; what is important is that each paragraph be consistent in its style and subject matter and that, together, all paragraphs form a unified whole.

Paragraph Coherence

Each paragraph consists of sentences related to one another so that each paragraph forms a single coherent part of a larger unit, your essay. Sentences within a paragraph should be related in subject matter and tied together by logic and grammatical structure. In this way, a paragraph has unity.

Each paragraph typically contains a "topic sentence" which presents the overall point of that paragraph. The other sentences in that paragraph develop the topic sentence by presenting supporting, illustrative details, comparing or contrasting differences and similarities, or defining further the assertion of the topic sentence. Each of the paragraph's sentences should connect logically and smoothly.

Consider this paragraph:

Medicare covers people disabled for at least two years as well as people suffering from chronic kidney disease. Coverage will include nursing care if a nursing home is certified or if the physician certifies that nursing care is required. If requirements are met, the bill can be paid by Medicare. Medicare is a federal insurance program for people sixty-five and over. The Medicare patient is, however, under constant review by a committee of physicians.

Notice that while all the sentences are related, each dealing with Medicare, the fourth sentence is not in logical order; it would be better placed at the beginning of the paragraph. This misplaced sentence destroys the coherence of the paragraph.

Paragraph coherence also requires a unity of tone. Regardless of whether you are writing with authority, or wit, or sarcasm, try to keep your tone constant throughout so that your paragraphs form a consistent whole.

Smooth Transitions

Paragraphs should not just end and another begin. Rather, paragraphs should flow smoothly, one into the next. For example, consider these three paragraphs taken from an essay:

Early man accepted the viewpoint that his behavior was accounted for in terms of inner agents or spirits. From the immobility after death, for example, it was assumed that the spirit had left. This spirit, which lacks physical dimensions, came to be known as the soul, or "psyche" in Greek, the word from which psychology derives its name.

In time, every aspect of behavior was attributed to a corresponding feature of the mind. To some, the inner man was seen as driving the body, much as a person drives a car, and speculation on the nature of this inner person was given considerable attention. Furthermore, how the mind, or inner man, related to the physical body became an important point of departure for those seeking answers to man's nature.

Gradually, in the course of inquiring into the nature of the universe, there arose the question "How can we know?" The philosophers of the time . . .

Notice how the second paragraph changes time period, moving to a later time. Notice how the phrase "In time" helps to make a smooth transition between the first and second paragraphs. So too, the word "Gradually" creates a smooth transition between the second and third paragraphs, where there is another move in time.

This is one example of how paragraphs require smooth transitions or linking expressions so that the reader can easily follow the line of thought from one to the next. Paragraphs often begin with words or phrases such as these: first, finally, accordingly, nevertheless, on the contrary, in this way, however. These are but a few of the many transitional devices used to help paragraphs form a unified, coherent whole.

LEGIBILITY

While handwriting is not graded and does not constitute part of your overall score, your essay must nevertheless be readable. If it cannot be deciphered, it cannot be scored. Form all letters distinctly, with clearly crossed t's, clearly dotted i's, and conspicuous capital letters. Leave uniform margins, indent only for each paragraph, and follow other forms of normal manuscript form. If your handwriting is hard to read, you may consider printing if that is more legible.

If you decide to delete a word or phrase written in pen, simply draw a horizontal line through it. If you wish to make a brief insertion, write it above the line and indicate the point of insertion with a caret ($\wedge$) below the line.

SCORING

Each essay is typically scored by two people, each of whom is unaware of the other's score. If their scores on a single essay diverge widely, a third reader may be asked to score the paper. The final score may be the total (or, in some cases, the average) of all the readers' scores.

The common method for scoring is to assess the essay "holistically." That is, each essay is graded on overall, or general, competence in the aforementioned areas (fullness of response, development, language, organization) rather than on tiny details such as an occasional punctuation error. A reader will not expect a perfectly polished essay, since under time constraints, even the best writer's effort will be somewhat flawed.

Numerical scoring scales vary from program to program. Some programs use a 0-to-6 or 1-to-6 scale, the lowest score (0 or 1) being a poorly written essay and 6 being a superior essay. Other programs may use a 1-to-4 scale, or a 1-to-8 scale, with the lowest scores indicating poor and the highest scores superior. Typically the upper-half scores are considered passing (for example, 5, 6, 7, and 8 on the 1-to-8 scale; 3 and 4 on the 1-to-4 scale) and the lower-half scores (1, 2, 3, and 4 on the 1-to-8 scale; 1 and 2 on the 1-to-4 scale) are considered failing.

While the scales may differ numerically, the same guidelines for requirements pertain.

TYPICAL SCORING GUIDE

A simple way of understanding how a reader scores an essay holistically is to separate essays into several categories. A 0-to-6 scale breakdown follows. Scores of 4, 5, and 6 are considered passing; scores of 0, 1, 2, and 3 are failing.

Passing Scores

6—Superior: Such an essay is exemplary in all requirements. It clearly and thoroughly addresses all parts of the topic; demonstrates strong essay and paragraph organization; develops by use of extensive specific and appropriate detail; exhibits proficient grammar, usage, and sentence structure; and is legible to the reader. Occasional errors may exist, but they are minor.

5—Proficient: This essay fulfills all the requirements for a passing essay but exhibits some weaknesses in one or more areas. Organization is effective but not necessarily strong. It may competently use supporting detail and specific examples, but it may lack skillful execution and insight inherent in a superior essay. Its tone may not be consistent throughout. Occasional minor errors in grammar, sentence structure, or usage won't mar an otherwise sound paper.

4—Adequate: This minimal-pass essay demonstrates adequate sentence structure, grammar, and usage, but its errors are not major enough to distract the reader or indicate serious problems in standard written English. It shows adequate use of specific examples and detail but is not as fully developed as a more well-written essay. It may lack insight, be repetitive or simplistic, or lack consistent tone. It may fail to address all parts of the assignment or incompletely address one or more parts.

Failing Scores

3—Inadequate: This essay is clearly inadequate in one of the required elements or partially inadequate in more than one requirement. It may fail to address a major part of the assignment. It may lack supporting details or examples and thus have little or no development. It may fail to exhibit correct paragraph or essay form. It may demonstrate consistent and serious errors in grammar, usage, and sentence structure. It may be barely legible.

2—Weak: This essay shows an inability to address the topic in a consistent, correct manner. It may be badly marred by errors in grammar, usage, and sentence structure, enough to distract the reader or suggest serious problems in standard written English. It may be thin in supporting detail and content and flawed in organization. Any strengths are obscured by its severe and pervasive weaknesses. Despite any competence, this essay is clearly inadequate.

1—Incompetent: This effort demonstrates little ability to address the topic or use correct standard written English. The essay has little or no development, major flaws in organization and focus, and errors in mechanics so serious and frequent as to affect understanding.

0—No credit: This essay does not address the topic or may be totally illegible.

ESSAY CHECKLIST

The following checklist may help you evaluate your written essays in a more detailed manner.

HOW EFFECTIVELY DOES YOUR ESSAY . . .

Address the Topic?	Excellent	Average	Poor
1. Does it focus on the assigned topic?	1.		
2. Does it complete all tasks set by the assignment?	2.		
3. Are such topic words as "either," "or," "and," etc., correctly addressed?	3.		

EVALUATION

Organize Its Thoughts?	Excellent	Average	Poor
4. Is there an effective introduction?	4.		
5. Are the paragraphs logically arranged?	5.		
6. Does each paragraph focus on one main idea?	6.		
7. Are there smooth transitions between paragraphs?	7.		

Support Its Points?	Excellent	Average	Poor
8. Are there sufficient specific details for each point?	8.		
9. Are the examples given relevant to the issue?	9.		
10. Are the examples fully developed?	10.		
11. Are paragraphs full rather than skimpy?	11.		

Use Language Correctly?	Excellent	Average	Poor
12. Is language mature and varied?	12.		
13. Is punctuation correct?	13.		
14. Is spelling correct?	14.		
15. Are grammar and usage correct?	15.		

Present Itself?	Excellent	Average	Poor
16. Is the handwriting legible?	16.		
17. Is the paper neat?	17.		

PLAN OF ATTACK

For any timed writing task, the writer should envision three "steps" leading to the finished product:

1. Preparing to write (prewriting)
2. Writing
3. Proofreading (editing)

PREPARING TO WRITE

NOTING TIME AND SPACE CONSTRAINTS

Before you begin analyzing the topic itself, you should be aware of the amount of time allotted for the assignment as well as the amount of paper available on which to write your essay. This will help you assess not only how much time you'll have to organize and write the essay, but also how long the essay should be and how much development it requires.

The following chart gives you some basic guidelines, *although these will vary depending on the length of the prompt and the topic type.* Remember, long prompts may take five minutes to read.

Minutes for Entire Essay	Minutes for Prewriting	Minutes for Writing	Minutes for Proofreading
45	6–10	30	3–5
60	10	45	5
75	12–13	55	5–7
90	14–15	65	7–10
120	16–20	90	10
150	20–25	115	10–15
180	20–30	140	10–20

READING THE TOPIC

Next, read and understand the topic. A major mistake is to give too little time and attention to this task. Remember that if you address the topic incorrectly, or even partially, your score is significantly lowered, no matter how well the essay is organized, supported, and written. Therefore, you must spend adequate time carefully reading and understanding the topic and its exact requirements.

Pay special attention to key words in the directions, like "describe," "compare," "explain," "contrast." Be aware that "or" requires a choice, whereas "and" requires several elements. For example, "Present your opinions for or against . . ." means take one point of view, not both, whereas "for and against" means present both sides. Be careful to assess completely all the tasks required by a directed topic.

You may find it helpful to read the topic several times. If you are permitted to write on the test booklet, circling or marking the key words or tasks may also be effective. For example, suppose your topic is

---

Topic—We have all faced challenges. Write an essay about the most difficult challenge you have faced. Discuss why that challenge was difficult, describe the way you prepared, and explain how you were successful or unsuccessful in meeting that challenge.

What would you mark or circle? Perhaps the words "challenge," "why . . . difficult," "way you prepared," "how successful *or* unsuccessful." Notice there are several tasks to address.

PLANNING: BRAINSTORMING / ORGANIZING

Remembering, inventing, and organizing information at short notice can be difficult unless you are prepared with an effective technique. Writing your essay immediately after reading the topic often results in a poorly organized, haphazard essay. If scratch paper is allotted for planning, take time to organize your thoughts on paper before writing.

Brainstorming

The process of creating and accumulating ideas, examples, and illustrations is called "brainstorming." Brainstorming is simply jotting down on scratch paper as many thoughts, ideas, and possibilities as you can remember, invent, or otherwise bring to mind in order to address the topic. Neatness, order, and spelling are unimportant at this point.

Organizing

After generating as many illustrations as you can within the time allotted, assess these ideas. Remembering that development relies on specific examples, decide which examples best enable you to support your points. Eliminate (cross out) those you don't wish to use, and number those you'll want to address in your essay. Add any notes regarding more specific details or new thoughts that come to mind. However, don't worry about developing everything completely, since these planning notes are (typically) not seen by your reader. Your time will be better spent developing these points in your writing and not in your notes.

Brainstorming and Organizing

Usually the process requires two steps: creating ideas and then organizing them. However, one technique will enable you to brainstorm *and* organize at the same time. This is called "clustering."

Clustering

One such idea-generating technique well suited to the timed essay is the "cluster." For example, suppose, as before, your topic is

---

Topic—We have all faced challenges. Write an essay about the most difficult challenge you have faced. Discuss why that challenge was difficult, describe the way you prepared, and explain how you were successful or unsuccessful in meeting that challenge.

After reading the topic, you decide to write about the challenge of running a ten-kilometer race ("10K," for short).

Step One: On your scratch paper, jot down the challenge you will discuss ("10K") and several aspects that made it difficult. These notes are typically not graded, or even seen by the reader, so don't worry here about neatness or spelling.

Step Two: Consider each of the three subareas of "Running a 10K" and quickly jot down, in a cluster, whatever comes to mind (see following).

Step Three: Add more information to what you have so far. The additional information can (1) answer the question "Why?" or "How?" or "So what?" and (2) give a concrete example or "for instance."

Here is a completed, thorough cluster for "Running a 10K." Had there been less time for planning, the cluster would not have been as extensive.

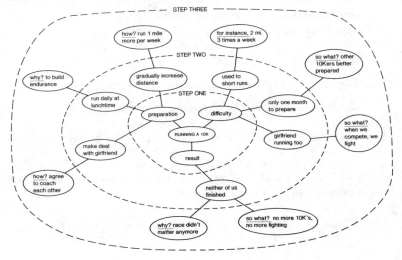

Mastering the cluster takes *repeated practice*. As you become more familiar with this technique, you should be able to jot down a wealth of information in a few minutes. (Note that you can use fragment sentences and abbreviations to save time.) Once your cluster is complete, you will have more than enough information, which will be clustered into categories for easy organization, and you will be ready to write your opening paragraph.

WRITING

OPENING PARAGRAPH

A strong opening paragraph is essential. One type of introduction, easy to master and very effective, is a GENERALIZE-FOCUS-SURVEY structure. This is a three- or four-sentence paragraph in which the first sentence generalizes about the given topic; the second sentence focuses on what you have chosen to discuss; and the last one or two sentences survey the particulars you intend to present.

Referring to the essay question and to your cluster, jot down (1) the central term from the given topic, (2) the term that names your subject, and (3) several aspects of your subject that you plan to discuss:

1. General term	difficult challenge
2. Focused term	running a 10K
3. Aspects to survey	increasing distance
	building endurance
	maintaining relationship

Step One: In your first sentence, use the general term.

Difficult challenges can be physical and emotional.

Step Two: In your second sentence, focus on the subject you have chosen to discuss.

When I took on a tough physical challenge, *running a 10K,* I did not expect it to be emotional as well.

Step Three: Finally, survey the aspects you will discuss.

Increasing my running distance and *building endurance* taxed me physically. At the same time, I faced the emotional challenge of *maintaining a relationship,* with my chief competitor, my girl friend.

An effective first paragraph tells your reader what to expect in the body of the essay. The GENERALIZE-FOCUS-SURVEY paragraph points toward the specifics you will discuss and suggests the order in which you will discuss them.

BODY

Writing the body of the essay involves presenting specific details and examples that are related to the aspects you have introduced. The body of the essay may consist of one longer paragraph or several shorter paragraphs. If you choose to break your discussion into several paragraphs, make sure that each paragraph consists of at least three sentences. Very short paragraphs may make your essay appear to be insubstantial and scattered.

Be realistic about *how much* you will be able to write. Your readers do not give more credit for longer essays. Although they want you to support your points adequately, they understand that you must write concisely in order to finish in time.

It will be important to provide at least one substantial example or "for instance" for each aspect you discuss in the body of your essay. Here is an example of a two-paragraph body:

About a year ago, I was a "jogger" but not a "runner." I jogged three times a week, two miles each time, but wondered whether I had the ability to endure a run of over six miles—the demanding 10K. With the Independence Day 10K only a month away, I began a very difficult training program. I began running three miles daily for a week, then four miles, then five miles. and a week before the race I was running six miles a day. My friends warned me that I was driving myself too hard, and my constant exhaustion told me that as well. But pushing myself this hard seemed like the best way to build endurance and increase distance by the time of the race.

The physical challenge was at least matched by the emotional challenge in dealing with my girl friend. She had decided to train for the race as well, and I was afraid that because we were both so competitive we would be fighting constantly. So, early on, I made a deal with Jane. She would help me and I would help her. We'd support each other. There were moments every day when cooperating seemed almost impossible. Tired and sweating, we began to grumble at each other. But both of us quickly remembered the deal and stopped a potential argument. But restraining myself from arguing was hard work.

Notice that so far this essay deals with two of the three parts of the question. It discusses the difficulty of the challenge and describes the preparation. Notice also that not all of the details that are in the cluster are in the essay. You should not expect to or try to use every detail. Also realize that as you write, new ideas and details will come up, and you should use them to your advantage.

CONCLUSION

As you prepare to write the conclusion, you should be paying special attention to time. You must allow enough time both to write the conclusion and to proofread. The conclusion may function to (1) *complete* your response to the essay question, (2) *add* information that was not introduced earlier, or (3) *point toward the future*. The following conclusion serves all three functions:

The day of the race arrived, and both of us were not really ready. We both felt that we had trained too hard and too often, and we were right. After running just three miles, we simply could not continue and dropped out. However, both of us agreed that learning to cooperate was more important than finishing the race. Once we dropped out of competition for the 10K, we stopped competing and fighting with each other as well.

Let's take a look at another sample:

Topic—Consider the following, written by Lewis Thomas:

"We learn, as we say, by 'trial and error.' Why do we always say that? Why not 'trial and rightness' or 'trial and triumph'? The old phrase puts it that way because that is, in real life, the way it is done."

Thomas suggests that learning is a result of making mistakes rather than doing things correctly. Decide whether Thomas is right or not, and support your decision by discussing the role of trial and error with reference to a particular modern problem.

First, *mark the key words* in the question. You must *decide* about Thomas and must *support* that decision by discussing a *particular modern problem*. To prepare to write, create a cluster:

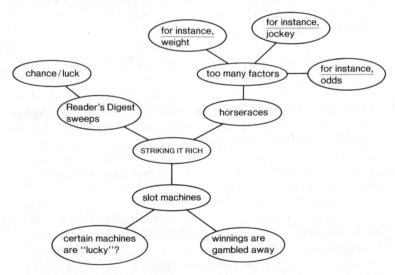

Notice several things about this cluster. First, it is much less extensive than the "Running a 10K" cluster. This writer, spending a few minutes jotting down ideas and examples, could not think of more information than that which appears here. Knowing that he must not spend excessive time on the outline and trusting that he will discover more ideas while writing the essay, this writer goes ahead to compose the first paragraph. The GENERALIZE-FOCUS-SURVEY introduction proceeds as follows:

1. General term   trial and error
2. Focused term   striking it rich
3. Aspects to survey   horseraces
                       Reader's Digest sweepstakes
                       slot machines

Following is a first paragraph based on this approach:

Lewis Thomas claims that we learn through *trial and error.* However, he seems to be forgetting a modern problem that thousands of people are struggling with every day—the problem of beating the odds and *striking it rich.* They place their bets at the *racetrack,* mail their entries to the *Reader's Digest sweepstakes,* and fill casino *slot machines* with coins, learning nothing new from losing time and time again.

Note that this writer has taken a novel approach to the question. Rather than worrying about whether the "modern problem" he chooses is serious or dignified enough and choosing something he feels uncomfortable with, this writer picks an "unexpected" subject for which he has something to say and makes it fit the question.

Here is an example of a one-paragraph body:

For every gambler's "trial," there is more often an "error" than a "triumph," so I would agree with Thomas that trial and error go together. Whether we "learn" from gambling losses is another matter. Conducting "research" at the Santa Anita race track this summer, I found that although every gambler was trying to pick a winner, and trying to keep relevant factors— weight, jockey, odds—in mind, most groaned at the finish and then groaned again at the end of race after race. There were no more winning bets in the ninth race than there were in the first. Nobody learned a thing. As the racing season ends, these gamblers migrate to Las Vegas, where they pour money into slot machines, conducting trial after trial and suffering error after error and going home busted. Sitting at home, dejected, they fill out entries to the *Reader's Digest* sweepstakes and any other sweepstakes game that comes in the mail, only to receive nothing in response for the umpteenth time.

In the following conclusion, this writer adds new information, a new perspective, which follows from what he has written but which was not included in the earlier material.

Perhaps gamblers do learn, or should learn, something from their errors. They learn that gambling is fundamentally a matter of chance and luck, even for professionals. And after years of errors and wasted money, some of us learn that we shouldn't gamble at all.

SAMPLES—FROM PLANNING TO FINISHED ESSAY

OUTLINING

Clustering is by no means the only way to plan before you write. Simple brainstorming, or jotting down random notes, can be effective if those notes are then numbered or ordered. Another technique is formal "outlining." A typical outline may look something like this:

I. Introduction (with thesis statement)
   A. point to be covered
   B. point to be covered
   C. etc.

II. Development (each subheading below may be one paragraph)
   A. discussion of point A, from above, with
      1. specific example supporting A
      2. specific example supporting A
   B. discussion of point B, from above, with
      1. specific example supporting B
      2. specific example supporting B
      3. specific example supporting B
   C. discussion of point C, from above, with
      1. specific example supporting C
      2. specific example supporting C

III. Brief conclusion or summary

Consider this topic:

Some have said that Americans are becoming a nation of spectators rather than a nation of doers. Others have argued the opposite, that Americans have become active participants rather than just passive observers. Write an essay to be read by a history teacher in which you take one side of the argument. Support your position using examples from your own experience, reading, and/or observations.

A simple outline for this sample might go something like this:

Americans—Spectators, Not Doers

I. Sporting events
   A. Attendance figures highest ever
   B. More teams being watched

II. Television and Films
   A. Homes with TVs
   B. TVs on more and more

III. Elections
   A. Only half of eligible voters vote
   B. More watch on TV than participate

OR

Americans—Doers, Not Spectators

I. Recreation—More popular than ever
   A. More sporting equipment sold than ever before
      1. Athletic shoes: its own industry
      2. Athletic outfits
   B. On weekends, parks are filled
      1. Tennis courts hard to get
      2. Ballfields always used

II. Public involved in fundraisers
   A. For social concerns
      1. Aid to Africa
      2. Farm Aid

    3. Comic Relief
    4. Door-to-door for diseases
  B. For political candidates

Sample Essay

   A sample essay from the first outline might go something like
this:

   It has been said that Americans are becoming a nation of
spectators, rather than a nation of participants. From my
observations, I can easily agree with this statement. In recent
years, Americans have increasingly demonstrated their passive,
nonparticipatory status. This is most apparent in the increase in
popularity of spectator sports, the rise of the visual media, and
unfortunately, the decline of electoral participation.
   The popularity of spectator sports has risen dramatically. The
number of sports teams has expanded and continues to grow. At
one time, there were only sixteen major-league baseball teams;
now there are twenty-seven. Once major-league football teams
played only in the East and Midwest; now they include the major
cities in the South and West as well. Professional hockey once
consisted of only six major-league teams; now there are almost
two dozen. Total attendance has likewise grown. It is impossible
to get tickets to some football games, as they are sold out
months, sometimes years, in advance. If you don't have season
tickets, you may not be able to get in the stadium. Sell-outs, once
uncommon, are an everyday event. Each year, total attendance
for individual sports breaks the previous year's records.
   The rise of the visual media is also indicative of a more passive
society. Nearly every home has at least one television set, if not
more. Recent studies have found that watching television, a
passive entertainment (unlike reading or card playing), con-
sumes hours of the average American's day. Once there were
only about a half-dozen television stations available to any
individual; now there are dozens, including cable films, twenty-
four-hour sporting events, and many more yet to come. Americans' appetite for television appears to be insatiable.
   Unfortunately, the increasingly passive nature of the Ameri-

can citizen is also reflected in the American electoral process. Fewer voters than ever take the time to fulfill their responsibility to vote. In the last presidential election, nearly half of the eligible voters stayed home instead of going to the polls. It was estimated that more Americans *watched* the election on television than voted. Sad to say, but the growing passivity of the American character may have grave consequences for the future of our democracy.

American passivity is exemplified by the recent growth of spectator sports and television and the decline of participatory electoral democracy. Hopefully, however, this trend is only a temporary one.

Following are two more methods for approaching essay topics:

THE "STORY FORMULA"

One good way to approach a question that asks you to *describe one experience* is through the use of the "story formula." The story formula consists of

1. Setting—where and when the story took place
2. Main characters—the people in the story
3. Plot—the problem in the story or the crisis to be overcome
4. Climax—the turning point in the story
5. Resolution—the ending or how you are now as a result of the experience

So, in the sample essay—

Paragraph 1—introduce the setting and the main characters in the story
Paragraph 2—introduce the plot ⎫   number of paragraphs
Paragraph 3—introduce the climax ⎭   may vary
Final paragraph—introduce the resolution

The story formula allows you to describe one experience in detail using clear transitions while keeping a unifying theme throughout your essay.

Topic—Some students can look back on their years in school and pinpoint one particular course or one particular teacher most

instrumental in shaping their lives.
Reflect on your own school years and focus on one such
instructor or course. Describe the conditions or qualities that
made that particular experience or teacher special.

Your cluster might look like this:

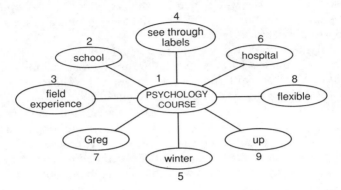

Notice, in this cluster, that the writer decided to number the
material to help put it in order.

The Finished Essay

Here's the finished essay in "story formula."

Ten years ago, I was twenty-one and a junior at California
State University at Long Beach. My schooling had been quite
traditional and because of this I regarded my college experience
as a necessary means to an end and rarely educational. Shortly
after I began my second semester in the Education Department,
however, I took a course in abnormal psychology that became
most instrumental in shaping my life.

On a cold blustery winter day, as I drove to my part-time job
at the neuropsychiatric hospital, I had a nagging feeling that the
psychology class I enrolled in was slowly changing my point of
view. As I drove onto the damp parking lot and walked in the
doorway to the children's unit, my professor's words haunted me:
"The challenge of the new psychology is to look beyond the
'labels' given to people and to see for oneself the human being

that is there." I mulled over in my mind whether this day would bring me any closer to that goal.

That day a new patient arrived. He was a four-year-old child pinned tightly with the label of "autistic." His name was Gregory, and in him I saw immediately all that I had previously only read about. He had all of the usual behaviors of a child who was autistic. He would not respond to touch or affection, engaged in constant finger flicking and hand gazing, and seemed to withdraw into his own world.

In the days that passed I spent much time with Gregory, involving him in whatever I was doing, always maintaining some physical contact with him. It was not until the fourteenth day that I dropped my ever-so-precious label.

Gregory and I frequently engaged in games, but his favorite game was entitled "Up." In this game I was to lift Gregory into the air as he gleefully shouted out, "up, up!" After several times, my arms grew weary, and instead of putting him down, I held Gregory in my arms. There we stood in an embrace of trust—an opening to a place beyond his label. My tears flowed freely as he calmly touched each one with his fingers, smiling as their wetness served to cement our relationship. Somehow, in that moment, all of what I had read mattered little compared to what I now knew. As my professor had warned us in class, "The labels only serve to make things easy—it is up to you to discover the truth."

Each day I went to the nueropsychiatric institute filled with a joy I had never known, yet in one sharp moment it was all shattered. On December 26, 1972, Gregory was transferred to a state mental institution. Over the advice of the staff and the doctors, Gregory was taken to a place where he would wear his label forever.

The next few weeks at the hospital seemed empty to me. A challenge by a professor to see through the labels and the willingness and trust of a four-year-old child enabled me to learn a lesson that I shall never forget. For the first time a college course provided me with a real learning experience; all of the coursework that I had taken never touched me as a deeply as this one course.

THE "WHY" ESSAY

One good way to approach a question which asks you to explain, analyze, or evaluate is to use a "why" essay format. A "why" essay is built around a thesis sentence. The thesis sentence begins with your opinion, followed by the word *because* and then a list of the most important reasons the opinion is valid, reasonable, or well founded.

The "why essay" format could look like this in outline form:

Paragraph	*"Why" Essay Format*
1	Introduction—Thesis Sentence
2	Reason 1
3	Reason 2
4	Reason 3
5	Conclusion

Each paragraph should contain at least three to five sentences. The introduction invites the reader to read on. Your reasons (three are often sufficient) that follow should give examples or evidence to support each reason. Your concluding paragraph summarizes your reasons and restates the thesis statement.

Topic—A recent movement in education has been called "Back to Basics." Its proponents argue that the curriculum should concentrate only on reading, writing, and mathematics skills and completely ignore such courses as sociology, art appreciation, and drama.

Imagine that you are a school principal faced with the task of making policy for your school. Present your argument(s) either for or against "Back to Basics."

This is what the cluster for this topic might look like.

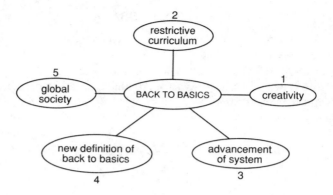

Now using the "why" formula, the finished essay might look like this:

The Finished Essay

As principal of your school, I have seen many educational movements come and go. Some are worthy of the attention given to them, and others should be ignored because of their devastating effect on the educational system. One such movement that falls into the latter category is the "Back to Basics" movement. Its proponents argue that education should concentrate on reading, writing, and mathematics skills and completely ignore such courses as drama, art appreciation, and sociology. I am against the "Back to Basics" movement because it inhibits creativity, fails to recognize the importance of the arts, and restricts the curriculum.

The enhancement of creative thinking is primal to the advancement of any educational system. To create, to invent, or to discover, one needs to have not only freedom of thought but also the exposure and application of that creativity to all areas of the curriculum. To concentrate on only reading, writing, and mathematics would restrict thinking to a narrow focus. The future needs thinkers who can create in the widest spectrum so as to be able to meet the challenge of a global society.

The "Back to Basics" proponents also fail to see that a restrictive curriculum on only mathematics, reading, and writing fails to support the many great advancements made in our culture by those whose first exposures to art, drama, or sociology took place in the schools. The great artists who have changed the way people see; the great dramatists who have told their stories worldwide; and the great sociologists who have helped us to understand social relations, organizations, and changes in our culture have all been products of an education that included the arts as basic to a well-rounded education.

Finally, the "Back to Basics" supporters fail to see in their narrow view of education that the basics *include* art, drama, and sociology as well as music, dance, and computer literacy. "Basics," by definition, means that knowledge which is needed by children in our society in order to compete and simply survive in that society. The "Back to Basics" movement is an attempt to take education back to a time that has long since passed. The narrow focus of the movement also overlooks the integrative value of reading, writing, and mathematics throughout all curriculum areas and especially in the arts.

The "Back to Basics" issue is a sad attempt to restrict the information that children need for their future. It will stifle creativity in those knowledge areas upon which our society is dependent. So, as your principal, I hope that you on the school board continue to support an education for the future—an education that defines the "basics" as those curriculum areas beyond the courses of reading, writing, and mathematics. We must meet the future with an education that *includes* art, drama, and sociology.

PROOFREADING

Always allow a few minutes to proofread your essay for errors in grammar, usage, and spelling. To make sure that you do not proofread hastily, try this: With a sheet of paper, cover all but the first line of your essay. Read that line carefully. Then reveal and read the second line, and so forth. Using this method, you are more assured of focused and careful proofreading.

If you detect an error, line it out carefully and insert the correction neatly. Keep in mind, both while you are writing and while you are correcting, that your handwriting must be *legible*.

Following are more essay topics, following by typical clusters, completed essays, and reader comments. For example, the sample topic we encountered earlier, in a slightly different form:

ESSAY 1

Topic—Cities have been criticized for being centers of crime, for overcrowding, for extremes of poverty and wealth. But cities have their advantages, too—advantages in employment, in education, in opportunity for entertainment and intellectual growth.

You live in or near a large metropolitan area. From what you have experienced, observed, or read, what advantages do you think city life has to offer? Write a focused, developed, organized essay in which you discuss two or three specific advantages and explain why they are advantageous.

Your cluster could look like this:

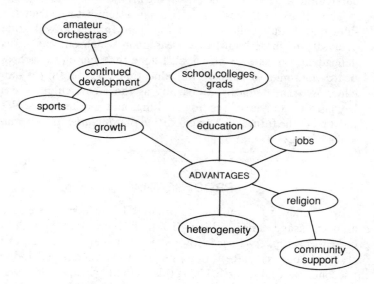

The Finished Essay

Overpopulation, poverty, and crime have always plagued large cities, and twentieth-century America is no exception. But urban life also offers many distractions and entertainments and many opportunities—employment possibilities, for example—that would be unavailable in a rural area or small town. Particularly in the area of personal growth and development, cities offer an exciting and rewarding environment.

The educational opportunities of the city extend from grade school to university. Instead of the limited choice of elementary and secondary schools provided by a country town, the city offers an array of schools, from those that specialize in the performing arts, to military academies, liberal arts colleges, preparatory high schools, and business magnets. Furthermore, the proximity of the city, with its diverse possibilities for field trips and cultural outings, enriches any of these educational choices. Certainly, a tour of one of the city's art museums brings alive the work of the classroom; seeing a professional production of *Romeo and Juliet* can only illuminate the discussion of the play in class; visiting municipal government offices transforms the poltical-science textbook into reality. And the opportunities extend through college to graduate school. Especially beneficial to adults who want to continue their education and who cannot give up their jobs or move their families, city colleges and universities provide them with courses and degrees in new career fields or enable them to extend their understanding and job opportunities in their own fields.

In a city, individuals can continue to grow outside of a school setting also. Depending on their abilities and inclinations, people can develop their talents in a number of ways. From dance to yoga, cooking classes to amateur musical groups, Sunday softball teams to drawing courses, city dwellers can continue to grow and become the best they can be. The city can support and thus attracts talented instructors, and in such numbers that along one stretch of a major Los Angeles boulevard alone, eleven ballet schools offer classes from morning until night, from beginning stretches to advanced choreography.

But probably the most important opportunity for personal growth and development comes from the city's tolerance for diversity. It is difficult becoming the best self one can become in a small town if that self is "different," for the pressure to conform in a small community can be intense to the point of intolerance. While the diverse educational opportunities encourage and generate multiple ways of thinking, the very different racial, ethnic, and religious populations in a large city help to work against ignorance and smallmindedness. Thus, minority groups of various kinds find the city a more comfortable place in which to live and grow. The racially mixed couple is accepted, or at least ignored; the observant Jew's celebrations are supported and shared by a large religious community; the Mexican-American feels encouraged by the city's large Hispanic population and its bilingualism to continue to cherish its language and cultural uniqueness. The city's diversity is indeed advantageous—educationally, culturally, and personally.

Reader Comments

The essay effectively responds to the question. Personal observation, since it was invited by the question, was used to generate "two or three specific" examples of the thesis, that city life offers advantages.

First paragraph: Briefly summarizes the condition posed by the question and offers a restatement of the question's central assertion—city life has advantages. In response to the question's request for two or three particular advantages, the last sentence states, as the thesis that will control the essay, a restriction of the assertion: "Particularly in the area of personal growth and development, cities offer an exciting and rewarding environment."

Second paragraph: The first sentence serves as topic sentence for the entire paragraph and states the first particular advantage of city life. All the specifics that follow—kinds of schools, particular cultural opportunities—develop that statement. Notice the use of concrete examples to prove more general assertions: for example, *Romeo and Juliet* to illustrate "professional production." Note also the transitions within the paragraph, providing coherence among the various facets of the central assertion in this paragraph: for example, "Furthermore," "Certainly," "And," "Especially beneficial."

Third paragraph: The first sentence, the topic sentence, asserts another advantage of city life; the "also" makes it transitional, referring the reader to the advantage proposed by the preceding paragraph. Again, note the concrete examples of general assertions; while the list of activities catalogued in the third sentence proves diversity—"a number of ways"—the illustration of ballet schools proves abundance.

Fourth paragraph: Again, the first sentence is the topic sentence, for it controls the entire paragraph; again, it is transitional—note "the most." It again asserts an advantage of city living, a third response to the question's request for specific examples. Much in the paragraph serves to create coherence by referring to points made earlier in the essay; "the best self" refers to the point made in the third paragraph. The new point here—racial, ethnic, and religious diversity—is supported with various specific examples. The final sentence of this paragraph serves as the conclusion of the essay; it summarizes the whole and points to and rephrases the thesis, the answer to the question.

ESSAY 2

Topic—The relief one feels when an anticipated disaster or disappointment does not occur has been described as the greatest of all human emotions. Whether this claim is accurate or not, most people have experienced this type of relief. For the essay, select one experience or person that you expected to be a bore, a disappointment, an aggravation, a nightmare, a fate worse than death, but later turned out to be a high point in your life. You may select any experience or person so long as the negative anticipation has a positive outcome.

You might select a birthday celebration, a holiday, a party, a dinner, a classroom presentation, a test or project, a date or blind date, an athletic event, a job, and so on.

The purpose of your essay is not merely to describe your anticipation and its aftermath, but also to explain why you had a negative expectation and how the positive result occurred. In

developing your argument, you should use as many concrete and specific details as possible.

Your cluster could look like this:

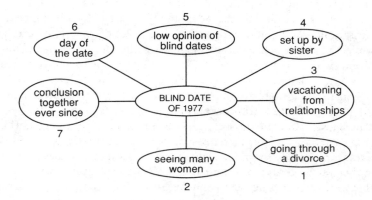

The Finished Essay

What a great relief when the expected nightmare turns out to be a beautiful dream, when the anticipated disappointment becomes the pleasant surprise. Being pleasantly surprised was exactly my experience back in 1977 when I was set up with my first and last blind date. My life at that time made me an unlikely candidate for a blind date, but I found myself on one nonetheless.

In 1977 my life was in a state of great change and fleeting relationships. I was going through a divorce and selling my home of five years. Furthermore, the divorce was painful and hostile, which encouraged me to avoid my ex-wife at every opportunity. What is it about divorce that brings out the predator in people? One of the ways I escaped was by dating women widely and variously with a high concentration on fun and enjoyment. In fact, I dated so frequently and quickly that I often wound up on dates with women I had absolutely nothing in common with. In almost every case, I would finally realize I often did not like the person and had very little to say to her. I was just not being careful about getting to know them. For example, one woman I dated was quite shocked at my comments and general behavior, but I was so unaware that I interpreted her reactions as amusement. The date itself was stiff and unpleasant. Another woman I dated was desperate to get married, and before I realized it, I had proposed marriage to her even before my divorce was final. She sued me for breach of promise when I broke it off. Finally, I once made three dates with three different women for the same day. They all fell through and I was grateful. I finally decided to take a vacation from these fleeting relationships so my life could calm down.

It was during this calm period in my life that I was set up with a blind date. A friend of a friend of mine told me his girl friend's sister was looking for a nice guy to date. He said the sister had recently graduated from college and was tired of frivolous men. I accepted the date, but in my mind I was only being polite. My real feelings were a combination of disgust, smugness, and pity: I was disgusted at the idea of a blind date; I was smug about being considered eligible; and I felt pity for any girl whose younger sister had to get dates for her. When he left the room, I asked George what she looked like. His reply was, "To me she is ugly." His response confirmed my prejudice. I planned to honor the commitment, but I was in no hurry.

After breaking the date twice in a row with lame excuses (I did not feel she rated a carefully thought-out lie), I decided to go meet my blind date. I dressed very casually and decided to just be myself; I was not going to impress anyone. When I arrived, her sister said, "I'll go wake her up." That statement caught me off guard. It was not consistent with my image of her as a desperate, ugly little milkmaid anxiously awaiting her handsome blind date. Was she as indifferent as I was?

Her name was Cheryl, and my first thought was, "She's a little skinny but not unpleasantly so." From that moment on, we fell into an easy conversation and comfortable feeling about one another that kept increasing as the evening wore on. She had just returned from France (another violation of my previous image of her—milkmaids were not world travelers), and I soon discovered she had a classical, liberal-arts education similar to my own. As we got to know each other further through conversation, I realized we saw the world quite similarly. We liked similar movies, food, values, and entertainment and believed in openness and honesty. We were made for each other. And contrary to

George's opinion, she had the skin and beauty of an unspoiled princess. We have been together ever since that day and now are approaching our thirteenth year of marriage—and we are still on that first date.

I was prepared for a nightmare and an extremely boring evening with a charity case. Instead I found the woman of my dreams. And to think I broke the date twice. The blind date was all right after all—what a relief.

Reader Comments

Introduction: Immediately addresses the topic question and quickly narrows it to a specific experience.

Second paragraph: Provides general background information which explains why he developed a cautious and cynical attitude toward dating.

Third paragraph: Introduces the blind date and reveals the cynical expectations of the writer.

Fourth paragraph: Provides the first suggestion that the writer's prejudices may be exploded. His smugness is being challenged before meeting his blind date.

Fifth paragraph: Summarizes the meeting. The writer falls into an easy relationship and apparently falls in love.

Conclusion: Brief, returning the reader to the topic and reminding the reader of the main idea of the essay.

ESSAY 3

Topic—Identify a group you belong to that is often stereotyped. Describe the stereotype and discuss where/how we see the depiction—that is, TV commercials or programs, popular songs, newspaper cartoons, books, movies, etc. Be specific. Then, show that the stereotype is just or refute it as unjust.

Your cluster and notes could look like this:

1. coeds stereotyped as airheads
2. where and how depicted
3. unjust!

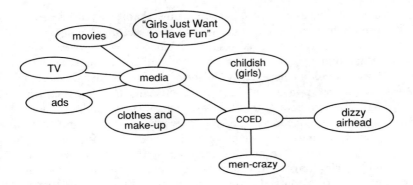

The Finished Essay

As a young, female college student, I often feel that people put me in the "Party-going coed" category and dismiss me as an incompetent, self-absorbed airhead, concerned only with looking good for men. Most men, initially at least, respond to me flirtatiously, as though the only reason I took the trouble to look attractive was to please a man. Others, men and women, respond to me as though I was a pretty but not-very-bright youngster, with the kind of indulgence adults reserve for children. Or, if I'm asking for information—directions in a department store, for example—they treat me with impatience, as though the answers to the questions I ask them were obvious to any thinking person. In all these cases, however, I sense that people are responding out of preconceived ideas to an image, a stereotype, not to me.

This stereotype is depicted by all the media. Popular songs such as "Girls Just Want to Have Fun" reinforce the idea that women, after all, are actually "girls" whether they are under or over twenty years old and therefore capable of only girlishly frivolous interests. Advertisements such as "Give her Chocolates and Diamonds" remind us that young women are not only brainless pleasure-seekers but also insatiable consumers, who need to be bought with candy and jewelry. TV sitcoms have been doing their part for quite awhile, featuring situations in which only two types of young women exist: the cheerleader and the student. One precludes the other; popular girls are not studious in the world of TV and Hollywood movies, and the few who are interested in their studies, who are bright and socially concerned, are outsiders and marked in some unmistakable way as "weird," usually by wearing glasses or having buck teeth.

Such stereotyping is insulting, harmful, and inaccurate. While many young women enjoy dressing up and looking their best, they don't necessarily do so to "catch a man." Nor does their interest in a pleasing appearance mean nothing else is important to them or that they are incapable, somehow, of more substantial concerns. The young women I know, including myself, take their college education and their futures very seriously. They are actively involved in their course work, in considering important career choices, and at the same time in helping to support themselves at outside jobs. Considering a person as only a member of a group already described by the media prevents us from actually seeing the individual behind the label.

Reader Comments

This is a clear and well-organized answer to the question, and it deals with all parts of the question: identifying a group that is stereotyped and describing the stereotype, discussing where and how that stereotype is depicted by the media, and evaluating the justice or injustice of the stereotype. The essay is carefully written and generally error free.

First paragraph: Introduces the topic by addressing the question's first concern—the identification of a group—thus assuring the reader that the writer has read and understood the question. Specific examples of stereotyped responses follow. The last sentence of this paragraph serves as a kind of thesis statement, summarizing the writer's attitude toward stereotyping.

Second paragraph: Note the transitional topic sentence. "This" refers to the last sentence of the first paragraph, and "is depicted" looks ahead to the subject of the second paragraph, the second concern of the question. Specific examples are given of media depictions of the stereotype.

Third paragraph: Again, the topic sentence of this paragraph is transitional, referring back to the "stereotyping" discussed in paragraph two and forward to the subject of the final paragraph and the final concern of the question, the justice/injustice of the stereotype. The final sentence of the essay echoes, while elaborating on, the thesis.

ESSAYS TO EVALUATE

On the next few pages are several student-written essays. Noting the requirements of a well-written essay—fullness of response, adequate development, sound organization, and skillful language— evaluate each of them, paragraph by paragraph and overall, and rate each as an upper-half (passing) essay or a lower-half (failing) essay. Use the space provided following each essay to write your comments. Then compare your comments to the following remarks made by an English instructor scoring the same essays holistically.

ESSAY 1

Topic

Identify a group you belong to that is often stereotyped. Describe the stereotype and discuss where/how we see the depiction—that is, in TV commercials or programs, newspaper cartoons, books, movies, etc. Be specific. Then, show that the stereotype is just or refute it as unjust.

Essay

As human beings we all belong to an enormous list of groups that are often stereotyped. But the group that I belong to that causes a smile to crawl across most peoples' faces is the group known as the Boy Scouts of America. At parties or gatherings I am often asked what I do with my spare time. When I mention that I like to help with my old Scout troop as an Assistant Scoutmaster, the first question I usually encounter is, "Helped any old ladies cross the street lately?" Boy Scouts are characterized as these little guys who help people cross the street, learn knots that have no purpose or sing songs around campfires.

These images have worked their way into the unconsious mind of America. Children's cartoons show Scouts attacking old ladies and dragging them across streets. Family shows have shown Scouts practicing their knot-tying abilities by tying up their Scoutmaster. Scouts are shown as these white-faced little angels who go around quoting the Scout law to all their less-than-perfect friends and family

67

who have the misfortune of knowing a Scout. Scouts are stereotyped by second-hand images. Due to copyright laws or something like that, the Scout symbol, uniform, and all the rest of Scouting's paraphernalia are proteced from general use or misuse in movies. So we get clubs in movies, books and television like the Badgers or the Chipmunks, that are poor copies of the Scouts.

No one ever mentions the hundreds of miles of mountain trails that scouts have built with shovels, saws and countless gallons of sweat. Or the fact that more than one of the men captured in Vietnam survived on the skills and ideas that he learned in scouting. Scouting teaches young men self reliance, teamwork, authority, and respect for themselves and their country. The simple skills that teach boys to survive in the woods help them realize that they have, or can learn, the skills to survive in the everyday world. As Scouts, boys meet peers that they might not encounter otherwise. They establish another group of friends that they can rely on. A brotherhood is established that stretches across 3,000 miles of land and the diverse cultural melting pot of the United States. This brotherhood unites boys in a spirit of friendship, learning, and fun that few organizations have matched. In truth this brotherhood stretches around the world. Scouting is a world-wide organization.

Unfortunately, Scouting in the United States receives only a fraction of what the program receives in other countries. The Scouting organization has been so stereotyped as a bunch of kids doing nothing in particular in some dumb uniforms that the boys that so sorely need that kind of guidance Scouting can offer are afraid of being laughed at by their friends. Imagine, an organization that helped mold the minds of presidents, the men who landed on the moon, outstanding film makers (the list goes on and on) lacks the respect enough to win members. Boys feel that they can't risk their reputation, no matter how much they are attracted to Scouting. Parents even discourage their son's interest because, due to their own ignorance, they think Scouts are a bunch of wimps.

While Scouting has won the support of many people, it lacks the support of the entertaiment media. Scouts are portrayed as a pack of wormy brats who lack discipline. The entertainment industry makes these statements so powerfully that the Scouts have little hope of rebutting. Only the news media gives Scouts some coverage, but it usually comes off a condescending, "ain't they cute," time killer.

The Scouting program has so much to offer and has helped millions of boys to grow into responsible citizens. It is a crime that so many people lack respect for it and cling to the stereotypes that have been set up for the organization.

Your Comments

Paragraph 1:

Paragraph 2:

Paragraph 3:

Paragraph 4:

Paragraph 5:

Paragraph 6:

General Comments and Rating:

Reader Comments

Paragraph 1: Good thesis statement followed by examples of the stereotype. More development of the examples is needed.

Paragraph 2: Good examples of media stereotyping, but the point about copyright laws and the Badger and Chipmunk "copies" is not clear, and the writer does not connect it with the thesis.

Paragraph 3: A transition is needed to signal this switch in approach. The writer should mention the *specific* skills and ideas learned in Scouting that would help men captured in Vietnam and the *specific* skills that boys learn in Scouting that prepare them to survive in the everyday world. The comments on brotherhood are redundant and also suffer from the lack of specifics.

Paragraph 4: The point of this paragraph is unclear and off topic. Word choice is vague.

Paragraph 5: Summarizes points made earlier, but not particularly strongly.

Paragraph 6: Adequate conclusion, restating the injustice of the stereotype.

General Comments and Rating: The writer's diction is by no means sophisticated, but it's certainly not dull—it's colloquial and vigorous, sometimes very effectively—"bunch of wimps," "pack of wormy brats." At the same time, it suffers from vagueness in places, off-topic digressions, and a lack of concrete examples. There are some diction errors ("unconscious mind"), spelling errors ("unconsious"), punctuation errors ("peoples'"), redundancies ("diverse . . . melting pot"), but they are not extensive enough to seriously downgrade the essay. This is a marginally upper-half essay and would probably receive a passing grade.

ESSAY 2

Topic

The Los Angeles Board of Education recently voted to reverse the requirement that a student maintain grades of "C" or above in order to engage in such school-related, extracurricular activities as sports and drama. The Board decided that a student could have one "D" or "F" and still engage in such activities. Write a well-organized, well-developed essay in which you agree or disagree with this ruling.

Essay

The recent ruling by the Los Angeles Board of Education, that a student may have one "D" or "F" and still engage in extracurricular activities is a sad testamonial to the state of our society today. Such misplaced emphasis as this ruling represents forms the backbone of the current down-spiraling of the level of education being offered at our public schools.

We live in a culture where Michael Jackson is far more recognized than the late Dr. Martin Luther King, Jr. Television has replaced books. Actors and popular sports figures are far more important to the general public than the important political figures in the world today. Education is not an emphasis. In the United States, money triumphs over knowledge; popularity eclipses ability. Our system of public education feeds this growing emphasis on such goals by glorifying athletics and failing to assert the importance of knowledge. The boards ruling serves to further uphold the importance of such extracurricular activities as sports and drama. Students may choose, and in some cases are encouraged, to forego studying in favor of practices, workouts, or rehearsals. It is reinforcement of this kind that by this action the Board is providing, and it is reinforcement of this kind that procreates the above named anomalies in the student communities of today.

Our schools are far from as effective as they could be. Teachers are underpaid in relation to other occupations in the workplace. Our society has become quite apathetic to public education in general, despite the common belief that a college education is a desirous, albeit monetarily profitable, thing. All of the most popular aspects of schooling in this nation (i.e., extracurricular activities) have formed a sort of leash by which those in control of these most sought after areas have gained control over most of the rest of each of their particular institutions. More money is spent on football gear and set decoration while out-of-date textbooks, worn and battered, clutter the shelves. The status quo proliferates. Those in control remain in control while others fade farther and farther into the background of the budget, the focus, the emphasis. The Board's ruling serves to do nothing but strengthen the position in which those who hold the leash now reside.

It is a sad society that relegates achievements of the mind to the job of one self alone. It is a sad school system that supports these sentiments. The Los Angeles Board of Education has done so; and all the football players and actors of the future will be examples not only of the result of this situation but also of its cause.

Your Comments

Paragraph 1:

Paragraph 2:

Paragraph 3:

Paragraph 4:

General Comments and Rating:

Reader Comments

Paragraph 1: Good introductory paragraph in that it addresses the question directly and states its thesis clearly. The effect is, however, spoiled to some degree by the confused metaphor: a "down-spiraling" would not have a "backbone."

Paragraph 2: Poor organization. This paragraph makes several complaints (repeated in the next paragraph) but handles each only sketchily, providing little specific supporting detail. "Procreate" is a wrong word choice, as is "anomalies." The logical point that the writer should make is that they are *not* anomalies.

Paragraph 3: This paragraph is partially off topic. It is not clear how the complaints pertain to the question of grading and extracurricular activities. The "leash" metaphor is poorly constructed and confusing.

Paragraph 4: The parallelism of "It is a sad . . ."/"It is a sad . . ." is effective. But the final sentence is vague and makes little sense as stated.

General Comments and Rating: The essay uses a reasonable four-paragraph organization: the first paragraph states a thesis, the second links the ruling with criticism of the values of the general culture, the third links the ruling with a decline of academic values in the schools, and the concluding paragraph brings together the two topics—society and the school system. However, the essay is badly marred by fuzzy diction and vagueness of message. This is a very marginal essay and would probably receive a lower-half grade.

ESSAY 3

Topic

The Los Angeles Board of Education recently voted to reverse the requirement that a student maintain grades of "C" or above in order to engage in such school-related, extracurricular activities as sports and drama. The Board decided that a student could have one "D" or "F" and still engage in such activities. Write a well-organized, well-developed essay in which you agree or disagree with this ruling.

Essay

Why do we send our kids to high school? One general answer that might be received is, "for education." Where does Joe's education start and pure pleasure begin? Recently the Los Angeles Board of Education reversed the rule of all students to have a "C" or above in all of their class to participate in extracurricular activities. Not only is this a reward for attending, but encourages the students to widen their horizons.

In the Los Angeles county, there has been a constant-struggle to keep kids in school. Not only to educate them, but also to keep them off the streets. By theory, it is great to only those with C's or better to enjoy the other facets of the school, but to blatantly ignore them until they receive proper grades is more harmful than helpful. Say Johnny wants to be a basketball player when he grows up, but his mathematics skills are not up to par. It is not fair to Johnny to disassociate him from his peers because he excels in every academic subject besides math.

There are other occasions for one poor grade besides the student and subject, there is the teacher. Especially in the LAUSD, where there is a shortage of teachers capable of teaching the subjects they were given. I went through the Los Angeles system and had college level math teacher explain beginning geometry. Needless to say, the teacher went over everyone's head from day one, and more than half of the class got lower than a C in the class.

One more aspect on why the school district should allow students with a non-passing grade participate in extracurricular activities is to keep them busy. Anyone who has made a shift in the amount of classes they take will note that the busier they are, the more efficient they become. When one balances out his or her time with many different forms of education or enjoyment-type activities, they learn to make the most of their time and in turn, concentrate more on their studies.

I still ask, "Why do we send our children to high school?" To get an education? To get an education in life, is my answer. In life, people mess up. People make mistakes or are put in a situation where it is close to impossible to succeed. Just because this happens in the real world does not mean we have all other forms of education, teamwork, and mental focusing are taken away. Just because a child gets one non-passing does not mean he is a failure, nor should be treated like one.

Your Comments

Paragraph 1:

Paragraph 2:

Paragraph 3:

Paragraph 4:

Paragraph 5:

General Comments and Rating:

Reader Comments

Paragraph 1: The point of the second sentence is unclear. Why is "education" necessarily opposed to "pure enjoyment"? Three of the four sentences in this paragraph are awkward or unclear.

Paragraph 2: The second sentence is a fragment. The third sentence is unclear; it has no connection with the first sentence of the paragraph. The last sentence is illogical, jumping without basis to a mention of disassociation from peers.

Paragraph 3: The first sentence is incorrectly structured; the second is a fragment. The point in this paragraph seems to be that poor teachers may be the cause of low grades, but the focus shifts from sentence to sentence, so the force of the argument is lost.

Paragraph 4: The meaning here is unclear. The writer first suggests that students should be kept "busy" and then suggests that the busier they are the more efficient they are—without saying what they are efficient at or how the two things connect. Nor does the writer make clear what is meant by "different forms of education."

Paragraph 5: Sentence 6 is nearly unintelligible. The final sentence effectively restates the position.

General Comments and Rating: The essay is riddled with awkward and ungrammatical constructions. The organization is *potentially* effective. If the writer had used clear topic sentences and planned more carefully, the essay might have succeeded. But because of the consistent problems here, this essay would probably receive a lower-half score.

ESSAY 4

Topic

The Los Angeles Board of Education recently voted to reverse the requirement that a student maintain grades of "C" or above in order to engage in such school-related, extracurricular activities as sports and drama. The Board decided that a student could have one "D" or "F" and still engage in such activities. Write a well-organized, well-developed essay in which you agree or disagree with this ruling.

Essay

The Los Angeles Board of Education's recent decision to reverse their policy which banned students with a grade below a "C" from extracurricular activities is a positive step towards keeping minority students in school, and improving the overall education of students in general.

Considering that the Los Angeles County High School drop out rate is close to forty percent, it just cannot make any sense to deny a student who is failing one class the right to participate in the one thing which may keep them in school: extracurricular activities like sports. Many high school students of all races could be encouraged to stay in school by being allowed to participate in sports.

Sports give a young person a sense of accomplishment and a feeling of belonging to the group. Both these positive feelings need to be nurtured for the potential drop-out to stay in school.

What is a drop-out? Merely a person who suffers from low self esteem, fueled by successive failures. The sense of well-being that comes from mastery of an athletic skill is just the confidence builder a young, developing mind needs to learn to tough it out in all of life's arenas, including the classroom.

For some high school males, the prestige which accompanies playing on the school team could be one of the few bright spots in their lives. It would be wrong to take it away.

The team spirit fostered by groups of young people while playing together helps to develop trust, cooperation, and a sense of responsibility to the group something essential to building the community. The entire concept of school extracurricular activities is to develop the socialization skills, the skills which are lacking in the high school drop-out. It is no surprise that such dejected youths would quit school altogether if they were denied the social pleasure and prestiege of participation in the schools group events.

Minority students who are dropping out could be encouraged to stay by the possibility of playing sports. Not only varsity sports, which can only accommodate the best athletes, but inter- and intra-mural programs which accommodate all skill levels, could be seen to significantly affect the drop-out figures now that students can stay and play despite a low grade. This is a serious social problem which needs to be addressed. Young people of inner-city need to be drawn away from the attractions of street-life, crime, and drugs. What they need is an outlet to channel their tremendous energies of adolescence; sports are the answer. A boring history or math class won't win out over the glitz of fast money and chemical highs, but sports can.

Even the middle-class students can benefit from the reversal of this assine rule. If an aspiring computer programmer or electrical engineer who also plays sports decides not to take a hard calculus class because he may jeapordize his right to play ball, his or her education has been hampered by a rule whose intention was originally to make jocks study. With the change of the rule, an academically successful athlete won't be discouraged from challenging him or herself in search of their full potential.

It is depressing to think of how many young lives were adversely affected by the discriminatory policy. How many energetic, but confused youths of Los Angeles were balancing precariously on the dividing line between school-life and street-life, when they were pushed into making the wrong choice by an irrational rule which took away the only positive aspect which kept them in school? It is about time this policy relaxed, less young students of tomorrow suffer the same fate.

Your Comments

Paragraph 1:

Paragraph 2:

Paragraph 3:

Paragraph 4:

Paragraph 5:

Paragraph 6:

Paragraph 7:

Paragraph 8:

Paragraph 9:

General Comments and Rating:

Reader Comments

Paragraph 1: Effective introduction which addresses the question and states a position clearly.

Paragraph 2: States the central thesis—the need to cut the drop-out rate. The writer makes good use of evidence.

Paragraph 3: This paragraph needs development with specific examples.

Paragraph 4: This is simply repetition of the general point. The paragraph needs examples.

Paragraph 5: Another undeveloped paragraph. Better planning could have improved the organization here and avoided repetition.

Paragraph 6: The argument that extracurricular activities keep potential drop-outs in school and help them develop social skills is a logical one.

Paragraph 7: This paragraph is also somewhat repetitive. The need to draw inner-city youth away from the streets might better have been handled in a separate paragraph. The assumption that "minority" students necessarily equate with "inner-city" students is not logical.

Paragraph 8: Makes a strong point—that generally capable student athletes might be deterred from taking challenging courses for fear of a bad grade. However, the assumption that capable students are necessarily "middle-class" is also illogical.

Paragraph 9: Strong close. The writer is effective in language use in "were balancing . . . were pushed."

General Comments and Rating: The sentences are generally clear and grammatical, with only minor spelling and punctuation problems. The essay is, however, undermined by an accumulation of trite expressions ("positive step," "make any sense," "sense of accomplishment," "sense of well-being," "tough it out," "suffer the same fate"). The organization is adequate, but the essay would benefit from the deletion of paragraphs that are repetitive and the expansion of other paragraphs with more specific detail. This essay would clearly receive a passing grade but not the highest.

ESSAY TOPICS FOR PRACTICE

The following sample topics are provided to give you practice. They are categorized into the four general types:

You may wish to focus on the particular topic type(s) appropriate to your program.

- Descriptive/Narrative
- Analytical/Expository
- Compare/Contrast
- Argument/Persuasion

DESCRIPTIVE/NARRATIVE

Topic 1

"Youth is wasted on the young."

The old adage seems to imply that young people don't appreciate youth, that they take for granted their energy, their good health, and their many years left to live.

Consider someone you know who is young. Describe your observations of his or her behavior, and explain how that behavior either affirms or contradicts the above quotation. Discuss whether or not you would feel comfortable behaving in such a manner.

Topic 2

Currently, many college students seem to feel that, having worked hard during the school year, they deserve to be able to "let loose" during their spring break. In fact, recent excesses of college students during spring break parties have resulted in vandalism and arrests, and many therefore have urged this practice of spring break be discontinued.

Write an essay in which you

1. Identify the current situation.
2. Describe any changes you would make.
3. Explain what results you would expect to occur from these changes.

Topic 3

Write a fully developed essay of no less than 300 words on the topic below. During writing, remember to keep to your thesis.

While we are still children, we are taught how to do hundreds of things. We are taught how to tie our shoelaces, to brush our teeth, to ride a bike, to mow the lawn, to read, and to write. Some of us are taught how to swim, to dance, to play piano, to speak a new language, or to ride a horse.

Write an essay in which you describe some activity or skill that you were not taught as a child but now wish you had been. Discuss what the value would be to you or others if you had been taught it.

Topic 4

It has been said that each of us is not an owner, but a caretaker, of this earth. We do not possess the world and its resources, but rather our task is to hold them in safekeeping for the generations which follow.

Write an essay in which you

1. Describe some resource which you feel warrents protection for future generations.
2. Explain how that resource has, or has not, been adequately protected.
3. Tell how you would advise future generations to best care for that particular resource.

Topic 5

A Chinese philosopher, in explaining that learning best occurs when the student is actively involved, once wrote

> I hear, and I forget.
> I see, and I remember.
> I do, and I understand.

Write an essay in which you

1. Describe one experience you had in school in which learning the material was particularly difficult.

2. Explain why it was so difficult to learn the material.
3. Tell how you might have changed that situation to make learning the material easier.

Topic 6

A noted essayist once wrote

"Many good movies help you escape from your troubles; a few great ones help you face them."

Write an essay in which you

1. Describe a movie which had a strong influence on you.
2. Explain how your viewing of this movie influenced your viewpoint.
3. Tell why you think this movie had such a significant effect on you.

Topic 7

A celebrated essayist once wrote

"Send yourself packing! Traveling to new places is the surest cure for chronic boredom."

Write an essay in which you

1. Describe a place you have visited which has made a strong impression on you.
2. Explain how visiting this place influenced your attitudes or views.
3. Tell why you think this place had such a strong impact on you.

Topic 8

Describe a situation in your life when you had difficulty making a particular choice. Examples: deciding which college to attend, deciding which automobile to purchase with your savings, deciding what to buy as a gift for a special friend, etc.

• Describe the choice you had to make and why it was difficult to make it.
• Tell what you finally decided and the outcome of your decision.

Topic 9

Describe a time in your life when something changed your life for the better. Examples: learning to dance made it easier for you when attending dances, getting the braces removed from your teeth made you less self-concious, getting your first automobile made dating more fun.

- Describe what happened.
- Tell how it made your life better.

Topic 10

It has been said that we learn more from our worst enemies than from out closest friends. Our friends usually mirror our values, our likes and dislikes; our friends tend to share out beliefs and our prejudices. Our enemies, however, are usually different from us in important aspects. While we certainly may not wish to emulate our enemies, we can observe their behavior, values, and ideas which are quite different from ours and, in doing so, have a better perspective on our own behavior, values, and ideas.

Write a clear and fully developed essay giving an example or examples which demonstrate what this statement means:

"We learn more from our worst enemies than from our closest friends."

Your example(s) might be taken from your personal experiences or drawn from situations you have heard or read about.

In your essay you should

1. Describe your experience(s) or example(s) with specific details.
2. Explain why or how your example(s) or experience(s) show what the statement means.

Topic 11

It has been said that wishing for something and not getting it can be upsetting, but wishing for something and actually getting it may be even more upsetting. Some people, for example, may wish to be financially wealthy and then, through circumstances, find that being wealthy creates even bigger problems for them. Others may wish for a love relationship with a certain person and find that once they've attained that relationship, it unfortunately isn't what they envisioned it to be.

Write a clear and fully developed essay giving an example or examples which demonstrate what this statement means:

"Wishing for something and getting it can sometimes be more upsetting than wishing for something and not getting it."

Your example(s) might be taken from your personal experiences or drawn from situations you have heard or read about.

In your essay you should

1. Describe the experience(s) or example(s) with specific details.
2. Explain why or how the example(s) or experience(s) show what the statement means.

Topic 12

Most of us would love to have the power to change things—either in our own life situation or in the world in general. Imagine you had the power to alter one event in history. What would you change?

Choose one particularly historic event that you would change if you could. Write a well-organized essay in which you describe the event as it occurred, how you would change it, and the impact of those changes.

Topic 13

Issue: Television affects our lives in a variety of ways.

Directions: Write an essay in which you examine the effects of television upon society or upon private lives.

(Students from other countries may choose to refer to their experiences in their own countries in answering this question.)

Topic 14

Identify an instructor you have had whose teaching style you wished were different. Write a well-organized essay in which you explain that instructor's teaching style, the way(s) in which you would have it be different, and the reasons these changes are desirable.

Topic 15

Artists and writers occasionally compare people to animals. Because of a particular quality or qualities, some human beings are described as lions; others are depicted as mice. Stories and novels have envisioned people as eagles, or foxes, or rabbits.

Think of a person you know well, and choose an animal this person most resembles. The resemblance should not be based upon appearance, but upon their most striking qualities or characteristics.

You have two tasks:

• Describe that person and his or her most striking qualities.
• Explain how those qualities would lead you to depict that person as a certain animal.

Topic 16

We all have had the occasion to say to someone, "I know what you are going through. The same thing happened to me." Imagine you are writing a handbook to help people understand and cope with a difficult life situation which you have already experienced. Be sure to choose a life situation which, although difficult for you, you managed to overcome. You may choose from any number of common life situations—such as the death of a relative, the break-up of a relationship, the transition from high school to college, or the trauma of being fired from a job.

You have two tasks:

• Describe the difficult life experience you faced.
• Explain in detail how you could assist, advise, and encourage someone who is undergoing a similar experience.

Topic 17

We all wish now and again that things might go back to the way they were "in the good old days." Consider one present-day activity or practice which you feel was handled or carried out better in the past. You may choose anything from how advertisers sell products or how politicians campaign for office to how professional athletes conduct business or how couples approach dating and courtship.

You have two tasks:

- Describe the present-day practice and also how it used to be carried out or handled.
- Explain in detail how you would go about bringing back or renewing the past practice.

Topic 18

A writer once wrote, "It is a rare person who has no regrets." Think of an incident or time, either in your own life or in history, which you regret having occurred.

You have two tasks:

- Describe the incident or time which you regret.
- Explain in detail how you would have changed your behavior or (if it were possible) the behavior of others to alter that particular incident or time.

Topic 19

You will be asked to write one essay on an assigned topic, to test how well you can write, not how much you know. The topic calls for an essay in which you try to convince the reader to accept a particular argument or point of view. You are expected to assemble and organize examples, facts, and details to make your argument or point of view clear and convincing. You may also draw upon personal experiences and observations to support your points.

The topic:

It has often been said that "misery loves company." For this essay, select one time in your life, or someone else's life, when you or another was feeling particularly depressed and wanted the company of another or others.

There are no restrictions on whom you choose or why that person was feeling so low, except that whoever was feeling sad wanted the company of others.

You might select a time when you or another was physically ill, had been disappointed by an event or another person, and so on.

The purpose of your essay is not merely to describe but to demonstrate how "company" (being with others) helped someone who, for whatever reasons, felt miserable. In developing your argument, you should use as many specific details as possible.

Topic 20

Identify a particular law which you would either enact or repeal if you had such power. Explain how and to what extent this law's being enacted or repealed would benefit society.

Topic 21

Write a paper describing a particular location which had a significant impact on your college life (for example, the gym where you spent hours training, the student union where you worked, the movie theatre in town where you spent your spare hours, the school newspaper offices where you edited the school paper, the computer room where you wrote most of your papers, etc.). Explain how and to what extent this particular location affected your college years.

Topic 22

It has often been said that a good way to measure whether a particular college stimulates learning would not be to analyze the curriculum taught, but rather to eavesdrop on the student conversations in the dormitories and student center.

How effectively do campus conversations reflect the learning occurring on campus? How would you evaluate the quality of conversations you have had on campus? Are they indicative of the quality of your education?

Topic 23

Someone once wrote that the impact of a teacher depends as much on fortuitous timing as on a teacher's talents. For instance, if a student has an inspirational instructor during the particular time when that student needs inspiration, that teacher will be important for that student. But that same teacher may have little effect on another student who at that time in his or her life may need something else—for example, discipline or a challenge. Thus it is foolish to judge a teacher's worth solely on talent.

How has timing affected a particular teacher's impact on you? How would you evaluate the different impacts teachers have had on you during your school years? Was the importance of certain teachers in your life as much affected by timing as by the teachers' individual talents?

Topic 24

"Law is the protector of the weak."

—Frederick Schiller

It has been said that "justice is blind"—that the law treats everyone as equal, whether rich or poor, black or white, young or old. If that's true, the weak can certainly see the law as their protector. However, some people maintain that the law, as it is practiced in the United States, is actually the tool of the rich and mighty.

Reflect on your own observations of the law. In a well-organized essay, identify one situation, discuss its effects, and explain how it supports, or doesn't support, the quotation above.

ANALYTICAL/EXPOSITORY

Topic 1

Write a fully developed essay of no less than 300 words on the topic below. During writing, remember to keep to your thesis.

Many young people still enjoy hard rock music, and their parents still cannot understand why. Also, an increasing number of parents are getting worried about their children's music heroes. In recent months, there has been renewed controversy over the effects of hard rock music on young listeners. Parents of a Nevada teenager claim that their son shot himself because he listened to "subliminal," or buried, messages about death in a rock band's recorded music.

Write an essay in which you discuss why you believe rock music continues to be popular with young audiences and explain whether or not you believe hard rock music has any harmful effects on listeners.

Topic 2

Most people like to believe that if they have talent and work hard, they will be recognized for their ability and effort and duly rewarded. Write an essay in which you discuss your views about what it takes to get ahead. Make sure that you consider how much of getting ahead depends on knowing the "right" people and taking advantage of connections.

Topic 3

"Time is our most precious commodity, for once it is lost, it can never be regained."

In a well-organized essay explain how—because of people's different behaviors—time can appear to be precious to some but seemingly not to others. Explain how some people may use time better than others. Support your statements by citing specific examples.

Topic 4

Many people claim that any organization, business, or even community is like a living organism. It has its own "brain," or command center, its own means of protecting and defending itself, its own hungers and desires.

For this essay, select an organization, business, or community that you feel can be compared to a living organism. In your essay, use specific examples to show how your choice reflects many of the functions and activities of a living organism. You may consider other functions besides those mentioned above.

The purpose of your essay is not only to describe the activities of that particular organization, business, or community, but also to demonstrate how those activities are similar to those of a living organism.

Topic 5

Recently, a newspaper was critical of California's lottery. Its editorial stated that the average lottery-ticket buyer is poor and, while a few do hit the jackpot, the overwhelming majority of them are just tossing their money away on the extremely slim chance of hitting it big. Their money, the newspaper said, would be more wisely put into savings.

Writing Assignment:
• Do you agree or disagree with the newspaper's editorial?
• Explain your reasons.
• Provide examples to support your view.

Topic 6

A noted educator once remarked that most children learn "in spite of school." What he meant was that our public educational system actually discourages true learning but that most students learn despite the school's influence.

Writing Assignment:

• Do you agree or disagree with the statement?

• Explain your reasons.

• Provide examples to support your view.

Topic 7

Passage to Consider:

A recent study of American attitudes about the environment found that 71% of those polled responded that the environment must be protected even at the cost of increased spending and higher taxes. Also in the same poll, 56% responded that the environment must be protected even it it means jobs in the local community are lost. Despite this apparently overwhelming concern for protecting the environment, America's elected leaders consistently vote in favor of industry to the detriment of the environment. In fact, the first major congressional bill in ten years on "Clean Air" was considerably weakened as senators appeased the concerns of big industry, either because of special interests in their local districts or because of the influence of PAC money donated to their campaigns.

Directions for Writing:

Discuss one or more of the problems—either human or political— revealed above, and how lawmakers, or citizens, might address them.

Topic 8

Passage to Consider:

A recent study has indicated that the American dream of owning one's own home will not be possible for most of the next generation of college students. Not only have prices of homes skyrocketed in the past decade, but also the earning power of the average American worker is actually decreasing in comparison to the incomes of twenty years ago, relative to inflation. Even those families with two wage earners will be hard pressed to afford housing in most American metropolitan areas in the coming decades. In fact, the expense and difficulty of finding good child care will require one parent to stay home and tend to the children, making it even more difficult for those families to afford to own their own homes.

Directions for Writing:

Discuss one or more of the problems revealed above, and how elected representatives, or citizens, might address them in order to make home ownership more available to average Americans.

Topic 9

Passage to Consider:

The business of pet care in the United States is worth over $12 billion. Around half of the money goes to feeding our dearly beloved dogs, cats, fish, and other animals we call pets. The fact is, we spend nearly $4 billion more on pet food than we do on baby food. If we figure in the price of medical care for cats and dogs, our grand total now approaches $17 billion. $1.7 billion more goes into the purchase of pet gear.

Directions for Writing:

Discuss what this passage reveals about U.S. attitudes toward pets and evaluate whether spending billions of dollars on pet care is justified in a society with many neglected social needs.

Topic 10

Passage to Consider:

Travel industry experts predict that in the 1990s it will be more common for American vacationers to take short-term, adventure-oriented trips. Travelers also will seek out more remote locations; many will prefer vacations in Fiji to those in Hawaii. Furthermore, although American travelers will still enjoy a bargain, they won't skimp on comfort or mind paying for some frills.

Directions for Writing:

Discuss what you believe are the societal or other reasons which could account for the American travel patterns and preferences described in the passage.

Topic 11

In an essay of at least 500 words (three to four pages), write a clear, well-organized response to the following:

It used to be the director's job to yell, "Cut!" But now it's the movie censor's. Films have been exploitive—racier and grittier only in order to sell more tickets. Therefore, we need the censor to put a stop to this subversion of values.

However, critics of film censorship claim that the new Hollywood is only doing what it has always done: holding a mirror up to society. Since the times have changed, so must the movies. Therefore, the censor has no place in American films.

For your essay, explain whether or not you believe American films are more exploitive now because of the desire to increase ticket sales or because their creators sincerely wish to examine and depict modern society. Choose one or more films that reflect this new look to argue either for or against having movie censors.

Topic 12

It is estimated that almost eight million children in the United States suffer from some form of mental distress or disorder. Between 1980 and 1986, there was a nearly forty percent increase in admissions of children and teenagers to psychiatric hospitals. Many researchers say the reason for these alarming statistics is that children are not able to deal with the pressures of living in today's society.

In your essay, briefly describe what you believe to be the single greatest pressure a child must face in growing up, explain the remedy you would offer to help the child cope with the pressure, and explain why you believe your remedy would be effective.

COMPARE/CONTRAST

Topic 1

Please read and think about the following two quotations:

(A) "Any homeless person could get a job if he really wanted to work."

(B) "Most homeless people were once normal working citizens who were let down by society."

Write an essay in three parts on the above two statements as follows:

1. Compare the statements. Explain how the two statements are similar or share things in common.
2. Contrast the statements. Explain how the two statements differ.
3. Take a position with respect to the two statements by defending one of them or mediating between them, and justify your defense with an example from your own observation or experience.

Topic 2

Please read and think about the following two quotations:

(A) "Legalizing the use of marijuana in this country would be equivalent to promoting its use."

(B) "If marijuana use were made legal, companies would rush to have their marijuana cigarette be the first commercially available one on the market."

Write an essay on the above two statements in three parts as follows:

1. Compare the statements. Explain how the two statements are similar or share things in common.
2. Contrast the statements. Explain how the two statements differ.
3. Take a position with respect to the two statements by defending one of them or mediating between them, and justify your defense with an example from your own observation or experience.

Topic 3

Some students say that attending a local community college is tantamount to not attending college at all, that community college is more like an extension of high school.

Write an essay describing your personal feelings about the above statement. In it, compare and contrast the experiences one might encounter in a high school and a community college.

Topic 4

Japanese and U.S. business styles, although they have some similarities, also are said to differ in certain basic ways. While the American ethic promotes independence of thought and entrepreneurial flair, the Japanese value loyalty to company and group consensus. While American businesses concentrate on marketing and sales, Japanese companies place an equal, if not greater, value on production and on research and development.

Write an essay comparing and contrasting the two business styles and the results each is likely to achieve. Include your personal feelings about the effectiveness or lack of effectiveness of each style.

Topic 5

Please read and think about the following two quotations:

(A) "Save for a rainy day."

(B) "Sacrificing for the future is fine for many, but for some of us, it may never come. Enjoy the present, for it is the only thing of which we *all* are certain."

Write an essay on the above two statements in three parts, as follows:

1. Compare the two statements. Explain what they may have in common and how they may overlap.
2. Contrast the statements. Explain how the two statements differ.
3. Take a position with regard to the two statements by choosing one or mediating between them, and support your view with an example from your own observations or experience.

Topic 6

This examination is based on two essays: Mary Stewart Van Leeuwen, "A View from Other Cultures: Must Men Fear 'Women's Work'?"; and Debbie Taylor, "Domestic Chores Weren't Always Women's Work." It is expected that you have already read the essays and will incorporate ideas and quotations from them into your written examination.

You will have two hours for planning, writing, revising, and proofreading your essay response to the writing topic. Be sure to respond to all aspects of the topic. Responses that do not cover each aspect with care will not pass, even if portions of your essay are well written.

Your essay will be graded with respect to your

1. Ability to distill your understanding of the essays into a written summary, to analyze the essays critically, and to incorporate ideas and passages from the essays into your own essay.
2. Ability to compose a coherent essay in which you develop and support a central idea.
3. Ability to make proper use of source material: to use an established and consistent format for documenting your sources and to use quotations to reinforce your ideas, not to replace them.
4. Ability to deal directly with a specific topic in clear prose free of mechanical or grammatical errors which would impede one's reading.

Writing topic: Briefly summarize the main points made in each essay and compare how each writer explains men's reluctance to share more responsibility for domestic work with women. Giving (and documenting) specific citations from the essays, discuss how at least two of the theories of male dominance given in Van Leeuwen's essay can be used to explain certain historical occurrences related by Taylor in her essay. Finally, discuss to what extent men and women can and should transform their own gender roles.

A VIEW FROM OTHER CULTURES: MUST MEN FEAR "WOMEN'S WORK"?

Anthropologists have found that around the world whatever is considered "men's work" is almost universally given higher status than "women's work." If in one culture it is men who build houses and women who make baskets, then that culture will see house-building as more important. In another culture, perhaps right next door, the reverse may be true, and basket-weaving will have a higher social status than house-building. Anthropologists agree that biology is not a sufficient explanation of male dominance. Following are three different theories anthropologists have suggested to account for the universality of male dominance and female subordination.

Nature Versus Culture: In all cultures women are seen as closer to nature than men, whereas men are seen as more involved with culture than women. Since the culture is universally valued more than the merely natural, women, by being closer to nature, are therefore devalued.

Women are considered closer to nature than men because their bodies share the same reproductive functions as nonhuman female mammals. These involve more time, energy, and bodily risk than men's reproductive role. Men therefore have more freedom and energy to invest in technology, trade, games, arts, politics, and religion.

And since women spend more time with young children, who are born incontinent and unsocialized and thus seem more like animals, women are also seen as more connected to nature because of their care of "unacculturated" children. Because of this, women are often seen as more "childlike" themselves.

Domestic Versus Public: Although women's reproductive activities do not inevitably force them to keep their activities close to home, women are more apt than men to do domestic tasks that are easily combined with child care. For the same reason men are more likely to engage in "public" activities that take them out of the home and away from the children. These public, male-dominated activities almost always have commanded more cultural respect than the domestic, less visible activities of women.

Object Relations and Family Life: Psychologists have traced the process by which children become aware of being male or female. It is not until around age three that a child is able to reason that he or she is either a boy or a girl, and always will be. From that time on, one of a child's developmental tasks is to become emotionally secure and happy about being either a boy or a girl.

Here is where the role of mothers as almost exclusive child rearers begins to matter. Both little girls and little boys are naturally attracted by the nurturance and apparent power of the mother, and want to be like her. But a little boy soon finds out that he can't grow up to be like Mommy. He must be like Daddy—the big male person he sees only a short time mornings and evenings.

The boy is caught in a double-bind in that he cannot stay attached to his mother, yet his role model for imitation is largely absent. Thus his sense of being securely male is less solid and he may nurse deep and unconscious doubts about his ability to cope with the male role.

But as the boy grows older, he begins to realize that being male is supposed to be a privilege, and if men are "real men" they are socially more important than women. Already somewhat insecure in his masculinity, he must now try all the harder to prove to himself and the world that he is a real man.

How to do this? The safest way is to have as little to do with women and their activities as possible, to repress and deny any "womanly" qualities or impulses in himself. In extreme cases he may do this by openly scorning or even mistreating women. Or a man may simply avoid women except when he has domestic and sexual needs to be filled, spending the rest of his time in visibly and exclusively male groups. Or paradoxically, he may idealize women, "placing them on a pedestal." This too keeps them at a safe distance, but is often accompanied by impossible demands of "womanly perfection" from them as well.

In some cultures, men may seesaw between attitudes of scorn and idealization, a common feature of the "machismo" cult in many Latin American societies. In such cultures, aggressive displays of masculinity may alternate with reverence for the Virgin Mary and heavy-handedness toward the women in one's own family.

Whatever strategies are used, they allow an insecure man to mask what amounts to an unconscious "dread of women." His earliest associations are still of a mother who seemed all-powerful. When combined with his early deprivation of an available male role model, the result may be a deeply repressed yet powerful conviction that women can somehow strip him of his masculine identity.

In this way we can see how masculine insecurity perpetuates itself from generation to generation. The underfathered boy develops a fragile, ambivalent male identity. To compensate for this insecurity in adolescence and adulthood, he distances himself from women and "women's work." And what is most obviously women's work? Caring for young children. So he avoids nurturing contact with his own sons and unwittingly contributes to *their* development of insecure masculinity, dread of women, and woman-rejecting behavior.

Is there any escape from this vicious circle? Since cultures differ in the extent to which they emphasize the private/public split, it may be instructive to look at one culture that minimizes the gender roles between men and women. I will draw on my own research experience with the Pygmy nation of Central Africa, who live as hunter-gatherers.

Among the Pygmy there are some gender role differences, but the smallness and mobility of the group require close cooperation among all members. Women and children help with some of the hunting, and a woman can call on her husband to care for an infant while she is cooking. Grandparents of both sexes care for toddlers while both parents hunt and gather. Here the public/private split has very little relevance.

Of particular interest is the fact that hunter-gatherers' flexibility in gender roles and cooperation is accompanied by greater intellectual similarity between men and women.

What can we learn from this about our own situation? Some cultural anthropologists say that it is imperative to move in two different directions: Men must be integrated into the domestic sphere, sharing the socialization of children and performing domestic tasks; and women must participate equally with men in the public world of work and culture. Only then can women's status be elevated.

Such changes do not turn men into women and women into

men. What is vital in upgrading the status of women's work is not eliminating the presence of gender roles, but rather the degree of proximity, cooperation, and role flexibility that men and women share. In fact, even when men and women do perform a common task—such as child care—they approach it rather differently, and many of these stylistic differences turn out to be very much worth preserving.

DOMESTIC CHORES WEREN'T ALWAYS WOMEN'S WORK

In January 1973 a young criminal named Paul Giles was ordered by a British magistrate to clean an elderly person's house as a punishment for his offense. On hearing this, women around the world might be forgiven for wondering just what heinous crimes *they* must have committed to justify their life sentences of housework.

Women in the industrialized world did not gather together over tea one afternoon and agree to work unpaid at cleaning, cooking, laundry, child care, and nursing out of the sheer kindness of their hearts. No, they were given little choice. They were, as Ivan Illich put it, "flattered and threatened, by capitalist and cleric" into their current situation.

A number of authors have investigated the history of housework and have discovered that the housewife role is a very recent one indeed—and confined to industrialized societies. As sociologist Anne Oakley put it: "Other cultures may live in families but they do not necessarily have housewives. They have women, men, and children whose labor is woven together to create a home and livelihood for the whole family."

As a woman in Kenya, for instance, starts to untie the shawl securing a baby to her back so she can wield her hoe with more freedom among the maize stalks, another child will be there to take the baby from her. While she works, her daughters will be pounding sorghum and fetching water for the evening meal, her sons driving goats and cattle to fresh grazing, her husband sinking wooden poles into the ground for a new house.

All of these activities are work, but those that we would term housework are so intricately interwoven with agriculture that it is difficult to tease them apart. The growing of food and the growing of children are both vital to the family's survival. Without children the food cannot be grown; without food there can be no children. Who would dare make the judgment that holding your youngest baby on your lap is less important than weeding a few more yards in the maize field? Yet this is the judgment our society makes constantly. Production—of autos, canned soup, advertising copy—is important. Housework—cleaning, feeding, and caring—is unimportant. How did this degradation of domestic work come about? And how is it that women in our societies are expected to do all this work alone?

Well, according to Oakley, Illich, and other historians, this situation set in with the growth of the cities, factories, and mines in the early 19th century. By 1850 half of the United Kingdom population were living in cities. In those days factory and mine owners did not care who did their work for them and hired whole families to dig coal or weave cloth in the textile mills. It might have continued that way, too, except for two reasons.

First was the extraordinarily high infant mortality rate in the dreadful city slums where the workers lived. This came about largely because attention to domestic chores among the new proletariat had been reduced to an absolute minimum, crowded out by the demands of wage labor. Babies were left untended in filthy hovels with no water or sanitation and weaned onto gruel as soon as they were born, to free their mothers for work in the factories. The general "condition of the working class" became a cause for serious concern among capitalists. Malnourished, disease-ridden, stunted, and crippled by the conditions in which they lived, the workers were less and less able to do a good day's work.

Meanwhile, as machines became efficient, fewer workers were needed to work them—which was the second factor contributing to the creation of the housewife.

(At this point the story starts to read like a conspiracy—though, in fact, capitalism tends to operate more by trial and error, rather like Darwinian evolution, with the "fittest," by which I mean the most cost-effective for capitalists, economic arrangements surviving.) It turned out that the most cost-effective way to run a work force was to remove women from the factories and put them to work on improving the conditions in their homes. This had the added advantage that only one wage would need to be paid—to the man of the house—to support a working-class family.

Both women and men protested vigorously; the women because they were accustomed to providing for themselves; the men because they resented being made suddenly responsible for their wives and children (compulsory education and child labor laws had barred children, too, from the factories). "The plebeians rioted," says Illich. "And the crowd was led, more often than not, by its women."

The rioting went on until what Illich mischievously calls "the enclosure of women"—the transformation of women into house-wives—was completed. In 1737, more than 98 percent of married women in England worked outside the home. By 1911, more than 90 percent were employed solely as housewives. And this pattern was repeated throughout the industrialized world.

Perhaps if women had enjoyed the support of their men from the beginning, they might have been able to resist the pressures on them to provide free domestic services. But the industrial revolution created a split between working-class men and women by, as Illich put it, "making working men wardens of their domestic women." A similar antagonism between the sexes can be observed today in developing countries where the introduction of cash crops and wage labor has given men—but not women—access to money. The men feel the money is theirs; the women resent their lack of control over the family's income.

Today the carrots and sticks used to force women into domestic work are no longer necessary. We are trained for specific gender roles from the day we are born. So powerful is our training that even the massive influx of women back into the labor force in recent years has had little effect on the division of labor in our homes.

This is because women are trained to *take care* of their loved ones. This means that the housewife role includes much more than the sheer drudgery of providing clean socks. It is also a cool hand on a feverish forehead in the early hours; boiling his eggs exactly the way he likes them; flowers on the table; organizing a treasure hunt for Easter eggs. . . . Domestic labor has become fused in our minds with love.

It is probably not necessary to point out here that *men* do not appear to have the same problem with limiting their devotion. While this is lamentable in many ways, there is a part (a very small part) of me that sympathizes with them. Men perceive that equating love and domestic work is a trap. They fear that to get involved with housework would send them hurtling into the bottomless pit of self-sacrifice that is women's current caring role. As soon as they do attempt a smidgin of housework, they often find themselves caught up in a wrangle with women about "standards" of cleanliness—a wrangle that is really about deciding when enough is enough. If housework really were only about providing clean socks, then men *might* be more prepared to do their share.

Women have to unpick this confusion of domestic labor (which has its limits) and love. This is not to suggest that we should stop loving. Just that we should stop equating loving with unpaid domestic service as if the two were interchangeable. Ironing shirts yet more perfectly does not increase the sum of human happiness.

Topic 7

This examination is based on two essays: Michael Castleman, "Cures for the Common Cold: A Consumer Guide" and Dana Ullman, "The Revival of Homeopathy." It is expected that you have already read the essays and will incorporate ideas and quotations from them into your written examination.

You will have two hours for planning, writing, revising, and proofreading your essay response to the writing topic. Be sure to respond to all aspects of the topic. Responses that do not cover each aspect with care will not pass, even if portions of your essay are well written.

Your essay will be graded with respect to your

1. Ability to distill your understanding of the essays into a written summary, to analyze the essays critically, and to incorporate ideas and passages from the essays into your own essay.
2. Ability to compose a coherent essay in which you develop and support a central idea.

3. Ability to make proper use of source material: to use an established and consistent format for documenting your sources and to use quotations to reinforce your ideas, not to replace them.
4. Ability to deal directly with a specific topic in clear prose free of mechanical or grammatical errors which would impede one's reading.

Writing topic: Briefly summarize the main points made in each essay and compare how homeopathic medicine differs from conventional medicine in its response to illness. Giving (and documenting) specific citations from the essays, discuss what you perceive to be the major differences in aims and approaches between "orthodox," or conventional, medicine and alternative medicine. Discuss the dangers which each author associates with alternative approaches to medicine; then state whether you believe that either author would discourage readers from using alternative medicine. Finally, discuss the claim made by futurists that "21st century medicine will include new and more powerful drugs and various innovative technological interventions," and give reasons why this may or may not be a hopeful future.

CURES FOR THE COMMON COLD: A CONSUMER GUIDE

There's an old saying that, if left untreated, colds last a week, but when treated aggressively, they clear up in just seven days. Such pessimism is understandable. Most cold remedies spell relief. Yet even hardened cynics rarely leave their colds untreated.

According to orthodox medicine, there is no cure for the common cold. Although practitioners of alternative healing arts would disagree, the standard medical view is that the only real cure is time. Over a week or so, the immune system attacks, contains, and finally defeats the cold virus. In the meantime, orthodox medicine's goal is "symptomatic relief"—alleviation of discomfort until the body heals itself.

The vast majority of colds may be treated safely at home without consulting a health professional. However, good medical self-care involves recognizing situations that call for a physician. People over age 70 or under 10, those who are pregnant or nursing, or who have heart disease, asthma, emphysema, diabetes, serious allergies, liver or kidney disease, a history of stroke, or other significant health problems should consult a physician before using the remedies discussed here.

The Over-the-Counter Cold Medicine Remedy

When colds strike, millions of Americans immediately reach for an over-the-counter (OTC) cold medicine. Especially popular are the heavily advertised, multisymptom cold formulas. Americans spend more than $1 billion a year on these products, but *none* of the cold researchers or clinical authorities I consulted recommended them—including the Food and Drug Administration (FDA) 1976 Advisory Review Panel on Over-the-Counter Cold, Cough, and Allergy Products. The experts unanimously recommend single-symptom generic drugs. Single-action generics cost much less and pose no risk of side effects from extra drugs that are unnecessary for the cold sufferer's specific symptoms.

Single-symptom over-the-counter drugs—especially generic drugs sold under their chemical names instead of the more familiar brand names—can save you a great deal of money. The cost of advertising a multisymptom cold formula is incorporated into its price. Today it's easier than ever to buy generic drugs—which are as pure and effective as their brand-name counterparts—for *25 to 90 percent less*.

"Effectiveness" of cold medications is a matter of sometimes passionately divided opinion. Some FDA-approved cold remedies—dextromethorphan for cough, for example—are backed by usassailable evidence of effectiveness. But others—for example, antihistamines—are surprisingly controversial; they may or may not be effective. FDA approval hinges more on safety than effectiveness.

Any cold symptom might signal an illness more serious than the common cold. Over-the-counter cold remedies should not be used more frequently or at higher doses than their packaging indicates.

Beware of the many cough medicines that contain both an expectorant (typically guaifenesin or terpin hydrate) and a cough suppressant (codeine or dextromethorphan). This is an irrational drug combination. The expectorant is supposed to make respiratory mucus easier to cough up; the cough suppressant stops coughing. Thus any loosened mucus falls into the lower respiratory tract, possibly contributing to bronchitis.

Also beware of hidden ingredients in cold remedies. A surprisingly large proportion of multisymptom cold pills contain caffeine; many liquid cold formulas contain a large amount of alcohol. Some as as much as 80 proof, the equivalent of gin, vodka, or scotch. Alcohol has no effect whatsoever on cold viruses.

The best argument against cold medications, however, is that most over-the-counter medicines (and some folk and herbal remedies as well) achieve their efforts by interfering with the immune system's battle against the viral invasion. Cold symptoms are produced not by the cold virus, but by the immune system's fight against it. Cold symptoms are part of the healing process. No studies show that taking cold remedies significantly prolongs colds, but given their effects on the immune system, that might well be the case.

The Doctor's and Grandmother's Remedy

The more scientists learn about the common cold, the more they agree that Grandma was right about how to treat one. In 1984 Kaiser-Permanente, the nation's largest health maintenance organization, consulted experts on colds and flu at several leading medical centers. Here is their advice for self-treatment:

•**Rest.** The effort required to fight a cold, especially during the first few days, is the equivalent of hard physical labor, which is why colds cause lethargy.

•**Bundle up.** Keeping warm helps alleviate the chills associated with fever.

•**Stop smoking.** Smoking irritates the inflamed nasopharynx, depresses blood levels of vitamin C, and paralyzes the respiratory cilia, which move mucus out of the infected area.

•**Drink hot liquids**—eight ounces every two hours. Hot fluids sooth an irritated throat, help relieve nasal congestion, and prevent dehydration. Don't drink cold beverages. One study shows they impede the movement of nasal mucus and contribute to congestion.

•**Gargle with warm salt water** for a sore throat. It also helps to suck on hard candies and increase relative humidity.

•**Avoid aspirin.** For fever, headaches, and body aches, try a cool cloth on the forehead or use acetaminophen or ibuprofen. Aspirin increases viral shedding, and should be avoided. Seek professional help for fevers above 101° F; fevers above 100° F that last more than two days; or any fever with rash, stiff neck, severe headache, and/or marked irritability or confusion.

•**Use a vaporizer** for nasal congestion. Also try taking a hot bath or shower. At night use extra pillows to elevate the head.

•**Use disposable tissues.** Cold viruses cannot survive long in paper tissues. But cloth handkerchiefs harbor live virus and recontaminate the fingers with virus each time they are used. Wash your hands after blowing your nose or after wiping a child's nose.

•**Do not suppress productive coughs.** For dry coughs, use a vaporizer, take hot showers, suck on hard candies, or ask your pharmacist for the least-expensive over-the-counter drug with dextromethorphan.

•**Don't use antibiotics.** They are powerless against colds. Penicillin and other antibiotics kill bacteria, but not cold viruses.

The Homeopathic Remedy

Although homeopaths recognize the common cold and flu as viral infections, they do not believe that viruses alone make people sick. They view disease ecologically, saying that pathogens cause illness only when the host's immune system has been weakened enough to permit infection. The allopathic (or traditional medical) goal is to eliminate pathogens. Homeopaths strive to boost the immune response so that the body can heal itself.

Because of the dilution of homeopathic medicines, these remedies pose no overdose hazard when used as recommended. Even harsh critics concede that homeopathic medicines are non-toxic.

To be effective, the medicines must be matched as closely as possible to the patient's symptoms. Homeopaths claim that if cold symptoms have been matched accurately with the right medicine, the cold should clear up after a night's rest. If not, try a different medicine. However, most homeopaths discourage the use of more than three medicines during any acute illness.

These are some homeopathic remedies as they are commonly matched with specific cold symptoms:

•For colds characterized by sore throat and patchy, flushed face, without restlessness or loss of mental sharpness, take ferrum phos.

•For colds involving tearing eyes, burning nasal discharge, and frequent sneezing aggravated while indoors, in warm rooms, and in the evening, use Allium cepa—Latin for onion, a traditional cold remedy in large non-homeopathic doses.

•For colds with burning tears and non-irritating nasal discharge, which feel worse outdoors, in the morning, and when lying down, try Euphrasia. Euphrasia is a microdose of eyebright, a plant used since the Middle Ages to treat vision problems and other ailments, though sources dispute its safety and effectiveness in non-homeopathic doses.

•For late-stage colds with runny nose, thick stringy mucus, and possibly sinus headache, use Kali bichromium. This medicine is also known as bichromate of potash.

•For colds characterized by chest congestion, thirst, and coughing aggravated by talking or motion, take Byronia. The common name for Byronia is wild hops, which is different from the hops used in brewing beer. Large, non-homeopathic doses are toxic. *Do not exceed the recommended dose.*

•For colds with thirst and nasal congestion that alternate with thick nasal discharge, with symptoms aggravated in warm rooms, try Pulsatilla.

THE REVIVAL OF HOMEOPATHY

At the end of the 19th century, homeopathy was a respected branch of medical science, taught in 22 homeopathic medical schools and practiced by 15 percent of U.S. physicians. Now, as it gains a new popularity as a natural way to boost the body's defense system, this controversial 200-year-old medicine may once again force the medical establishment to re-examine some of its basic assumptions about fighting disease.

Based on principles developed in the late 1700s by German physician Samuel Hahnemann (1755–1843), homeopathy—

with its twin principles of "like cures like" and "less is more"—
stands in marked contrast to today's conventional (or allopathic)
approach to health, which often seems preoccupied with merely
counteracting the symptoms of disease. And while even proponents will concede that some of homeopathy's concepts seem to
defy the laws of science as we know them, they argue that results
are what matter. Results are apparently why it has won such
influential adherents as Britain's royal family and, proponents
say, help explain why it has been seen as a threat to be eradicated
by the medical and pharmaceutical establishment.

Supporters are now looking to the role homeopathy will play
in treating what appear to be the chronic diseases of the future,
diseases against which the machines and chemicals of allopathic
medicine have so far been largely ineffective.

We have already observed some significant changes in the
'80s that portend what health problems lie ahead. Diseases of the
immune system—not just AIDS—have reached epidemic pro-
portions, and growing numbers of viral conditions, such as
Epstein-Barr virus and cytomegalovirus, aren't responding to
conventional therapy. Most bacterial infections are becoming
resistant to antibiotics and therefore require stronger ones,
which are still not always successful. Allergies to foods and new
chemicals are becoming more prevalent. Chronic disability is
affecting people at younger ages, and mental disease is affecting
more people.

Futurists generally assume that 21st century medicine will
include new and more powerful drugs and various innovative
technological interventions. They tend to forget, however, the
serious problems presently arising from conventional medications and therapies, which can cause serious side effects, particularly when used in combination. According to 1986 statistics, the
average American receives 7.5 prescriptions a year. Since most
drugs have side effects, some of which are quite serious, and
since the sick person is often prescribed several drugs at the same
time, any combination of which may have even greater potential
for side effects, it is no wonder that 50 percent of the time people
do not even get their drug prescriptions filled. Additionally,
various studies have indicated that 25 to 90 percent of the time
patients make errors in administering the medicines.

Homeopathic medicine offers an alternative. Instead of giving a person one medicine for headache, one for constipation, another for irritability, and yet another to counteract the effects of the other medicines, the homeopathic physician prescibes one medicine at a time to stimulate the person's immune and defense capacity and to bring about an overall improvement in health. The procedure by which the homeopath finds the precise substance is the very science and art of homeopathy.

Too often physicians and patients alike assume that a person's symptoms *are* the disease and that simply treating these symptoms is the best way to cure. Such treatment is on a par with unplugging a car's emergency oil light because it is flashing.

Recent research has shown that fever, for example, is the effort of the organism to heal itself—that the body prepares itself to resist viral or bacterial infection by creating a fever, and then is better able to produce interferon (an antiviral substance). Fever also increases white blood cell mobility and activity, instrumental factors in fighting infection.

Thus, while many conventional drugs work by controlling or suppressing symptoms, these drugs may well *inhibit* the body's defense and immune processes. Such drugs should be avoided, except in special circumstances.

Homeopathic practitioners seek to find a substance that in large doses would cause symptoms similar to those a sick person is experiencing. When the match is made, that substance is then given in very small, safe doses, often producing dramatic effects. Homeopaths define the underlying principle for this matching process as the "law of similars." This law is not unknown to conventional medicine—immunization and allergy treatments are based on similar principles.

Homeopathic medicines are powerful tools, but they are not effective in treating all kinds of diseased states. Some conditions do not respond to microdoses because they require surgical intervention; others need immediate and certain relief of symptoms; others are addressed by simple nutritional or lifestyle changes; and still others are relieved only upon reduced exposure to certain environmental stresses.

Homeopathic medicines may not be appropriate for symptoms that require immediate, sometimes drastic treatment. Certain cases of asthma in which breathing is sigificantly impaired; meningitis, which requires immediate antibiotic treatment to avoid brain damage or death; and various other conditions require conventional medical treatment to assure survival.

This isn't to say that homeopathic medicines are of *no* value in these situations. In fact, they may reduce the need for conventional medical treatment—including surgery—even in difficult cases. Microdoses may effectively treat a severe attack of asthma, may cure serious infection without the need for antibiotics, and may rapidly relieve various other life-threatening symptoms. However, since homeopathic medicines require strict individualization to obtain the best results, one cannot always depend on them for rapid, effective relief. There is general consensus among practitioners that homeopathic medicine can nevertheless be used in emergencies—on the way to the doctor or the hospital—in conjunction with conventional medical treatment.

Probably the greatest frustration to the homeopath (and to the patients as well) are those people, who, for uncertain reasons, do not respond to homeopathic treatment. Homeopaths initially assume they have not correctly analyzed the case and thus are not giving the correct medicine. Experienced homeopaths know, however, that certain other medicines are sometimes useful when the indicated one isn't working. Since it is generally recommended to try homeopathic medicines one at at time (with sometimes a month or more between them), finding an effective remedy may take some time. When people with chronic indigestion, headaches, arthritis, or other persistent symptoms do not improve with conventional drugs, delay isn't a major problem, since they have been waiting for curative care for years or even decades. But a patient in pain and discomfort might understandably seek an alternative to homeopathic care before a "similimum" (most similar medicine) is found.

With this in mind, it is sometimes confusing to go to a health food store or pharmacy and see homeopathic medicines sold for specific conditions. Most homeopathic manufacturers make mixtures of three to eight substances commonly given for a certain condition. It is assumed that this new medicine will be helpful to a broad number of patients suffering from a specific complaint. Although many consumers find these medicines to be helpful, there is a general consensus in the homeopathic community that the individually chosen medicine works more often and more effectively.

The greatest danger of homeopathic medicines is widely recognized to be ineffective medicines that delay the application of other potentially effective treatments. Since most homeopaths are medical doctors or other licensed medical professionals, they generally know when conventional medical care is required or when referral to a specialist is indicated.

ARGUMENT/PERSUASION

Topic 1

Some school boards are proposing that elementary and secondary schools in their districts be kept open year-round. They see it as a way to combat the problem of overcrowding in classrooms. Many parents are furious over this proposal and do not want their children obligated to attend school in the summer months.

For your essay, discuss why you believe many parents are angry about plans for year-round schooling. Then argue your own position for or against the proposal.

Topic 2

Many college scholarships are given on the basis of a standardized-test score, like the SAT or ACT. Some educators contend that most college scholarships should be based on past academic performance rather than standardized-test scores.

Write an essay briefly discussing the pros and cons of each method, and then make a strong argument for your own position on the subject.

Topic 3

The policy of the armed forces in the United States is to bar women from assignments which would place them in combat situations. Proponents of this policy feel that if women were allowed to participate in combat, the result would be a decrease in efficiency of the male personnel because of their cultural bias toward protecting women and because women may not have the physical strength to accomplish necessary combat tasks. Opponents of the policy, on the other hand, feel that such restrictions are discriminatory, unfairly depriving well-qualified women of leadership positions, positions that often result in promotion for their male counterparts.

Write an essay briefly discussing the pros and cons of the exclusionary policy. Then make a strong argument for your own position on the subject.

Topic 4

Read the following selection by John Fowles carefully. Then write an essay in which you argue for *or* against the writer's position on games and human nature. Support and illustrate your argument with evidence drawn from your reading or experience.

Games, sports, and pastimes that require rules and social contact have become increasingly significant in the last century. It was calculated that something like one hundred and fifty *million* people watched on television the final of the football World Cup in 1966. As with art, we may tend to regard games as a rather unimportant leisure activity. But as leisure increases, so does their influence on our lives.

Games are far more important to us, and in far deeper ways, than we like to admit. Some psychologists explain all of the symbolic values we attach to games, and to losing and winning them, in Freudian terms. But for most players and spectators a much more plausible explanation is the Adlerian one, that a game is a system for achieving superiority. It is moreover a system (like money getting) that is to a certain extent a human answer to the inhuman hazard of the cosmic lottery; to be able to win at a game compensates the winner for not being able to win outside the context of the game. This *raison d'être* of the game is most clearly seen in the games of pure chance; but many other games have deliberate hazards; and even in games technically free of hazards, the bounce, the lie, the fly in the eye exist. The evil is this: From instituting this system of equalizing hazard, man soon moves to regard the winner in it as not merely lucky but in some way excellent; just as he now comes to regard the rich man as in some way intrinsically excellent.

The prestige coveters have always tried to seize sport as their province. This is especially so in times of peace. Much has been made of the nobility of the early Olympic Games, in the sixth and seventh centuries before Christ, and of their later corruption under the Romans. But the sprig of olive was already too large a prize. Competition, the need to keep equal and the drive to do better, haunts mankind. But there are plenty of real fields for competition without inventing artificial ones.

Sport is an opportunity for personal pleasure, a situation where beauty may arise. But what is being contested is never prestige. Simply the game. The winner has more skill or more luck; by winning he is not in any sense in any game necessarily a better human being than the loser.

Topic 5

Some educational and social policy experts claim that, aside from teaching reading and writing, our present system of education does not prepare students for jobs in today's markets. They believe that we need to consider a major change in our approach to educating students such that more job opportunities are available to more students. Such an approach would significantly change the focus of higher education away from the general, liberal-arts course and toward a more specific vocational emphasis.

Write a well-organized essay in which you include the following:
- Identify and describe the present system of education, as you view it.
- Argue for or against the proposal to move from a more general education to a more specific vocational emphasis.

Topic 6

Read the following passage, "On Individuality" by John Stuart Mill, carefully. Then write an essay in which you defend or argue against Mill's ideas. Support your case by using specifics from this passage and from your own experience and reading.

I have said that it is important to give the freest scope possible to uncustomary things, in order that it may in time appear which of these are fit to be converted into customs. But independence of action and disregard of custom, are not solely deserving of encouragement for the chance they afford that better modes of action, and customs more worthy of general adoption, may be struck out; nor is it only persons of decided mental superiority who have a just claim to carry on their lives in their own way. There is no reason that all human existence should be constructed on some one or some small number of patterns. If a person possesses any tolerable amount of common sense and experience, his own mode of laying out his existence is the best, not because it is the best in itself, but because it is his own mode. Human beings are not like sheep; and even sheep are not undistinguishably alike. A man cannot get a coat or a pair of boots to fit him, unless they are either made to his measure, or he has a whole warehouseful to choose from; and is it easier to fit him with a life than with a coat, or are human beings more like one another in their whole physical and spiritual conformation than in the shape of their feet?

If it were only that people have diversities of taste that is reason enough for not attempting to shape them all after one model. But different persons also require different conditions for their spiritual development; and can no more exist healthily in the same moral, than all the variety of plants can in the same physical atmosphere and climate. The same things which are helps to one person towards the cultivation of his higher nature, are hindrances to another. The same mode of life is a healthy excitement to one keeping all his faculties of action and enjoyment in their best order, while to another it is a distracting burthen, which suspends or crushes all internal life. Such are the differences among human beings in their sources of pleasure, their susceptibilities of pain, and the operation on them of different physical and moral agencies, that unless there is a corresponding diversity in their modes of life, they neither obtain their fair share of happiness, nor grow up to the mental, moral, and aesthetic stature of which their nature is capable.

Why then should tolerance, as far as the public sentiment is concerned, extend only to tastes and modes of life which extort acquiescence by the multitude of their adherents? Nowhere (except in some monastic institutions) is diversity of taste entirely unrecognized; a person may, without blame, either like or dislike rowing, or smoking, or music, or athletic exercises, or chess, or cards, or study, because both those who like each of these things, and those who dislike them, are too numerous to be put down. But the man, and still more the woman, who can be accused either of doing "what nobody does," or of not doing "what everybody does," is the subject of as much depreciatory remark as if he or she had committed some grave moral delinquency. Persons require to possess a title, or some other badge of rank, or of the consideration of people of rank, to be able to indulge somewhat in the luxury of doing as they like without detriment to their estimation. To indulge somewhat, I repeat: for whoever allow themselves much of that indulgence, incur the risk of something worse than disparaging speeches— they are in peril of a commission *de lunatico,* and of having their property taken from them and given to their relations.

Part III: Grammar and Usage

This section deals with questions of grammar and usage that are tested by multiple-choice exams at several schools. Even if the exam at your school does not have a multiple-choice section, you should review grammar and usage carefully, since your essays will be judged, in part, by their grammatical correctness and variety.

MULTIPLE-CHOICE QUESTION TYPES

The following section gives examples of all of the question types used in the multiple-choice sections of the examinations. A diagnostic test follows it.

TYPE 1

This type of question tests your ability to identify errors of standard written English as they appear in sentences. Each sentence may contain one error in grammar, usage, idiom, or diction (word choice). You are to mark the letter (A, B, C, or D) of the part of the sentence which is incorrect. If no part of the sentence is incorrect, mark letter (E).

It is important to remember that you are looking for errors in standard *written* English, not conversational English, and that the parts not underlined in the sentence are correct. *Thus you must use the nonunderlined part to help you determine which underlined part may be wrong.* For example:

1. Each boy in the third and fourth sections of the class
   A   B
   gave their reasons for liking sports. No error.
   C   D   E

Note that *Each boy* is not underlined, so the subject of the sentence is singular. Therefore, *their* is incorrect. It should be *his* to agree with the singular subject. The incorrect part of the sentence is (C).

Other agreement errors in standard written English may include *subject–verb errors* such as

2. The wandering pack of dogs, first seen by the citizens many
   A   B
   years ago, were feared by all who lived in the town. No error.
   C   D   E

Here, since the subject of the sentence is *pack* (singular), the verb must also be singular, *was*. The incorrect part of this sentence is (C).

Other errors may include *faulty parallelism:*

3. Ernie's diligence <u>in studying every night</u> allowed him to
                              A
   score <u>high grades,</u> to gain the respect <u>of his peers,</u>
              B   C
   and <u>admission</u> to college. <u>No error.</u>
            D   E

The final part of the series is not in the same form as the first two
parts. It should be something like *to earn admission* or *to win
admission,* so that it parallels the form of the other items—*to score*
and *to gain.* Choice (D) should be chosen.

You may also find an error in *idiom* (nonstandard usage):

4. <u>Compromising over</u> a number of delicate issues, the members
        A
   <u>of the school board</u> <u>successfully</u> resolved <u>their</u> problems.
            B   C   D
   <u>No error.</u>
       E

The expression *compromising over* is unidiomatic. It should be
compromising on. Part (A) is not correct standard written English
and therefore is the correct answer.

TYPE 2

In this question type, you must choose the best of five different
versions of a sentence. If the original sentence most fully meets the
requirements of correct and effective English, choice (A), which
repeats the underlined portion exactly, is correct. If the underlined
part is incorrect, awkward, or ambiguous, you must pick the version
that best corrects it and retains the meaning of the originally
underlined phrase. Again, you must assume that any part of the
sentence not underlined is correct and cannot be changed.

An example:

1. The rigors of high office often demand <u>stamina, persistence, and having great patience.</u>
   (A) stamina, persistence, and having great patience.
   (B) stamina, persistence, and great patience.
   (C) that a person has stamina, persistence, and patience.
   (D) having stamina, persistence, and having great patience.
   (E) having stamina, being persistent, and having patience.

The correct answer is (B). The underlined part contains *faulty parallelism*. The last item in the series should not be preceeded by *having* but should be in the same form as *stamina* and *persistence*. By omitting the word *great,* choices (C) and (E) slightly change the meaning of the original and also have errors of parallelism.

Another example:

2. Rushing to avoid being late, <u>Bill's head collided with the cabinet door which was open.</u>
   (A) Bill's head collided with the cabinet door which was open.
   (B) Bill's head hit the open cabinet door.
   (C) Bill's head collided with the open cabinet door.
   (D) Bill hit his head on the open cabinet door.
   (E) Bill hit the cabinet door, having been opened.

The correct answer is choice (D). The sentence begins with an *-ing* phrase, which modifies what immediately follows the comma. In the original, *Bill's head* follows the modifying phrase. Was Bill's head doing the rushing? Certainly not. The sentence should read, *Rushing to avoid being late, Bill hit his head ... Bill* should follow the modifying phrase because he, not his head, was doing the rushing.

TYPE 3

Another kind of question prints complete paragraphs and requires you to determine if part of a sentence is incorrect and then to correct it, if necessary, by choosing from among several choices. If the underlined part is correct and makes sense with the rest of the passage, choose the answer that says "NO CHANGE."

You should assume that any part of the passage not underlined is correct and that the requirements are of *standard written English, not conversational English.* For example:

Furthering one's goals may require more effort than one had originally intended. However, a man may under-estimate <u>their</u> capacity for work when 　　　　1 setting out to accomplish some task.	1. A. NO CHANGE 　　B. its 　　C. ones' 　　D. his

Since the subject of the second sentence is *a man* (singular), *their* (plural) is incorrect. The pronoun must be singular to agree with *man.* Choice (D) properly corrects the error.

Punctuation may also need to be corrected. For example:

When packing for a hiking trip, you should insure that the following items are included in your <u>backpack; insect</u> 　　　　　　　　　　　2 spray, a good compass, a map, and a bottle of water.	2. A. NO CHANGE 　　B. backpack, insect 　　C. backpack: insect 　　D. backpack. Insect

The correct punctuation preceding a list is a colon. Therefore choice (C) is correct.

TYPE 4

In this question type, four possible corrections and a NO CHANGE option follow a single sentence. For example:

1. Sue is the woman who has been elected mayor this fall.
   (A) if a comma should be inserted after <u>woman</u>.
   (B) if <u>who</u> should be changed to <u>whom</u>.
   (C) if <u>has</u> should be changed to <u>have</u>.
   (D) if <u>fall</u> should be capitalized.
   (E) if <u>NO CHANGE</u> is necessary.

The sentence is correct as it stands, so (E) is the right answer. Notice that this question form may be used to test mechanics like punctuation or capitalization.

TYPE 5

In this question type, used often to test the recognition of verbose writing, the most effective sentence must be chosen from five possibilities. It is possible here to have two or more sentences that are grammatically correct, but one will be clearly better because it is clearer or more concise. For example:

1. (A) Because of the influenza epidemic, the office party was canceled.
   (B) The cancellation of the office party was because there was an epidemic of influenza.
   (C) Due to the fact of the influenza epidemic, the office party was canceled.
   (D) Being as there was an influenza epidemic, the office party was canceled.
   (E) On account of there was an influenza epidemic, the office party was canceled.

Choice (A) is the best response; it correctly expresses the thought clearly in the fewest words.

TYPE 6

These questions have only four choices. Though printed differently, the question type is like Type 2.

1. I was afraid I would miss my _____.
   (A) plane; but I arrived with ten minutes to spare.
   (B) plane, however, I arrived with ten minutes to spare.
   (C) plane however I arrived with ten minutes to spare.
   (D) plane; I arrived with ten minutes to spare, however.

The correct answer is (D). The two independent clauses are joined by the semicolon. In (A), the correct punctuation with the conjunction *but* would be a comma.

TYPE 7

In these questions, three of four sentences illustrate a similar error. Though you do not have to define what the error is, the questions are much easier to answer if you can recognize the repeated lapse. You must select the sentence that is correct. For example:

1. (A) Hoping to make money in gold, South African mining shares were the broker's choice.
   (B) Eating in restaurants five nights each week, a home-cooked meal was a special treat for the salesman.
   (C) Having stayed up until two studying for the test, I was too tired to concentrate properly.
   (D) Leaving the game ten minutes before the quarter ended, the parking lot was not overcrowded.

The correct answer is (C). All four sentences begin with participles. In (C), the understood subject of the participle immediately follows. The participial phrases in (A), (B), and (D) all dangle.

TYPE 8

Another grammar and usage question gives a sentence and asks you to rewrite the sentence in a different order without changing its meaning. Having rewritten the sentence in your head, you are asked to identify one of the four phrases that will occur in your revision. An example will make this clearer.

1. Eager to arrive before the concert began, we wisely allowed more than an hour on the bus.

   Rewrite, beginning with <u>Because</u> ... The next words will be

   (A) we wisely allowed
   (B) we were eager
   (C) eager to arrive
   (D) we are eager

The correct answer is (B). Your rephrased sentence should read "Because we were eager to arrive before the concert began, we wisely allowed more than an hour on the bus." This sentence contains the correct answer, (B), *we were eager*. A sentence in which the words next to *Because* were those of (A), (C), or (D) would change the meaning of the original sentence (A) or be poorly written (C or D).

TYPES 9 AND 10—STRUCTURE

In addition to questions about grammar and usage, there are two kinds of questions about the structure of the paragraph. In the first, you are given four sentences and asked to arrange them in the most logical order. In the second question type, you are asked to choose from among four sentences the one that best completes a given paragraph from which one sentence is missing.

Type 9

Choose the most logical order.

1. (1) The riddle of the Sphinx that Oedipus solved asked what walks on four and two and three legs.
   (2) In old age, he walks with the aid of a cane.
   (3) In maturity, he walks upon two legs.
   (4) The answer was man, whose first movement, as a baby, is to crawl on all fours.

   (A) 1, 2, 3, 4
   (B) 1, 4, 2, 3
   (C) 1, 4, 3, 2
   (D) 4, 1, 2, 3

The correct answer is (C), the sentence order—1, 4, 3, 2—that would form the most logical paragraph. It begins with the riddle and then gives an explanation of each of the parts following the order of the riddle and the progress of man from infancy to old age.

Type 10

Choose the sentence to fill the blank at the beginning of the following paragraph.

1. _____. All cacti are succulents, but not all succulents are cacti. It is the flower, not the leaf or stem that determines the family of a plant. Since we so rarely see the flowers of a cacti, it is no wonder we have trouble separating them from the larger group, succulents.

    (A) It is not surprising that there is some confusion between cacti and succulents.

    (B) Cacti are increasingly popular house plants.

    (C) Succulents, like the jade plant, are among the hardiest plants.

    (D) For apartment dwellers with forgetful habits, cacti are the ideal house plants.

The correct answer is (A), which defines the subject of the paragraph as the distinction between cacti and succulents. The three less effective sentences deal with cacti or with succulents, but not with both and their likeness.

SPELLING, PUNCTUATION, AND VOCABULARY

Several of the multiple-choice exams may incidentally test punctuation. Only one, Fresno, has items exclusively concerned with spelling, punctuation, and diction, or vocabulary. Samples of these questions follow the Grammar and Usage Diagnostic Test.

GRAMMAR AND USAGE DIAGNOSTIC TEST

ANSWER SHEET FOR GRAMMAR AND USAGE DIAGNOSTIC TEST
(Remove This Sheet and Use It to Mark Your Answers)

TYPE 1

1 Ⓐ Ⓑ Ⓒ Ⓓ Ⓔ
2 Ⓐ Ⓑ Ⓒ Ⓓ Ⓔ
3 Ⓐ Ⓑ Ⓒ Ⓓ Ⓔ
4 Ⓐ Ⓑ Ⓒ Ⓓ Ⓔ
5 Ⓐ Ⓑ Ⓒ Ⓓ Ⓔ
6 Ⓐ Ⓑ Ⓒ Ⓓ Ⓔ
7 Ⓐ Ⓑ Ⓒ Ⓓ Ⓔ
8 Ⓐ Ⓑ Ⓒ Ⓓ Ⓔ
9 Ⓐ Ⓑ Ⓒ Ⓓ Ⓔ
10 Ⓐ Ⓑ Ⓒ Ⓓ Ⓔ
11 Ⓐ Ⓑ Ⓒ Ⓓ Ⓔ
12 Ⓐ Ⓑ Ⓒ Ⓓ Ⓔ
13 Ⓐ Ⓑ Ⓒ Ⓓ Ⓔ
14 Ⓐ Ⓑ Ⓒ Ⓓ Ⓔ
15 Ⓐ Ⓑ Ⓒ Ⓓ Ⓔ

TYPE 2

1 Ⓐ Ⓑ Ⓒ Ⓓ Ⓔ
2 Ⓐ Ⓑ Ⓒ Ⓓ Ⓔ
3 Ⓐ Ⓑ Ⓒ Ⓓ Ⓔ
4 Ⓐ Ⓑ Ⓒ Ⓓ Ⓔ
5 Ⓐ Ⓑ Ⓒ Ⓓ Ⓔ
6 Ⓐ Ⓑ Ⓒ Ⓓ Ⓔ
7 Ⓐ Ⓑ Ⓒ Ⓓ Ⓔ
8 Ⓐ Ⓑ Ⓒ Ⓓ Ⓔ
9 Ⓐ Ⓑ Ⓒ Ⓓ Ⓔ
10 Ⓐ Ⓑ Ⓒ Ⓓ Ⓔ

TYPE 3

1 Ⓐ Ⓑ Ⓒ Ⓓ
2 Ⓐ Ⓑ Ⓒ Ⓓ
3 Ⓐ Ⓑ Ⓒ Ⓓ
4 Ⓐ Ⓑ Ⓒ Ⓓ
5 Ⓐ Ⓑ Ⓒ Ⓓ
6 Ⓐ Ⓑ Ⓒ Ⓓ
7 Ⓐ Ⓑ Ⓒ Ⓓ
8 Ⓐ Ⓑ Ⓒ Ⓓ
9 Ⓐ Ⓑ Ⓒ Ⓓ
10 Ⓐ Ⓑ Ⓒ Ⓓ
11 Ⓐ Ⓑ Ⓒ Ⓓ
12 Ⓐ Ⓑ Ⓒ Ⓓ
13 Ⓐ Ⓑ Ⓒ Ⓓ
14 Ⓐ Ⓑ Ⓒ Ⓓ
15 Ⓐ Ⓑ Ⓒ Ⓓ
16 Ⓐ Ⓑ Ⓒ Ⓓ
17 Ⓐ Ⓑ Ⓒ Ⓓ
18 Ⓐ Ⓑ Ⓒ Ⓓ
19 Ⓐ Ⓑ Ⓒ Ⓓ
20 Ⓐ Ⓑ Ⓒ Ⓓ

TYPE 4

1 Ⓐ Ⓑ Ⓒ Ⓓ Ⓔ
2 Ⓐ Ⓑ Ⓒ Ⓓ Ⓔ
3 Ⓐ Ⓑ Ⓒ Ⓓ Ⓔ
4 Ⓐ Ⓑ Ⓒ Ⓓ Ⓔ
5 Ⓐ Ⓑ Ⓒ Ⓓ Ⓔ
6 Ⓐ Ⓑ Ⓒ Ⓓ Ⓔ
7 Ⓐ Ⓑ Ⓒ Ⓓ Ⓔ
8 Ⓐ Ⓑ Ⓒ Ⓓ Ⓔ
9 Ⓐ Ⓑ Ⓒ Ⓓ Ⓔ
10 Ⓐ Ⓑ Ⓒ Ⓓ Ⓔ

TYPE 5

1 Ⓐ Ⓑ Ⓒ Ⓓ Ⓔ
2 Ⓐ Ⓑ Ⓒ Ⓓ Ⓔ
3 Ⓐ Ⓑ Ⓒ Ⓓ Ⓔ
4 Ⓐ Ⓑ Ⓒ Ⓓ Ⓔ
5 Ⓐ Ⓑ Ⓒ Ⓓ Ⓔ
6 Ⓐ Ⓑ Ⓒ Ⓓ Ⓔ
7 Ⓐ Ⓑ Ⓒ Ⓓ Ⓔ
8 Ⓐ Ⓑ Ⓒ Ⓓ Ⓔ
9 Ⓐ Ⓑ Ⓒ Ⓓ Ⓔ
10 Ⓐ Ⓑ Ⓒ Ⓓ Ⓔ

TYPE 6

1 Ⓐ Ⓑ Ⓒ Ⓓ
2 Ⓐ Ⓑ Ⓒ Ⓓ
3 Ⓐ Ⓑ Ⓒ Ⓓ
4 Ⓐ Ⓑ Ⓒ Ⓓ
5 Ⓐ Ⓑ Ⓒ Ⓓ
6 Ⓐ Ⓑ Ⓒ Ⓓ
7 Ⓐ Ⓑ Ⓒ Ⓓ

TYPE 7

1 Ⓐ Ⓑ Ⓒ Ⓓ
2 Ⓐ Ⓑ Ⓒ Ⓓ
3 Ⓐ Ⓑ Ⓒ Ⓓ
4 Ⓐ Ⓑ Ⓒ Ⓓ
5 Ⓐ Ⓑ Ⓒ Ⓓ
6 Ⓐ Ⓑ Ⓒ Ⓓ
7 Ⓐ Ⓑ Ⓒ Ⓓ

TYPE 8

1 Ⓐ Ⓑ Ⓒ Ⓓ
2 Ⓐ Ⓑ Ⓒ Ⓓ
3 Ⓐ Ⓑ Ⓒ Ⓓ
4 Ⓐ Ⓑ Ⓒ Ⓓ
5 Ⓐ Ⓑ Ⓒ Ⓓ
6 Ⓐ Ⓑ Ⓒ Ⓓ

TYPE 9

1 Ⓐ Ⓑ Ⓒ Ⓓ
2 Ⓐ Ⓑ Ⓒ Ⓓ
3 Ⓐ Ⓑ Ⓒ Ⓓ
4 Ⓐ Ⓑ Ⓒ Ⓓ
5 Ⓐ Ⓑ Ⓒ Ⓓ

TYPE 10

1 Ⓐ Ⓑ Ⓒ Ⓓ
2 Ⓐ Ⓑ Ⓒ Ⓓ
3 Ⓐ Ⓑ Ⓒ Ⓓ
4 Ⓐ Ⓑ Ⓒ Ⓓ
5 Ⓐ Ⓑ Ⓒ Ⓓ

TYPE 1

Directions

Some of the following sentences are correct. Others contain problems in grammar, usage, idiom, or diction (word choice). There is not more than one error in any sentence.

If there is an error, it will be underlined and lettered. Find the one underlined part that must be changed to make the sentence correct, and choose the corresponding letter on your answer sheet. Mark (E) if the sentence contains no error.

1. His intention was not to establish a new sect or <u>in any way</u>
                                                          A
   <u>to decrease</u> the power of Canterbury but <u>in hope of making</u>
        B   C
   the bishops cut back their lavish <u>outlay</u> of church funds.
                                          D
   <u>No error.</u>
        E

2. <u>Despite</u> his poor start, Williams is the player <u>whom</u> I think
        A   B
   is most likely to win the batting <u>crown.</u> <u>No error.</u>
   C   D   E

3. <u>Most all</u> the instruments in the orchestra <u>are tuned</u> <u>just</u>
      A   B   C
   before the concert begins; the piano, <u>of course</u>, is an
                                               D
   exception. <u>No error.</u>
                   E

4. The <u>fall</u> in wheat prices, together with a decline in the demands
          A
   for beef, <u>have</u> <u>effected</u> a significant drop in <u>the value</u> of
                 B   C   D
   Swenson Company stock. <u>No error.</u>
                               E

131

5. The number of Irish immigrants in Boston was larger
   <u>A</u>   <u>B</u>
   than Italian or Scottish, but it was not until 1900 that
   <u>C</u>
   Boston's first Irish mayor was elected. No error.
                                    <u>D</u>   <u>E</u>

6. The trustees of the fund which determine the awarding of the
                         <u>A</u>   <u>B</u>
   grants are expected to meet in New York, not Washington.
         <u>C</u>   <u>D</u>
   No error.
   <u>E</u>

7. The increasing number of predators that carry infectious
                        <u>A</u>   <u>B</u>
   diseases to the herds of zebra and gnu are a serious concern
         <u>C</u>   <u>D</u>
   of park rangers. No error.
                    <u>E</u>

8. The humor of the fable on which these questions are based
                        <u>A</u>   <u>B</u>
   derive from a logical problem relating to the drawing of
   <u>C</u>   <u>D</u>
   conclusions from evidence. No error.
                             <u>E</u>

9. Everybody stationed at the American embassy in Moscow
   have been affected in some way by the radio waves, but there is
   <u>A</u>   <u>B</u>
   not yet any certainty about just what the effects have been.
                          <u>C</u>   <u>D</u>
   No error.
   <u>E</u>

10. The speaker discussed the difficulty of finding a <u>single job</u>
                                                          A
    <u>that</u> combines financial security, creativity, personal growth,
    B
    and <u>opportunities to help others</u> and <u>effect</u> social change.
                      C   D
    <u>No error.</u>
         E

11. Unaffected <u>by neither hunger nor cold</u>, Scott covered up to
                              A
    twenty miles on each of the days <u>that</u> the weather
                                        B
    <u>permitted him</u> to travel <u>at all.</u> <u>No error.</u>
          C   D   E

12. Among the pleasures <u>of the film is</u> the subtle performance <u>by</u>
                              A   B
    W. C. Fields and the <u>more boisterous antics</u> <u>of</u> the youthful
                                  C   D
    Mae West. <u>No error.</u>
                    E

13. I had no sooner picked up my spoon <u>to begin my soup</u> <u>when</u> the
                                              A   B
    waiter <u>descended on</u> me with <u>my</u> salad, main course, and coffee.
                  C   D
    <u>No error.</u>
         E

14. Hoping <u>to lie</u> as close <u>to</u> the water as possible, I <u>laid my</u>
                A   B   C
    towel on the sand, unpacked my sun lotion, and <u>settled down for</u>
                                                            D
    the afternoon. <u>No error.</u>
                        E

15. The altitude, temperature, and wind conditions of the plain
    <u>make</u> cattle raising impossible, and <u>this is why</u> protein
     A   B
    deficiency <u>is</u> <u>so</u> common among the villagers. <u>No error.</u>
                 C   D   E

TYPE 2

Directions

Some part of each sentence below is underlined; sometimes the whole sentence is underlined. Five choices for rephrasing the underlined part follow each sentence; the first choice (A) repeats the original, and the other four are different. If choice (A) seems better than the alternatives, choose answer (A); if not, choose one of the others.

For each sentence, consider the requirements of standard written English. Your choice should be a correct and effective expression, not awkward or ambiguous. Focus on grammar, word choice, sentence construction, and punctuation. If a choice changes the meaning of the original sentence, do not select it.

1. The reason the cat won't eat is <u>because he likes only liver-flavored cat food.</u>
   (A) because he likes only liver-flavored cat food.
   (B) that he liked cat liver-flavored food only.
   (C) on account of he only likes liver-flavored cat food.
   (D) that he likes only liver-flavored cat food.
   (E) because of liking only liver-flavored cat food.

2. <u>If you would have been more careful,</u> you would have broken fewer plates.
   (A) If you would have been more careful
   (B) If you had been more careful
   (C) If you would be more careful
   (D) Were you more careful
   (E) If you would have taken more care

3. Madame Arnot insisted <u>on me speaking only</u> in French.
   (A) on me speaking only
   (B) on me only speaking
   (C) on my speaking only
   (D) upon me speaking only
   (E) that only I speak

4. When she was only five, Janet's mother married for the third time.
   - (A) When she was only five, Janet's mother married for the third time.
   - (B) When only five, Janet's mother married for the third time.
   - (C) When Janet was only five, her mother married for the third time.
   - (D) When Janet's mother married for the third time, she was only five.
   - (E) Janet's mother married, when Janet was only five, for the third time.

5. We asked him about not only how he expected to reduce taxes, but his plans to increase employment.
   - (A) how he expected to reduce taxes, but his plans to increase employment.
   - (B) how he expected to reduce taxes, but also how he planned to increase employment.
   - (C) how he expects to reduce taxes, but also his plans to increase employment.
   - (D) how he plans to reduce taxes, but also about his plans to increase employment.
   - (E) how he expected to reduce taxes, but also about his plans to increase employment.

6. Although England and France believe the Concorde is the plane of the future, other countries, like the United States, is beginning to become concerned about the Concorde's effect upon the environment.
   - (A) is beginning to become concerned about the Concorde's effect upon
   - (B) are beginning to become concerned about the Concorde's affect upon
   - (C) are beginning to be concerned about the Concorde's affect on
   - (D) are beginning to become concerned about the Concorde's effect on
   - (E) is beginning to be concerned about the Concorde's effect upon

7. After he graduated from college, his parents gave him a new car, ten thousand dollars, and sent him on a trip around the world.
   (A) After he graduated from college, his parents gave him a new car, ten thousand dollars, and sent him on a trip around the world.
   (B) After graduating from college, his parents gave him a new car, ten thousand dollars, and sent him on a trip around the world.
   (C) After he had graduated from college, his parents gave him a new car, ten thousand dollars, and a trip around the world.
   (D) After he had graduated from college, his parents gave him a new car, ten thousand dollars, and sent him on a trip around the world.
   (E) After graduating from college, his parents gave him a new car, ten thousand dollars, and a trip around the world.

8. The difficulty with an inflated grading system is that everyone believes he or she is as good or better than everyone else as a student.
   (A) believes he or she is as good or better than everyone else as a student.
   (B) believes he or she is as good as or better than every other student.
   (C) believes he or she is as good as or better than every student.
   (D) believes they are as good as or better than every other student.
   (E) believes they are as good as or better than everyone else as a student.

9. When a halfback for the New York Jets, the records he set lasted fifteen years.
   (A) the records he set lasted fifteen years.
   (B) his records lasted fifteen years.
   (C) he set records that lasted fifteen years.
   (D) the records that he set lasted fifteen years.
   (E) he set records, and they lasted fifteen years.

10. <u>The shortstop threw late to the second baseman and missed the runner, which</u> allowed the batter to reach first base safely.

(A) The shortstop threw late to the second baseman and missed the runner, which

(B) The shortstop's throwing late to the second baseman and missing the runner

(C) By throwing late to the second baseman, the shortstop missed the runner which

(D) The shortstop throwing late to the second baseman missed the runner, and it

(E) The shortstop threw late to the second baseman and missed the runner, and this

TYPE 3

Directions

In the left-hand column, you will find passages in a "spread-out" format with various words and phrases underlined. In the right-hand column, you will find a set of responses corresponding to each underlined portion. If the underlined portion is correct as it stands, mark the letter indicating "NO CHANGE." If the underlined portion is incorrect, decide which of the choices best corrects it. Consider only underlined portions; assume that the rest of the passage is correct as written.

Passage I

Theodore Roosevelt was vice president when McKinley was assassinated in 1901. As the Republican candidate, he was elected <u>to be the president in</u>
                                   1

1. A. NO CHANGE
   B. to be president
   C. to the presidency
   D. to president

<u>1904, and</u> he declined to run
   2
for a third term. He supported Taft, the Republican nominee

2. A. NO CHANGE
   B. in 1904 and
   C. in 1904, and then
   D. in 1904, but

in 1908, and he was elected
        3
by a wide margin. By 1912,

3. A. NO CHANGE
   B. 1908; who
   C. 1908 who
   D. 1908, he

Roosevelt became dissatisfied
              4

4. A. NO CHANGE
   B. had become
      dissatisfied
   C. dissatisfied
   D. was unsatisfied

with Taft, and ran in
                5
opposition to Taft and Wilson
    5
as the candidate of a third
party, the Progressives.

5. A. NO CHANGE
   B. ran opposed to
   C. ran as opposition of
   D. opposed to

Wilson, the Democratic
            6
candidate, was the winner of the
        6
election of 1912, and he was
to win again in the election of

6. A. NO CHANGE
   B. (DO NOT begin new
      paragraph) The
      Democratic candidate,
      Wilson,
   C. (DO NOT begin new
      paragraph) The
      Democratic candidate,
      Wilson
   D. Wilson, the
      Democratic candidate

1916. Known best, perhaps, for
             7
his failure to persuade the
Senate to join the League of
Nations, Wilson's first term as
president was marked by reform.
Wilson's management of the war
was efficient and tactful, and he

7. A. NO CHANGE
   B. Perhaps known best
   C. Though he is,
      perhaps,
      best known
   D. Best known, perhaps,

won the backing both of business
                          8
and labor. He suffered the third
       8
of three strokes in 1919, and

8. A. NO CHANGE
   B. both of labor
      as well as business.
   C. of both business
      and labor.
   D. both of business
      as well as of labor.

thereafter he is without any
                    9
significant political influence.
     9

9. A. NO CHANGE
   B. was of no significant
   C. had no significant
   D. was without
      any significant

10. Which of the following additions could easily be made in order to
    strengthen the picture of Wilson?
    (A) more details about the League of Nations
    (B) specific examples of the reforms of Wilson's first term
    (C) additional details about Wilson's illness
    (D) additional details about Wilson's last year in office

11. Based on the content and organization of these two paragraphs,
    the paragraph that follows is probably about
    (A) Theodore Roosevelt.
    (B) Wilson.
    (C) the president elected in 1920.
    (D) the president elected in 1928.

Passage II

For two years—ever since
a Turkish sponge diver first
spotted it—a joint Turkish-
American team has been
excavating a shipwreck 150 feet
below the surface <u>off the</u>
12
<u>southern coast</u> of Turkey. The
12

12. A. NO CHANGE
    B. of the southern coast
    C. off of the
       southern coast
    D. off of the south coast

wrecked <u>ship, its</u> salvagers
13
surmise, was Greek. It probably
set sail from Syria with a cargo
of tin and glass from farther
east and stopped in Cyprus to
load three tons of copper ingots
and several crates of pottery.
It was headed for Greece <u>when</u>
14
<u>it was driven on the rocks and</u>
14
<u>sank.</u> The cargo wasn't salvaged
14
at the time because the ship's
owners didn't have the tech-

13. A. NO CHANGE
    B. ship, so its
    C. ship, it's
    D. ship, so it's

14. A. NO CHANGE
    B. when it was driven
       on the rocks and
       was sunk.
    C. when it was driven
       on the rocks and
       was sunken.
    D. sinking, when it was
       driven on the rocks.

nology <u>to do it.</u> That was about
15
3,400 years ago.

15. A. NO CHANGE
    B. to do that.
    C. to do so.
    D. to do this.

<u>Up to the present point in</u>
16
time, the salvagers have brought
16

16. A. NO CHANGE
    B. So far
    C. So far,
    D. Up to this time,

up <u>much of the cargo and of</u>
17
<u>the artifacts</u>, as well as
17
part of the keel and some
planking from the vessel itself.
"These bones of the wreck push
back our knowledge of Mediter-
ranean ship-building by nearly
a millenium," an archeologist
writes. He believes the copper
and tin <u>brought west</u> for
18
the express purpose of manu-
facturing bronze weapons and
tools. His team is salvaging

history <u>itself. The</u> evidence of a
19
flourishing international trade;
the mystery of eight stone
anchors each weighing 600
to 800 pounds, somehow loaded
on board before the invention of
block and tackle; the artifacts of
the maritime industry that was
at the heart of ancient Greek
civilization. They will keep
scholars and onlookers enthralled
for years.

17. A. NO CHANGE
    B. many cargo and
       artifacts
    C. much of the artifacts
       and cargo
    D. much of the cargo
       and many artifacts

18. A. NO CHANGE
    B. were brought west
    C. were being
       brought west
    D. was being
       brought west

19. A. NO CHANGE
    B. itself; the
    C. itself: the
    D. itself, the

20. Which of the following would be the best conclusion of the
    second paragraph?
    (A) NO CHANGE.
    (B) The salvagers expect the work to continue for two or three
        more years.
    (C) The cost of the salvage operation is more than one million
        dollars.
    (D) The cost of the salvage operation is being underwritten by
        three American and Turkish universities.

TYPE 4

Directions

Read the sentences below and decide whether a correction needs to be made.

1. Her memoirs, *Pulling No Punches,* (the title was suggested by Harry Truman) were published in 1982.
   (A) if the italics in *Pulling No Punches* should be omitted.
   (B) if title should be capitalized.
   (C) if the parentheses should be omitted.
   (D) if were should be changed to was.
   (E) if NO CHANGE is necessary.

2. Many buyers of the bonds have said that when they made the purchase they used to believe the bonds were backed by government insurance.
   (A) if have said should be changed to said.
   (B) if made should be changed to make.
   (C) if used to believe should be changed to believed.
   (D) if were backed should be changed to backed.
   (E) if NO CHANGE is necessary.

3. The older boy wanted vanilla ice cream, the little girl wanted chocolate, and the younger boy wants strawberry.
   (A) if older should be changed to oldest.
   (B) if the comma after cream should be omitted.
   (C) if younger should be changed to youngest.
   (D) if wants should be changed to wanted.
   (E) if NO CHANGE is necessary.

4. Delaying by one month the implementation of the new insurance law, the Commissioner hoped that the irate consumer's sense of fairness would win him their support.
   (A) if implementation should be spelled implimentation.
   (B) if the comma after law should be omitted.
   (C) if consumer's should be changed to consumers'.
   (D) if would should be changed to should.
   (E) if NO CHANGE is necessary.

5. The decision, at least for now, dashes the hopes of more than 500,000 foreign nationals who have been attempting to acquire resident status.
   (A) if the comma after <u>decision</u> should be omitted.
   (B) if <u>dashes</u> should be changed to <u>dash</u>.
   (C) if <u>foreign</u> should be spelled <u>foriegn</u>.
   (D) if <u>who</u> should be changed to <u>whom</u>.
   (E) if <u>NO CHANGE</u> is necessary.

6. Unlike Renoir, Georgia O'Keefe's paintings of flowers depend on the use of bold colors.
   (A) if <u>Renoir</u> should be changed to <u>Renoir's</u>.
   (B) if <u>paintings</u> should be changed to <u>painting</u>.
   (C) if <u>depend</u> should be changed to <u>depends</u>.
   (D) if <u>on</u> should be changed to <u>upon</u>.
   (E) if <u>NO CHANGE</u> is necessary.

7. The warning was addressed to surfers whom are usually undeterred by high winds, cold, or rain.
   (A) if a comma should be inserted after <u>surfers</u>.
   (B) if <u>whom</u> should be changed to <u>who</u>.
   (C) if <u>usually</u> should be changed to <u>usual</u>.
   (D) if the comma after <u>cold</u> should be omitted.
   (E) if NO CHANGE is necessary.

8. The cold weather improved the sale of firewood significantly, but the ice cream vendors couldn't find hardly any customers.
   (A) if <u>of</u> should be changed to <u>in</u>.
   (B) if <u>significantly</u> should be changed to <u>significant</u>.
   (C) if the comma before <u>but</u> should be omitted.
   (D) if <u>couldn't</u> should be changed to <u>could</u>.
   (E) if <u>NO CHANGE</u> is necessary.

9. In recent decades, mortality rates have declined for both white and nonwhite Americans, but the national averages obscures the extremely high rates in many inner-city communities.
   (A) if <u>have declined</u> should be changed to <u>has declined</u>.
   (B) if the comma after <u>Americans</u> should be changed to a semicolon.
   (C) if <u>obscures</u> should be changed to <u>obscure</u>.
   (D) if <u>extremely</u> should be changed to <u>extreme</u>.
   (E) if <u>NO CHANGE</u> is necessary.

10. If one is careful about how you keep records, you will not have any problems, even if you are audited by the I.R.S.
   (A) if <u>one is</u> should be changed to <u>you are</u>.
   (B) if the comma after <u>records</u> should be changed to a semicolon.
   (C) if the word <u>even</u> should be omitted.
   (D) if <u>I.R.S.</u> should not be capitalized.
   (E) if <u>NO CHANGE</u> is necessary.

TYPE 5

Directions

Which sentence below expresses the thought most effectively?

1. (A) Because he was from an uneducated family was why Akim was denied a fair hearing.
   (B) Due to his being from an uneducated family, Akim was denied a fair hearing.
   (C) Akim was denied a fair hearing because his family was uneducated.
   (D) The fact that his family was uneducated was the cause of Akim being denied a fair hearing.
   (E) Akim was denied a fair hearing, because of the fact that he came from a family that was uneducated.

2. (A) Without hardly a delay, the actor picked up the fallen chair and sat down.

   (B) Hardly delaying, the fallen chair was picked up and sat in by the actor.

   (C) Not hardly delaying, the actor picked up the fallen chair and sat down.

   (D) With hardly a delay, the actor picked up the fallen chair and sat down.

   (E) Sitting down without hardly a delay, the actor picked up the fallen chair.

3. (A) With the soup, a white wine was served by the waiter, and he served a red wine with the beef.

   (B) With the soup, a white wine was served by the waiter, and a red wine with the beef.

   (C) A red wine with the beef and a white wine with the soup was served by the waiter.

   (D) A white wine was served by the waiter with the soup, and with the beef, a red one.

   (E) The waiter served a white wine with the soup and a red with the beef.

4. (A) As a rule, gerrymandering to fragment a body of voters usually takes place in urban areas and cities.

   (B) Gerrymandering usually occurs in cities.

   (C) In cities and urban areas is where gerrymandering usually takes place.

   (D) Taking place in cities and urban areas is usual for gerrymandering.

   (E) It is in cities or in urban areas that gerrymandering occurs usually.

5. (A) Nelson passes more often and more accurately than any other quarterback in the league.
   (B) When he is compared to the other quarterbacks in the league, Nelson is the most frequent and the most accurate passer.
   (C) In passing, compared to the quarterbacks in the league, Nelson is the most often and most accurate.
   (D) Nelson's passing is more accurate and more frequent when it is compared to other quarterbacks in the league.
   (E) Compared to the other quarterbacks in the league, Nelson's passing is more accurate and more frequent.

6. (A) The primary purpose and chief function of the director is to oversee and supervise the traffic control officers.
   (B) Overseeing the traffic control officers is the director's primary purpose, chief function, and principal responsibility.
   (C) The primary purpose of the director is to supervise the traffic control officers.
   (D) To oversee and supervise the traffic control officers is the chief function of the director.
   (E) The director's chief function and principal responsibility is to supervise and oversee the traffic control officers.

7. (A) Paying no attention to the polls, and ignoring the predictions of increasing unemployment, the party is supporting higher military spending.
   (B) The party is going to support increasing spending on the military in despite of the predictions of increasing unemployment and what the polls say.
   (C) Ignoring the polls and the predictions which say unemployment will increase, the party is supporting higher military spending.
   (D) Ignoring the polls and the predictions of increasing unemployment, the party is supporting higher military spending.
   (E) Supporting higher military spending, the party is paying no attention to the polls and it is also ignoring predictions of increasing unemployment.

8. (A) A few white males have a fantasy life so strong that nothing can affect it.

   (B) There are a few white males who have a deep-seated fantasy life so inured that nothing can affect its continuance.

   (C) The deeply rooted fantasy life of a few white males is so powerful that nothing can be done about it.

   (D) A few white males' deep-seated fantasies are so well entrenched and established that there is nothing anyone can do to affect them.

   (E) The deep-seated fantasy life of a few white males is so entrenched and fixed that nothing can affect it.

9. (A) The interior prejudices within us may be more difficult to recognize than the external which is outside us in other people.

   (B) It may be more difficult to recognize our own prejudices than those of others.

   (C) Our own prejudices may be more difficult to recognize and see than the prejudices of other people.

   (D) Maybe it is more difficult to recognize our own interior prejudices than it is to see the prejudices of others.

   (E) It may be more difficult and harder to recognize our own prejudices than to see the prejudices of other people.

10. (A) How the forty-ton statues, huge and gigantic, were moved is an unanswered question that we cannot explain yet.

    (B) We still cannot explain how the huge forty-ton statues were moved.

    (C) How the huge and gigantic forty-ton statues were moved is a question which we still cannot answer.

    (D) How were the huge forty-ton statues moved is a question we cannot answer still.

    (E) The unanswered question still is how were the huge and gigantic forty-ton statues moved.

TYPE 6

Directions

In each of the following, select the best answer from the four suggested.

1. After dinner nowadays, gentlemen retire not to the library for cigars and port but _____.
   (A) the kitchen for washing dishes.
   (B) they go to the kitchen to wash the dishes.
   (C) to the kitchen for washing dishes.
   (D) the kitchen to wash dishes.

2. The senator admitted failing to report the acquisition of two pieces of property, pocketing over $5,000 in travel funds, and _____.
   (A) that he diverted campaign funds to his personal use.
   (B) that campaign funds were diverted to his personal use.
   (C) his having diverted campaign funds to his personal use.
   (D) diverting campaign funds to his personal use.

3. With a blood-alcohol level well above the legal minimum to show intoxication, _____.
   (A) the car was uncontrollable.
   (B) the driver could not control the car.
   (C) the car could not be controlled.
   (D) control of the car was impossible.

4. The weatherman predicted strong winds, rain, and high waves, _____.
   (A) which did not deter the surfers.
   (B) a forecast that did not deter the surfers.
   (C) but this could not deter the surfers.
   (D) and this did not deter the surfers.

5. If I can put an extra fifty dollars in the bank each month, by June
   I _____.
   (A) will have saved three hundred dollars.
   (B) have saved three hundred dollars.
   (C) will be saving three hundred dollars.
   (D) saved three hundred dollars.

6. According to a survey of high school seniors, Lincoln is more
   highly regarded _____.
   (A) than any other American president.
   (B) as any American president.
   (C) than any American president.
   (D) than any president.

7. She is the only candidate of the seven who have filed to run in
   November _____.
   (A) who have a chance to unseat the incumbent.
   (B) whom have a chance to unseat the incumbent.
   (C) who has a chance to unseat the incumbent.
   (D) by whom there is a chance that the incumbent will be
       unseated.

TYPE 7

Directions

In the following items, three of the four sentences illustrate a
similar type of error. Choose the correct sentence.

1. (A) The shoe's hard sole grip a rubberized track badly.
   (B) The record holders for the event, both from Romania, is not
       expected to compete.
   (C) There is, according to reports from London and Paris, no
       reasons to believe that shoes will increase in price.
   (D) There were, when Smith was just beginning to run long
       distances, no American runners able to equal the African
       and Swedish milers.

2. (A) We have no need to import fruits or vegetables because our climate permitted our growing them nearby.
   (B) The film opens in New York with some success, but it was not a money-maker in the rest of the country.
   (C) She bought ten dollars worth of groceries and then gave all the rest of her cash to a street person.
   (D) Scientists in Germany were enthusiastic about Darwin's ideas, but in France they are indifferent, if not hostile.

3. (A) To reach the restaurant by the shortest route, you should take the toll road.
   (B) To find the correct answer quickly, multiplication, not addition, should be used.
   (C) To make sure the plants are free from mildew, a sunny location is the best planting place.
   (D) To bring the story to an ending within the shortened time allowed, several implausible events were introduced in the last three scenes.

4. (A) The owners are apparently contemptuous for the public opinion.
   (B) He seems to be uncertain about the future of the play.
   (C) Forgetful to his dentist appointment, he went home after work.
   (D) He is anxious in his health, and so takes large quantities of vitamin pills.

5. (A) I had hoped the committee would agree to invite them, both him and her.
   (B) Between you and I, the food at the party was not good at all.
   (C) They may give two awards this year, to both you and I.
   (D) Edna, as well as her, was not invited to the awards dinner.

6. (A) He wrote a letter to his lawyer in Boston that was difficult to understand.
   (B) She bought a dress in a very expensive shop in Pasadena that didn't fit properly.
   (C) In the restaurant, he ordered a monk fish that was served with a white wine sauce.
   (D) I had a piece of apple pie for desert at lunch with ice cream on top of it.

7. (A) For near thirty hours, his body temperature was dangerously low.
   (B) Reading carefully between the lines, you can infer his really hostile attitude.
   (C) A good placed shot across the bow convinced the Captain to surrender without a fight.
   (D) A good question deserves a real thorough and accurate response.

TYPE 8

Directions

In this section, you are to rewrite sentences in your head. You will be told how to begin the new sentence. Keep in mind that your new sentence should have the same meaning and contain essentially the same information as the sentence given you.

1. The Portuguese have been in Africa for five centuries, their ships having anchored in ports along the northwest coast long before Columbus's time.

   Rewrite beginning with Having anchored in ports along the northwest coast long before Columbus's time, ... The next words will be

   (A) five centuries were
   (B) Columbus has
   (C) Portuguese ships
   (D) the Portuguese had been

2. You must use five different herbs and spices to make deviled crabmeat as it is served in New Orleans.

Rewrite, beginning with <u>As it is served in New Orleans,</u> . . . The next words will be

(A) deviled crabmeat
(B) you must
(C) five different
(D) using

3. The men's chorus, the marching band, and the rugby team are the three activities in which I plan to participate this semester.

Rewrite, beginning with <u>In addition to the men's</u>

(A) chorus and the marching band, the rugby team are
(B) chorus and the marching band and rugby team are
(C) chorus, the marching band and the rugby team is
(D) chorus, the marching band and the rugby team are

4. She encouraged other female writers to insist upon pay equal to that of the male writers, but had never done so herself.

Rewrite beginning with <u>Never</u> . . . The next words will be

(A) did she
(B) herself having
(C) having done it
(D) encouraging

5. The lands are fertile, well watered, and easily tilled.

Rewrite beginning with <u>Not only fertile, the lands</u> . . . The next words will be

(A) also were well watered
(B) also had been well watered
(C) well watered also
(D) were also well watered

6. Boone was unhappy in Philadelphia because he missed the sights and sounds of the forest.

Rewrite beginning with <u>Because he missed the sights and sounds of the forest,</u> . . . The next words will be

(A) was the reason for
(B) was the reason why
(C) Boone was
(D) caused Boone

TYPE 9

Directions

Choose the numbered sequence which rearranges the sentences in logical paragraph order. Even though you might prefer a sequence not listed, you must select one of these four answers.

1. (1) A challenge to the exemption in 1970 was turned aside.
   (2) Traditionally, churches have not had to pay taxes on their property or income.
   (3) The grounds were that the exemption did not subsidize religions because it covered all nonprofit groups, such as schools or hospitals.
   (4) Despite the exemption, California has collected sales tax on such items as T-shirts and coffee mugs sold through the mail by television evangelists.

   (A) 2, 3, 4, 1
   (B) 2, 1, 3, 4
   (C) 1, 4, 2, 3
   (D) 2, 4, 3, 1

2. (1) The last two lines rhyme with each other, and this rhyme of two adjacent lines is called a couplet.

   (2) In the first twelve lines, there are six different rhymes; line one rhymes with line three and two with line four.

   (3) The Shakespearean or English sonnet has fourteen lines.

   (4) The second quatrain (lines 5–8) and the third (lines 9–12) use two rhymes in a pattern like that of lines 1–4.

   (A) 2, 3, 1, 4
   (B) 3, 2, 1, 4
   (C) 3, 2, 4, 1
   (D) 2, 4, 1, 3

3. (1) She later served as an advisor to President Truman, and in 1952, she was nominated for vice president to run with Adlai Stevenson.

   (2) She entered politics in 1944 and by 1948 was a key member of the Democratic National Committee.

   (3) She declined the nomination but thirty years later was present when Geraldine Ferraro became the first female nominee.

   (4) Once a reporter and society editor for the Chicago *Tribune,* India Edwards was one of the first women to achieve political power.

   (A) 4, 2, 1, 3
   (B) 4, 2, 3, 1
   (C) 2, 1, 3, 4
   (D) 2, 1, 4, 3

4. (1) Creationists believe that the biology, geology, and physics of the earth can be explained by the Old Testament.
   (2) Their opponents claim the creationist argument leaves many questions unanswered.
   (3) The earth's geological state, they argue, was caused primarily by the flood of Noah described in the book of Genesis.
   (4) What was the source of all that water, and where did it all go after the flood?

   (A) 1, 2, 3, 4
   (B) 1, 3, 4, 2
   (C) 1, 4, 3, 2
   (D) 1, 3, 2, 4

5. (1) Firescaping, landscaping with fire-resistant plants, will reduce the risk of property damage in the most fire-prone areas.
   (2) While the natural fires that occur in chaparral country can never be fully controlled, homeowners can improve the chances of their homes surviving a fire.
   (3) But these places are the properties most endangered by wildfire.
   (4) In southern California, homes in the hills and canyons are among the most sought-after places to live.

   (A) 2, 1, 3, 4
   (B) 2, 4, 1, 3
   (C) 4, 3, 2, 1
   (D) 4, 2, 3, 1

156   GRAMMAR AND USAGE

TYPE 10

Directions

Each of the following items presents a paragraph in which a sentence is missing. Read each paragraph, and then choose, from the four sentences that follow it, the one that is most suitable as the missing sentence.

1. _____. Each winter, more than ten thousand gray whales migrate from the waters off Alaska to their breeding grounds off Baja California. Often, they pass less than a mile from the coast of southern California. The peak period of the migration is midmonth, when as many as two hundred whales have been sighted from the beach in a single day. From Point Loma or from one of the many excursion boats, a whale watcher in January can be sure of seeing whales as long as the visibility is clear.

(A) The Whale Watchers Society of California has more than eight hundred members.
(B) The best time to see a whale in California is in January.
(C) The Whale Watchers Society of California was established in 1943.
(D) Whale watching societies have existed in California since the 1940s.

2. _____. On one hand, it is the easiest way to earn money rapidly. An aircraft machinist, for example, can increase a $560 per week check to $980 by working overtime for twenty hours. The loss, of course, is free time. And this loss has led to a sharp increase in the number of broken homes among overtime workers. It is no wonder that many workers have mixed feelings about overtime.

(A) The American worker has a love-hate relationship with working overtime.
(B) Overtime is the best thing that can happen to a worker.
(C) Many companies are increasing the number of overtime hours their workers are permitted.
(D) Overtime is a danger to both the employer and the employee.

3. _____. Few restaurant-goers are ordering cocktails before dinner. Fewer still are ordering alcoholic drinks after dinner. The days of the cigar and brandy after dinner have gone. More rigorous drunk-driving laws and the greater consciousness of healthier eating habits have changed the drinking customs of American adults.

(A) These days, a liquor license is a very valuable property.

(B) Each year, only a small number of new liquor licenses are issued.

(C) The selling price of a license to sell alcoholic beverages is steadily declining.

(D) Alcohol sales are more profitable than food sales, as any restaurant owner knows.

4. _____. One predicts the discovery of artifacts from an alien spaceship on a sunken Spanish treasure ship. Another foresees the Russian cosmonaut's discovery of an abandoned space station, complete with the bodies of several E.T.'s. A third sees the capture of the Abominable Snowman and its public display at a zoo. But none of these soothsayers had been able to predict the events of the 1980s that might have been expected, like an oil spill or an earthquake.

(A) According to a recent poll, 65% of the American readers of tabloid magazines take the predictions by psychics "very seriously."

(B) The business of predicting the future by men or women claiming psychic powers is a very old one.

(C) The number of psychics seems to increase each year.

(D) Psychics' predictions for the 1990s published in tabloid magazines are stranger than ever.

5. _____. New York City voted overwhelmingly Democratic, but Republican majorities elsewhere in the state put New York in the Republican column. Similarly, in Illinois, the Republican vote throughout the state erased the wide Democratic lead in Chicago. In both of the cities, politicians have jokingly suggested that the quickest way to victory would be by forming a new state, composed only of the city.

(A) In the most recent election, the results in New York and Illinois were similar.

(B) In the most recent election, New York City was outvoted.

(C) The results of the recent election cannot have pleased the majority of the voters in New York City.

(D) The winners in the most recent election were the voters who live outside of New York City.

ANSWER KEY FOR GRAMMAR AND USAGE
DIAGNOSTIC TEST

Type 1	Type 3	Type 5	Type 8
1. C	1. C	1. C	1. C
2. B	2. D	2. D	2. A
3. A	3. A	3. E	3. D
4. B	4. B	4. B	4. B
5. C	5. A	5. A	5. D
6. A	6. A	6. C	6. C
7. D	7. C	7. D	
8. C	8. C	8. A	Type 9
9. A	9. C	9. B	1. B
10. E	10. B	10. B	2. C
11. A	11. C		3. A
12. A	12. A	Type 6	4. D
13. B	13. A	1. C	5. C
14. E	14. A	2. D	
15. B	15. C	3. B	Type 10
	16. C	4. B	1. B
Type 2	17. D	5. A	2. A
1. D	18. C	6. A	3. C
2. B	19. C	7. C	4. D
3. C	20. A		5. A
4. C		Type 7	
5. B	Type 4	1. D	
6. D	1. E	2. C	
7. C	2. C	3. A	
8. B	3. D	4. B	
9. C	4. C	5. A	
10. B	5. E	6. C	
	6. A	7. B	
	7. B		
	8. D		
	9. C		
	10. A		

SPELLING, PUNCTUATION, AND VOCABULARY
DIAGNOSTIC TEST

ANSWER SHEET FOR SPELLING, PUNCTUATION, AND VOCABULARY DIAGNOSTIC TEST
(Remove This Sheet and Use It to Mark Your Answers)

SPELLING TYPE 1

1 Ⓐ Ⓑ Ⓒ
2 Ⓐ Ⓑ Ⓒ
3 Ⓐ Ⓑ Ⓒ
4 Ⓐ Ⓑ Ⓒ
5 Ⓐ Ⓑ Ⓒ
6 Ⓐ Ⓑ Ⓒ
7 Ⓐ Ⓑ Ⓒ
8 Ⓐ Ⓑ Ⓒ
9 Ⓐ Ⓑ Ⓒ
10 Ⓐ Ⓑ Ⓒ

SPELLING TYPE 2

1 Ⓐ Ⓑ Ⓒ
2 Ⓐ Ⓑ Ⓒ
3 Ⓐ Ⓑ Ⓒ
4 Ⓐ Ⓑ Ⓒ
5 Ⓐ Ⓑ Ⓒ
6 Ⓐ Ⓑ Ⓒ
7 Ⓐ Ⓑ Ⓒ
8 Ⓐ Ⓑ Ⓒ
9 Ⓐ Ⓑ Ⓒ
10 Ⓐ Ⓑ Ⓒ

PUNCTUATION TYPE 1

1 Ⓐ Ⓑ
2 Ⓐ Ⓑ
3 Ⓐ Ⓑ
4 Ⓐ Ⓑ
5 Ⓐ Ⓑ
6 Ⓐ Ⓑ
7 Ⓐ Ⓑ
8 Ⓐ Ⓑ
9 Ⓐ Ⓑ
10 Ⓐ Ⓑ

PUNCTUATION TYPE 2

1 Ⓐ Ⓑ Ⓒ Ⓓ Ⓔ
2 Ⓐ Ⓑ Ⓒ Ⓓ Ⓔ
3 Ⓐ Ⓑ Ⓒ Ⓓ Ⓔ
4 Ⓐ Ⓑ Ⓒ Ⓓ Ⓔ
5 Ⓐ Ⓑ Ⓒ Ⓓ Ⓔ
6 Ⓐ Ⓑ Ⓒ Ⓓ Ⓔ
7 Ⓐ Ⓑ Ⓒ Ⓓ Ⓔ
8 Ⓐ Ⓑ Ⓒ Ⓓ Ⓔ
9 Ⓐ Ⓑ Ⓒ Ⓓ Ⓔ
10 Ⓐ Ⓑ Ⓒ Ⓓ Ⓔ

VOCABULARY TYPE 1

1 Ⓐ Ⓑ Ⓒ Ⓓ Ⓔ
2 Ⓐ Ⓑ Ⓒ Ⓓ Ⓔ
3 Ⓐ Ⓑ Ⓒ Ⓓ Ⓔ
4 Ⓐ Ⓑ Ⓒ Ⓓ Ⓔ
5 Ⓐ Ⓑ Ⓒ Ⓓ Ⓔ

VOCABULARY TYPE 2

1 Ⓐ Ⓑ Ⓒ
2 Ⓐ Ⓑ Ⓒ
3 Ⓐ Ⓑ Ⓒ
4 Ⓐ Ⓑ Ⓒ
5 Ⓐ Ⓑ Ⓒ
6 Ⓐ Ⓑ Ⓒ
7 Ⓐ Ⓑ Ⓒ
8 Ⓐ Ⓑ Ⓒ
9 Ⓐ Ⓑ Ⓒ
10 Ⓐ Ⓑ Ⓒ

SPELLING TYPE 1

Directions

Choose the correct spelling for the word parts combined below.

1. unlikely + hood =
   (A) unlikelyhood
   (B) unlikelehood
   (C) unlikelihood

2. change + ability =
   (A) changeability
   (B) changability
   (C) changebility

3. study + ing =
   (A) studyng
   (B) studing
   (C) studying

4. occur + ence =
   (A) occurrence
   (B) occurence
   (C) occurrance

5. true + ly =
   (A) truely
   (B) truly
   (C) truley

6. vary + able =
   (A) varyable
   (B) variable
   (C) varible

7. take + ing =
   (A) takeing
   (B) takking
   (C) taking

8. necessary + ly =
   (A) necessaryly
   (B) necessarily
   (C) necessarly

9. wrinkle + ing =
   (A) wrinkling
   (B) wrinkeling
   (C) wrinkelling

10. friendly + ness =
    (A) friendlyness
    (B) friendlness
    (C) friendliness

SPELLING TYPE 2

Directions

Choose the correct spelling.

1. (A) stupor
   (B) stuper
   (C) stoopor

2. (A) sychophant
   (B) psychophant
   (C) sycophant

3. (A) irritable
   (B) iritable
   (C) irratable

4. (A) clishay
   (B) cliche
   (C) clishe

5. (A) charleten
   (B) sharlatan
   (C) charlatan

6. (A) extrordinary
   (B) extraordinary
   (C) extraordinery

7. (A) occasionel
   (B) occassional
   (C) occasional

8. (A) pavilion
   (B) pavillion
   (C) pavilian

9. (A) villen
   (B) villian
   (C) villain

10. (A) obleke
    (B) oblique
    (C) obleek

PUNCTUATION TYPE 1

Directions

Choose the correct word to fill in the blank.

1. Show possession: The _____ hat was large.
   (A) ladies
   (B) lady's

2. Show possession: My _____ car is gray.
   (A) father's-in-law
   (B) father-in-law's

3. Prices are likely to rise _____ according to the broker.
   (A) soon
   (B) soon,

4. The broker ———————— prices to rise soon.
   (A) expects
   (B) expects,

5. You can enjoy surfing, ———————— sunbathing, and swimming.
   (A) rollerskating
   (B) rollerskating,

6. The skies were ———————— but the air was warm.
   (A) cloudy;
   (B) cloudy,

7. The air was ———————— the skies were cloudy.
   (A) warm;
   (B) warm,

8. I will buy nails, wallpaper, and ———————— repair the fence; and paint the cellar, when I can.
   (A) tile,
   (B) tile;

9. "Yes," he ———————— I will be there."
   (A) said: "
   (B) said, "

10. ———————— he asked.
    (A) "Why?"
    (B) Why,

PUNCTUATION TYPE 2

Directions

Decide what mark or marks of punctuation should be placed in the underlined space.

I. I hope she is satisfied now___she owns all the property

‎ 1

    on the street___

‎ ‎ ‎ ‎ ‎ ‎ ‎ ‎ ‎ ‎ 2

    (A) no punctuation
    (B) (,)
    (C) (:)
    (D) (;)
    (E) (.)

II. Find out how much it costs___then decide whether or not

‎ 3

     we can afford it___

‎ ‎ ‎ ‎ ‎ ‎ ‎ ‎ ‎ ‎ ‎ ‎ ‎ 4

     (A) no punctuation
     (B) (,)
     (C) (;)
     (D) (.)
     (E) (?)

III. The rules are as follows___first, roll the dice; then, move

‎ 5

      your token forward___unless the space is already taken;

‎ ‎ ‎ ‎ ‎ ‎ ‎ ‎ ‎ ‎ ‎ ‎ ‎ ‎ ‎ ‎ ‎ 6

      then, take a red card or a green card___

‎ 7

      (A) no punctuation
      (B) (,)
      (C) (:)
      (D) (;)
      (E) (.)

IV. The residents complained about these problems___the high
8
charges for electricity___the broken windows, and___the
9   10
weak pressure.

(A) no punctuation
(B) (,)
(C) (:)
(D) (;)
(E) (.)

VOCABULARY TYPE 1

Directions

Which word best fills the blank in the sentence below?

1. By choosing his words very carefully, the vice president was able
   to _____ about his position without actually lying.
   (A) prevaricate
   (B) equivocate
   (C) fib
   (D) lie
   (E) fabricate

2. Because of the storm, I had to _____ my visit to the
   dentist from Tuesday to Friday.
   (A) postpone
   (B) procrastinate
   (C) retard
   (D) adjourn
   (E) prolong

3. The _____ tastes of Cajun food probably account for its
   widespread popularity.
   (A) poignant
   (B) acrid
   (C) gamy
   (D) piquant
   (E) mordant

4. He was a pragmatist and an opportunist, a man who would do whatever was ——————— rather than what was right.
   (A) eligible
   (B) exigent
   (C) exclusive
   (D) expedient
   (E) explicit

5. After a trial of five months, the defendant was ——————— on all three count and set free.
   (A) exempted
   (B) convicted
   (C) adjudged
   (D) arraigned
   (E) acquitted

VOCABULARY TYPE 2

Directions

Choose the word division that shows the meaningful parts of the word.

1. predictable
   (A) pre/dic/table
   (B) pred/ict/able
   (C) predict/able

2. infallible
   (A) inf/all/ible
   (B) in/fallible
   (C) infal/ible

3. unquenchable
   (A) unquen/chable
   (B) un/quench/able
   (C) un/quen/chable

4. omnipotent
   (A) omni/potent
   (B) om/nip/otent
   (C) om/nipo/tent

5. periscope
   (A) peri/scope
   (B) per/is/cope
   (C) per/i/scope

6. welcome
   (A) we/lcome
   (B) wel/come
   (C) welc/ome

7. interdisciplinary
   (A) in/ter/dis/ciplin/ary
   (B) inter/disci/plinary
   (C) inter/disciplin/ary

8. locksmith
   (A) locks/mith
   (B) loc/ksmith
   (C) lock/smith

9. statesmanship
   (A) states/mans/hip
   (B) states/man/ship
   (C) state/smans/hip

10. outstanding
    (A) out/stand/ing
    (B) outs/tan/ding
    (C) out/stan/ding

ANSWER KEY FOR SPELLING, PUNCTUATION, AND VOCABULARY DIAGNOSTIC TEST

Spelling Type 1	Punctuation Type 1	Vocabulary Type 1
1. C	1. B	1. B
2. A	2. B	2. A
3. C	3. B	3. D
4. A	4. A	4. D
5. B	5. B	5. E
6. B	6. B	
7. C	7. A	**Vocabulary Type 2**
8. B	8. B	1. C
9. A	9. B	2. B
10. C	10. A	3. B
		4. A
Spelling Type 2	**Punctuation Type 2**	5. A
1. A	1. D	6. B
2. C	2. E	7. C
3. A	3. C	8. C
4. B	4. D	9. B
5. C	5. C	10. A
6. B	6. B	
7. C	7. E	
8. A	8. A	
9. C	9. B	
10. B	10. B	

ANSWERS AND COMPLETE EXPLANATIONS FOR GRAMMAR AND USAGE DIAGNOSTIC TEST

TYPE 1

1. (C) With the correlatives *not . . . but,* an infinitive must follow *but* to be parallel to the infinitive after *not* (*to establish . . . to make*).

2. (B) The *whom* should be *who,* subject of the clause *who is most likely to win.* The *I think* is parenthetical.

3. (A) The adverb *almost* should be used to modify the adjective *all.*

4. (B) The subject *fall* is singular. The correct verb is *has effected.*

5. (C) The comparison should be between *the number of Irish* and *the number of Italian or Scottish.*

6. (A) Since the trustees are humans, the pronoun *who,* not *which,* should be used. You might be tempted to choose (B), reasoning that the sentence should read *. . . the fund which determines . . .;* however, this choice would not use appropriate diction, suggesting that a *fund* (an inanimate thing) could *determine.*

7. (D) The singular *number* is the subject; the verb should be the singular *is.*

8. (C) The subject is the singular *humor;* the verb should be the singular *derives.*

9. (A) The singular *Everybody* should be followed by the singular verb *has been.*

10. (E) The sentence is correct as given.

11. (A) With the negative *unaffected,* the correlatives should be *either . . . or.*

174

12. (A) The compound subject (*performance* and *antics*) requires the plural verb *are*.

13. (B) The idiom is *sooner . . . than*.

14. (E) The sentence contains no error.

15. (B) The pronoun *this* has no specific antecedent. A phrase like *and it is for this reason that* would correct the sentence.

TYPE 2

1. (D) With the phrase *The reason is,* you must use the pronoun *that,* not the conjunction *because*. Choice (D) is preferable to choice (B) because of the two present tenses. Choice (B) shifts from present to past tense.

2. (B) The sentence is a contrary-to-fact construction requiring a past subjunctive (*had been*) in the *if* clause.

3. (C) The possessive *my* must be used with the gerund *speaking*.

4. (C) In all but choices (C) and (E), the pronoun *she* seems to apply to Janet's mother. Choice (E) awkwardly separates elements of the sentence.

5. (B) With the correlatives *not only . . . but also,* the structure *how he expected to* should be followed by the same structure, *how he planned to*.

6. (D) The plural *countries* requires the plural verb *are*. The noun *effect* is correct here.

7. (C) In choices (B) and (E), the participle dangles and seems to suggest that the *parents* have graduated from college. In choices (A) and (D), the three parts of the series are not parallel.

8. (B) The singular *everyone* requires the singular *believes he or she is*. Choice (A) omits the necessary *as* after *good*. Choice (C) omits the necessary *other*.

9. (C) In choices (A), (B), and (D), the initial phrase dangles and seems to refer to the *records*. Choice (E) is grammatically correct but wordier than choice (C).

10. (B) The pronouns (*which, it, this*) are all ambiguous. Choice (B) eliminates the ambiguous pronoun.

TYPE 3

Passage 1

1. (C) The more concise and more idiomatic phrase with *elected* is *to the presidency.*

2. (D) The *but* signals the change of direction in meaning more clearly than *and.*

3. (A) Only choice (A) has no punctuation error.

4. (B) The past perfect tense is necessary to indicate an action which took place before the past tense of *ran.*

5. (A) Only choice (A) is idiomatic.

6. (A) A new paragraph is necessary. The subject of the second paragraph is Wilson, not Roosevelt. The appositive after *Wilson* (*the Democratic candidate*) requires two commas to set it off.

7. (C) Only choice (C) avoids the dangling participle. The subject of the sentence is *Wilson's first term,* not *Wilson.* The sentence as given suggests that the *term* was *known best.*

8. (C) The *both . . . and* correlatives are used correctly and concisely in choice (C).

9. (C) Choice (C) provides the most concise expression.

10. (B) The presentation would be strengthened if details about his accomplishments were given.

11. (C) The paragraphs move chronologically from the election years of 1904 to 1916. The next election would be that of 1920.

Passage 2

12. (A) Choice (A) is both idiomatic and more concise than choices (C) and (D). Choice (B) distorts the meaning.

13. (A) Choice (A) is correct and concise. With the apostrophe, *it's* means *it is.*

14. (A) Choice (A) uses the verb tense correctly.

15. (C) None of the pronouns—*it, that,* or *this*—can be used here, since there is no specific antecedent for them to refer to.

16. (C) The phrase *So far* is more concise. It should be followed by a comma.

17. (D) The phrase *much of the* or *much* should precede *cargo;* *many* should precede *artifacts.*

18. (C) The plural subject (*copper* and *tin*) requires a plural verb (*were*). Since the action was incomplete, the correct tense is as given in choice (C).

19. (C) The series should be introduced by a colon.

20. (A) As it is written, the paragraph comes to a concluding climax. None of the three suggested additions follows logically from the preceding sentence. All have the effect of anticlimax.

TYPE 4

1. (E) No change is needed. The subject, *memoirs,* is a plural.

2. (C) The past tense *believed* is more concise and parallel to the past tense *made.*

3. (D) All three parts of the series of verbs should be parallel in tense.

4. (C) The use of *their* makes it clear that *consumers'* is a plural.

5. (E) No change is needed.

6. (A) *Renoir's* is parallel to *O'Keefe's.*

7. (B) The subject of the clause is *who.*

8. (D) The use of both *couldn't* and *hardly* is a double negative.

9. (C) The plural *averages* needs a plural verb, *obscure.*

10. (A) The pronouns must be consistent: *you are, you will, you are.*

TYPE 5

1. (C) Only choice (C) is concise and grammatically correct.

2. (D) Only choice (D) avoids the double negative and the dangling participle.

3. (E) Choice (E) avoids the wordier passive voice.

4. (B) Choice (B) avoids the repetitions of *city/urban* and *usually/as a rule*.

5. (A) Choice (A) is the most concise version.

6. (C) Choice (C) avoids the repetitions of *primary/chief, purpose/function,* and *oversee/supervise.*

7. (D) Choice (D) avoids the duplication of *paying no attention* and *ignoring.*

8. (A) Choice (A) is the most concise version.

9. (B) There are repetitions in *interior/within, recognize/see,* and *external/outside.*

10. (B) Only choice (B) is both concise and grammatically correct.

TYPE 6

1. (C) The correlatives *not . . . but* should be followed by parallel constructions.

2. (D) The present tense of the gerund keeps the three parts of the series parallel: *failing, pocketing, diverting.*

3. (B) It is the *driver,* not the *car* or *control,* with the high blood-alcohol level.

4. (B) By using *forecast,* you avoid the pronouns (*which, this,* or *that*) with no specific antecedents.

5. (A) The sense requires a future perfect tense.

6. (A) Since Lincoln was president, you should use *than any other.*

7. (C) The second *who* is the subject of the clause. Its antecedent is the singular *candidate*, so the correct verb is *has*.

TYPE 7

1. (D) The other three sentences have subject-verb agreement errors—*sole/grip, record holders/is, is/reasons.*

2. (C) The other three sentences have inconsistent verb tenses—*have/permitted, opens/was, were/are.*

3. (A) The other three sentences have dangling infinitives.

4. (B) The other three sentences have errors of idiom in the use of prepositions—*contemptuous for, forgetful to, anxious in.*

5. (A) The other three sentences have case—*her/she, me/I*—errors.

6. (C) The other three sentences place modifiers too far from the words they modify.

7. (B) The other three sentences have errors in the use of adverbs or adjectives—*near, good, real.*

TYPE 8

1. (C) The participle that begins the sentence will dangle if it is not followed by what had anchored, that is, the ships.

2. (A) The *it* in the opening phrase refers to *crabmeat.*

3. (D) The plural verb (*are*) with the plural subjects (*band* and *team*) is correct.

4. (B) The revised sentence will begin *Never herself having done so, she . . .*

5. (D) The correlatives *not only . . . also* require an adjective after *also* to parallel the adjective after *not only.*

6. (C) The reference of the pronoun *he* is made clear by placing *Boone* at the beginning of the main clause.

TYPE 9

1. (B) Sentence 3 must follow sentence 1, as it explains the challenge, and sentence 4 must follow sentences 1 and 3. Sentence 2 must go before sentence 1 to explain *this exemption.*

2. (C) The logical order of the paragraph follows the order of the fourteen-line poem: sentences 2, 4, 1. Beginning with sentence 3 is preferable to ending with it.

3. (A) Sentence 1 must follow sentence 2, and sentence 3 must follow sentence 1. Sentence 4 is the best choice for the first sentence.

4. (D) The *they* in sentence 3 must refer back to the *creationists* of sentence 1. Sentence 4 must follow sentence 2, giving examples of the *unanswered questions.*

5. (C) Sentence 3 must follow sentence 4, sentence 1 must follow sentence 2, and sentence 2 must follow sentence 3.

TYPE 10

1. (B) When and where whales are sighted are the issues here, not the societies that watch whales.

2. (A) The paragraph presents both good and bad sides of overtime.

3. (C) The paragraph stresses the decline in drinking; logically, the value of liquor licenses would decline.

4. (D) The paragraph gives examples of very unlikely predictions.

5. (A) The focus of the paragraph is on the similarity of the results in the two states.

GRAMMAR AND USAGE PRACTICE TEST

ANSWER SHEET FOR GRAMMAR AND USAGE PRACTICE TEST
(Remove This Sheet and Use It to Mark Your Answers)

TYPE 1

1. Ⓐ Ⓑ Ⓒ Ⓓ Ⓔ
2. Ⓐ Ⓑ Ⓒ Ⓓ Ⓔ
3. Ⓐ Ⓑ Ⓒ Ⓓ Ⓔ
4. Ⓐ Ⓑ Ⓒ Ⓓ Ⓔ
5. Ⓐ Ⓑ Ⓒ Ⓓ Ⓔ
6. Ⓐ Ⓑ Ⓒ Ⓓ Ⓔ
7. Ⓐ Ⓑ Ⓒ Ⓓ Ⓔ
8. Ⓐ Ⓑ Ⓒ Ⓓ Ⓔ
9. Ⓐ Ⓑ Ⓒ Ⓓ Ⓔ
10. Ⓐ Ⓑ Ⓒ Ⓓ Ⓔ
11. Ⓐ Ⓑ Ⓒ Ⓓ Ⓔ
12. Ⓐ Ⓑ Ⓒ Ⓓ Ⓔ
13. Ⓐ Ⓑ Ⓒ Ⓓ Ⓔ
14. Ⓐ Ⓑ Ⓒ Ⓓ Ⓔ
15. Ⓐ Ⓑ Ⓒ Ⓓ Ⓔ

TYPE 3

1. Ⓐ Ⓑ Ⓒ Ⓓ
2. Ⓐ Ⓑ Ⓒ Ⓓ
3. Ⓐ Ⓑ Ⓒ Ⓓ
4. Ⓐ Ⓑ Ⓒ Ⓓ
5. Ⓐ Ⓑ Ⓒ Ⓓ
6. Ⓐ Ⓑ Ⓒ Ⓓ
7. Ⓐ Ⓑ Ⓒ Ⓓ
8. Ⓐ Ⓑ Ⓒ Ⓓ
9. Ⓐ Ⓑ Ⓒ Ⓓ
10. Ⓐ Ⓑ Ⓒ Ⓓ
11. Ⓐ Ⓑ Ⓒ Ⓓ
12. Ⓐ Ⓑ Ⓒ Ⓓ
13. Ⓐ Ⓑ Ⓒ Ⓓ
14. Ⓐ Ⓑ Ⓒ Ⓓ
15. Ⓐ Ⓑ Ⓒ Ⓓ

TYPE 5

1. Ⓐ Ⓑ Ⓒ Ⓓ Ⓔ
2. Ⓐ Ⓑ Ⓒ Ⓓ Ⓔ
3. Ⓐ Ⓑ Ⓒ Ⓓ Ⓔ
4. Ⓐ Ⓑ Ⓒ Ⓓ Ⓔ
5. Ⓐ Ⓑ Ⓒ Ⓓ Ⓔ
6. Ⓐ Ⓑ Ⓒ Ⓓ Ⓔ
7. Ⓐ Ⓑ Ⓒ Ⓓ Ⓔ
8. Ⓐ Ⓑ Ⓒ Ⓓ Ⓔ
9. Ⓐ Ⓑ Ⓒ Ⓓ Ⓔ
10. Ⓐ Ⓑ Ⓒ Ⓓ Ⓔ
11. Ⓐ Ⓑ Ⓒ Ⓓ Ⓔ
12. Ⓐ Ⓑ Ⓒ Ⓓ Ⓔ
13. Ⓐ Ⓑ Ⓒ Ⓓ Ⓔ
14. Ⓐ Ⓑ Ⓒ Ⓓ Ⓔ
15. Ⓐ Ⓑ Ⓒ Ⓓ Ⓔ

TYPE 2

1. Ⓐ Ⓑ Ⓒ Ⓓ Ⓔ
2. Ⓐ Ⓑ Ⓒ Ⓓ Ⓔ
3. Ⓐ Ⓑ Ⓒ Ⓓ Ⓔ
4. Ⓐ Ⓑ Ⓒ Ⓓ Ⓔ
5. Ⓐ Ⓑ Ⓒ Ⓓ Ⓔ
6. Ⓐ Ⓑ Ⓒ Ⓓ Ⓔ
7. Ⓐ Ⓑ Ⓒ Ⓓ Ⓔ
8. Ⓐ Ⓑ Ⓒ Ⓓ Ⓔ
9. Ⓐ Ⓑ Ⓒ Ⓓ Ⓔ
10. Ⓐ Ⓑ Ⓒ Ⓓ Ⓔ
11. Ⓐ Ⓑ Ⓒ Ⓓ Ⓔ
12. Ⓐ Ⓑ Ⓒ Ⓓ Ⓔ
13. Ⓐ Ⓑ Ⓒ Ⓓ Ⓔ
14. Ⓐ Ⓑ Ⓒ Ⓓ Ⓔ
15. Ⓐ Ⓑ Ⓒ Ⓓ Ⓔ

TYPE 4

1. Ⓐ Ⓑ Ⓒ Ⓓ Ⓔ
2. Ⓐ Ⓑ Ⓒ Ⓓ Ⓔ
3. Ⓐ Ⓑ Ⓒ Ⓓ Ⓔ
4. Ⓐ Ⓑ Ⓒ Ⓓ Ⓔ
5. Ⓐ Ⓑ Ⓒ Ⓓ Ⓔ
6. Ⓐ Ⓑ Ⓒ Ⓓ Ⓔ
7. Ⓐ Ⓑ Ⓒ Ⓓ Ⓔ
8. Ⓐ Ⓑ Ⓒ Ⓓ Ⓔ
9. Ⓐ Ⓑ Ⓒ Ⓓ Ⓔ
10. Ⓐ Ⓑ Ⓒ Ⓓ Ⓔ
11. Ⓐ Ⓑ Ⓒ Ⓓ Ⓔ
12. Ⓐ Ⓑ Ⓒ Ⓓ Ⓔ
13. Ⓐ Ⓑ Ⓒ Ⓓ Ⓔ
14. Ⓐ Ⓑ Ⓒ Ⓓ Ⓔ
15. Ⓐ Ⓑ Ⓒ Ⓓ Ⓔ

TYPE 6

1. Ⓐ Ⓑ Ⓒ Ⓓ
2. Ⓐ Ⓑ Ⓒ Ⓓ
3. Ⓐ Ⓑ Ⓒ Ⓓ
4. Ⓐ Ⓑ Ⓒ Ⓓ
5. Ⓐ Ⓑ Ⓒ Ⓓ
6. Ⓐ Ⓑ Ⓒ Ⓓ
7. Ⓐ Ⓑ Ⓒ Ⓓ
8. Ⓐ Ⓑ Ⓒ Ⓓ
9. Ⓐ Ⓑ Ⓒ Ⓓ
10. Ⓐ Ⓑ Ⓒ Ⓓ

CUT HERE

ANSWER SHEET FOR GRAMMAR AND USAGE PRACTICE TEST
(Remove This Sheet and Use It to Mark Your Answers)

TYPE 7

```
1  Ⓐ Ⓑ Ⓒ Ⓓ
2  Ⓐ Ⓑ Ⓒ Ⓓ
3  Ⓐ Ⓑ Ⓒ Ⓓ
4  Ⓐ Ⓑ Ⓒ Ⓓ
5  Ⓐ Ⓑ Ⓒ Ⓓ
6  Ⓐ Ⓑ Ⓒ Ⓓ
7  Ⓐ Ⓑ Ⓒ Ⓓ
8  Ⓐ Ⓑ Ⓒ Ⓓ
9  Ⓐ Ⓑ Ⓒ Ⓓ
10 Ⓐ Ⓑ Ⓒ Ⓓ
11 Ⓐ Ⓑ Ⓒ Ⓓ
12 Ⓐ Ⓑ Ⓒ Ⓓ
13 Ⓐ Ⓑ Ⓒ Ⓓ
14 Ⓐ Ⓑ Ⓒ Ⓓ
15 Ⓐ Ⓑ Ⓒ Ⓓ
```

TYPE 8

```
1  Ⓐ Ⓑ Ⓒ Ⓓ
2  Ⓐ Ⓑ Ⓒ Ⓓ
3  Ⓐ Ⓑ Ⓒ Ⓓ
4  Ⓐ Ⓑ Ⓒ Ⓓ
5  Ⓐ Ⓑ Ⓒ Ⓓ
6  Ⓐ Ⓑ Ⓒ Ⓓ
7  Ⓐ Ⓑ Ⓒ Ⓓ
8  Ⓐ Ⓑ Ⓒ Ⓓ
9  Ⓐ Ⓑ Ⓒ Ⓓ
10 Ⓐ Ⓑ Ⓒ Ⓓ
11 Ⓐ Ⓑ Ⓒ Ⓓ
12 Ⓐ Ⓑ Ⓒ Ⓓ
13 Ⓐ Ⓑ Ⓒ Ⓓ
14 Ⓐ Ⓑ Ⓒ Ⓓ
15 Ⓐ Ⓑ Ⓒ Ⓓ
```

TYPE 9

```
1  Ⓐ Ⓑ Ⓒ Ⓓ
2  Ⓐ Ⓑ Ⓒ Ⓓ
3  Ⓐ Ⓑ Ⓒ Ⓓ
4  Ⓐ Ⓑ Ⓒ Ⓓ
5  Ⓐ Ⓑ Ⓒ Ⓓ
6  Ⓐ Ⓑ Ⓒ Ⓓ
7  Ⓐ Ⓑ Ⓒ Ⓓ
8  Ⓐ Ⓑ Ⓒ Ⓓ
9  Ⓐ Ⓑ Ⓒ Ⓓ
10 Ⓐ Ⓑ Ⓒ Ⓓ
```

TYPE 10

```
1  Ⓐ Ⓑ Ⓒ Ⓓ
2  Ⓐ Ⓑ Ⓒ Ⓓ
3  Ⓐ Ⓑ Ⓒ Ⓓ
4  Ⓐ Ⓑ Ⓒ Ⓓ
5  Ⓐ Ⓑ Ⓒ Ⓓ
6  Ⓐ Ⓑ Ⓒ Ⓓ
7  Ⓐ Ⓑ Ⓒ Ⓓ
8  Ⓐ Ⓑ Ⓒ Ⓓ
9  Ⓐ Ⓑ Ⓒ Ⓓ
10 Ⓐ Ⓑ Ⓒ Ⓓ
```

CUT HERE

TYPE 1

Directions

Some of the following sentences are correct. Others contain problems in grammar, usage, idiom, or diction (word choice). There is not more than one error in any sentence.

If there is an error, it will be underlined and lettered. Find the one underlined part that must be changed to make the sentence correct, and choose the corresponding letter on your answer sheet. Mark (E) if the sentence contains no error.

1. <u>Had you</u> paid very close attention to the shape of the gem, or
       A

   had you <u>looked</u> carefully at the <u>allegedly</u> sterling silver
          B   C

   setting, you <u>would of suspected</u> that the ring was not an
                   D

   antique. <u>No error.</u>
          E

2. If the election results are <u>as</u> Harris predicted, the new senator
                 A

   will be the man <u>whom</u> the people <u>believed</u> made the <u>better</u>
            B   C   D

   showing in the televised debate. <u>No error.</u>
                        E

3. None of sixty-five students <u>majoring in</u> economics
                 A

   <u>were prepared for</u> the teacher's <u>laying</u> a <u>trap</u> for them
         B   C   D

   in the comprehensive exam. <u>No error.</u>
                  E

4. If they <u>simply gave</u> the prize to <u>whoever</u> really deserves
         A   B

   it, the publishers who pay for publicity <u>would withdraw</u>
                          C

   <u>their support</u>, and <u>there would be</u> no award at all. <u>No error.</u>
       C   D   E

5. It must be <u>she</u> <u>whom</u> he had in mind when he spoke of a
        A   B
"well-trained, superbly conditioned athlete <u>who</u> <u>might have</u>
                                        C   D
<u>captured</u> a spot on the Olympic team." <u>No error.</u>
  D   E

6. The reasons for his success are <u>that he works hard,</u>
                                A
<u>his good looks,</u> <u>that he exercises regularly,</u> and <u>that his</u>
     B   C   D
<u>grandmother left</u> him four million dollars. <u>No error.</u>
     D   E

7. <u>You'd think</u> that people <u>smart and intelligent enough</u> to be in
   A   B
business <u>by themselves</u> would have the sense to know the
              C
value of monthly savings <u>at a guaranteed</u> high interest
                              D
rate. <u>No error.</u>
     E

8. The jury must first decide <u>whether or not</u> the defendant <u>was</u>
                           A   B
in New York on August third, and then, how <u>can he</u> have had
                                         C
the strength <u>to carry</u> a 200-pound body. <u>No error.</u>
            D   E

9. The art of American morticians <u>paints</u> death <u>to look like life,</u>
                                A   B
sealing <u>it</u> up in watertight caskets <u>and spiriting</u> it away to
       C   D
graveyards camouflaged as gardens. <u>No error.</u>
                                   E

10. <u>Anyone</u> of the compounds that can be <u>produced from</u>
     A   B
the leaves of this plant <u>is</u> dangerous, but the plant <u>itself</u> is not
                      C   D
poisonous. <u>No error.</u>
          E

11. None of the survivors <u>who have</u> now recovered consciousness
                           A
    <u>remember</u> <u>hearing</u> any unusual sound in the motor <u>just before</u>
       B   C   D
    the plane crashed. <u>No error.</u>
                           E

12. *The Destructors* is an <u>unusually</u> powerful film about a group
                              A
    of cruel and idle young boys <u>who destroy</u> an old man's home
                                    B
    for no other reason <u>but because</u> <u>it</u> is beautiful. <u>No error.</u>
                           C   D   E

13. <u>Hoping to both cut taxes and reduce unemployment,</u>
                           A
    the Senate has recommended a bill <u>that allows</u> married couples
                                          B
    <u>not to declare</u> the income of either the husband or the wife,
       C
    depending upon <u>which income is the lowest.</u> <u>No error.</u>
                      D   E

14. <u>It seems increasingly obvious</u> that men's clothes are designed
                   A
    not to please the men who will wear <u>them,</u> <u>but as status</u>
                                           B   C
    <u>symbols that impress</u> the people <u>who will see them.</u> <u>No error.</u>
       C   D   E

15. Unlike Monet, <u>Graham's oil paintings</u> have <u>few</u> bright colors,
                     A   B
    <u>are small,</u> <u>and depict</u> only urban scenes. <u>No error.</u>
       C   D   E

TYPE 2

Directions

Some part of each sentence below is underlined; sometimes the whole sentence is underlined. Five choices for rephrasing the underlined part follow each sentence; the first choice (A) repeats the original, and the other four are different. If choice (A) seems better than the alternatives, choose answer (A); if not, choose one of the others.

For each sentence, consider the requirements of standard written English. Your choice should be a correct and effective expression, not awkward or ambiguous. Focus on grammar, word choice, sentence construction, and punctuation. If a choice changes the meaning of the original sentence, do not select it.

1. That your horse won at Bowie is not an indication of Kentucky Derby quality.
   (A) That your horse won at Bowie
   (B) Because your horse won at Bowie
   (C) Your horse winning at Bowie
   (D) If your horse won at Bowie
   (E) Winning results at Bowie

2. Every one of the tickets that was reserved for parents has been sold.
   (A) that was reserved for parents has
   (B) reserved for parents have
   (C) that were reserved for parents have
   (D) that were reserved for parents has
   (E) reserved for parents had

3. Neither salad oils nor butter has less calories than margarine.
   (A) has less calories than
   (B) has fewer calories than
   (C) have fewer calories than
   (D) are less in calories than
   (E) are fewer in calories than

4. Manning's article on *Nicholas Nickleby* is both the most depend-
able account and shortest guide to this difficult novel.
   (A) is both the most dependable account and shortest guide to
   (B) is both the shortest and most dependable account to
   (C) both is the most dependable account and shortest guide to
   (D) is both the most dependable account of and shortest guide
to
   (E) is the most dependable account of and shortest guide to

5. Every one of the Socialist candidates have promised to support
whoever wins the primary.
   (A) have promised to support whoever wins
   (B) has promised to support whomever wins
   (C) has promised to support whoever wins
   (D) have promised to support whomever wins
   (E) had promised to support whoever wins

6. The symbolical and experimental nature of modern fiction
frequently relegates them to publication in magazines that have
limited circulation.
   (A) relegates them to publication in magazines that have limited circulation.
   (B) relegate them to publication in magazines with limited
circulation.
   (C) relegates them to publication in magazines of limited circulation.
   (D) relegates it to publication in magazines, which have limited
circulation.
   (E) relegates it to publication in magazines with limited circulation.

7. Lured by the Florida sun, Canadians by the thousands descend
annually into St. Petersburg each year.
   (A) Canadians by the thousands descend annually into St.
Petersburg each year.
   (B) St. Petersburg receives thousands of Canadians each year.
   (C) St. Petersburg annually receives thousands of Canadians.
   (D) Canadians by the thousands descend on St. Petersburg each
year.
   (E) thousands of Canadians descend into St. Petersburg each
year.

8. Like Switzerland, the mountains of Colorado and Wyoming keep their snows for ten months.
   (A) Like Switzerland,
   (B) As Switzerland,
   (C) Like those in Switzerland,
   (D) Like the mountains which are in Switzerland,
   (E) Switzerland, like

9. At the door to the kitchen, he stopped to wipe the mud from his boots, ran a comb through his hair, and knocks loudly at the door.
   (A) and knocks loudly at the door.
   (B) and knocks loud at the door.
   (C) and knocked loudly at the door.
   (D) and then knocks loudly at the door.
   (E) knocking at the door loudly.

10. Whoever makes the least mistakes or whoever the wind reaches first is likely to win the sailing trophy.
    (A) Whoever makes the least mistakes or whoever
    (B) Whoever makes the least mistakes or whomever
    (C) Whoever makes the fewest mistakes or whomever
    (D) Whoever can make the least mistakes or whoever
    (E) Whoever makes the fewest mistakes or whoever

11. I especially admire her eagerness to succeed, that she is willing to work hard, and her being optimistic.
    (A) her eagerness to succeed, that she is willing to work hard, and her being optimistic.
    (B) that she is eager to succeed, willing to work hard, and that she is optimistic.
    (C) her eagerness to succeed, her willingness to work hard, and that she is optimistic.
    (D) her eagerness to succeed, her willingness to work hard, and her optimism.
    (E) her being eager to succeed, her being willing to work hard, and her being optimistic.

12. Where the main purpose of the greenhouse is to raise half-hardy plants for planting out in the garden or to grow flowering plants in pots for cut flowers and for bringing into the house.
    (A) Where the main purpose of the greenhouse is
    (B) When the main purpose of the greenhouse is
    (C) The main purpose of the greenhouse is
    (D) The main purpose of the greenhouse are
    (E) Where the main purpose of the greenhouse are

13. With his new knowledge of the processes of cell formation and reproduction, nurserymen have now learned to induce sports or mutations in plants.
    (A) nurserymen have now learned to induce sports
    (B) science has now learned to induce sports
    (C) the nurseryman has now learned to induce sports
    (D) science has now learned how to induce sports
    (E) scientists have now learned how to induce sports

14. The city plans to dismantle and move a fourteenth-century English church to Arizona which will give it the oldest church in the Western Hemisphere.
    (A) which will give it
    (B) and this will give it
    (C) which will give the city
    (D) and this will give the city
    (E) to give the city

15. Banking regulators have seized a savings bank in Georgia and charged that the institution both used deceptive lending and business practices and it misled its stockholders.
    (A) both used deceptive lending and business practices and it misled
    (B) both used both deceptive lending and business practices and that it misled
    (C) used both deceptive lending and business practices, misleading
    (D) used deceptive both lending and business practices, and misled
    (E) both used deceptive lending and business practices and misled

TYPE 3

Directions

In the left-hand column, you will find passages in a "spread-out" format with various words and phrases underlined. In the right-hand column, you will find a set of responses corresponding to each underlined portion. If the underlined portion is correct as it stands, mark the letter indicating "NO CHANGE." If the underlined portion is incorrect, decide which of the choices best corrects it. Consider only underlined portions; assume that the rest of the passage is correct as written.

Passage I

Before the summer games of 1984, optimists believed the Los Angeles Olympiad would produce a small profit. But no
<u>1</u>

one guessed just how well the plan for private-sector financing would work. The latest audit shows that the summer games generated a whopping surplus of two hundred and <u>fifteen million</u>
<u>2</u>
<u>dollars, this sum will likely grow</u>
<u>2</u>
to two hundred and fifty million dollars as Olympic coin sales continue and two million dollars in interest is added to the total each month.

All of this money will be going to good <u>causes. The</u> U.S. Olympic
<u>3</u>

1. A. NO CHANGE
   B. will produce
   C. would deduce
   D. to produce

2. A. NO CHANGE
   B. fifteen million dollars
   C. fifteen million dollars;
   D. fifteen million dollars:

3. A. NO CHANGE
   B. causes; the
   C. causes, the
   D. causes including the following;

Committee, youth and athletic programs, and amateur American sports groups. In addition, the Los Angeles committee's board voted to donate seven million dollars to foreign Olympic committees, reimbursing them for their delegations' housing costs in
4
Los Angeles last summer.

4. A. NO CHANGE
   B. the costs for housing their delegations
   C. their delegations housing costs
   D. their delegation's housing costs

All of this stands in stark
5
contrast to the financing fiasco
5
in Montreal eight years before. Citizens there will be paying off their one billion dollar public debt for decades to come. And there was no surplus funds to
6
help sustain amateur athletics in Canada and Olympic committees elsewhere in the world. It is likely that in the future we will see fewer and fewer city govern-
7
ments taking on the financial risk of sponsoring the Olympic Games single-handed. The huge success of the 1984 summer games in Los

5. A. NO CHANGE
   B. in contrast starkly with
   C. contrasting to
   D. contrasting with

6. A. NO CHANGE
   B. there were no surplus
   C. they're were no surplus
   D. their were no surplus

7. A. NO CHANGE
   B. less and less
   C. a smaller and smaller number of
   D. a lesser and lesser number of

Angeles makes the privatization
8
option more attractive than ever.
8

8. A. NO CHANGE
   B. privatization options
   C. private financing
   D. the private financing

Passage II

These paragraphs may or may not be in the most logical order. The last item of this passage will ask you to choose the most logical order.

(1)

Many people mistakenly believe they have insomnia. Because they have not had eight full hours of sleep, they think that they are insomniacs. But there is no evidence to support the common belief that everyone has
9
to get eight hours of sleep

9. A. NO CHANGE
   B. everyone have
   C. everybody have
   D. that everybody have

nightly. In fact, a few people
10
habitually sleep as little as two hours a night and wake up feeling fine. A much larger

10. A. NO CHANGE
    B. OMIT and begin sentence with *A few*
    C. Move to after *habitually*
    D. As a matter of fact,

number requires only five hours
11
of sleep each night, while others must have ten hours to feel refreshed.

11. A. NO CHANGE
    B. requires
    C. only requires
    D. require only

(2)

Another type of insomnia occurs when something exciting
12
or something upsetting happens,
12
or is about to happen, in someone's life. Fortunately, this sort of insomnia is likely to disappear naturally after the

12. A. NO CHANGE
    B. something exciting or something upsetting happens
    C. something exciting or something upsetting happen,
    D. something exciting or upsetting happen

crisis has passed. When insomnia
does not go away, it is possible
that sleeplessness is a sign of
physical or emotional illness.
Awakening early in the morning,
for example, is sometimes a sign
of depression, <u>and this is a</u>
            13
potentially serious mental illness.

13. A. NO CHANGE
    B. OMIT
    C. which is
    D. that is

(3)
   There is a type of insomnia in
which people believe that they
have had only a few minutes of
sleep, or no sleep at all. Though
these sufferers have not slept
well, they have probably had
some sleep. Because periods of
light sleep and wakefulness are
often fused, the insomniac does
not realize that <u>they have been</u>
                14
<u>asleep.</u> It is harder to judge
14

14. A. NO CHANGE
    B. they were
    C. he or she has been
    D. he or she have been

time in a dark bedroom than in
the daylight, so it is easy to
overestimate the number of
wakeful hours and to under-
estimate those spent sleeping.

15. Choose the sequence
    of paragraph numbers
    that will make the
    essay's structure
    most logical.
    A. NO CHANGE
    B. 1, 3, 2
    C. 2, 1, 3
    D. 3, 1, 2

TYPE 4

Directions

Read the sentences below and decide whether a correction needs to be made.

1. The plastic bag, used only at Mead's Supermarket, is photodegradable.
   - (A) if bag should be changed to bags.
   - (B) if the commas should be deleted.
   - (C) if only should be deleted.
   - (D) if Mead's Supermarket should not be capitalized.
   - (E) if NO CHANGE is necessary.

2. Rockabye Records, the downtown record store, are having a sale of compact disks.
   - (A) if Records should not be capitalized.
   - (B) if the commas should be deleted.
   - (C) if are should be changed to is.
   - (D) if of should be changed to on.
   - (E) if NO CHANGE is necessary.

3. We listen to recordings of books as we drove to work each morning.
   - (A) if listen should be changed to listened.
   - (B) if recordings should be changed to recording.
   - (C) if a comma should be inserted after as.
   - (D) if as should be changed to when.
   - (E) if NO CHANGE is necessary.

4. Please give this completed application form to the man, who is seated at the desk in office B.
   - (A) if a comma should be inserted after this.
   - (B) if completed should be changed to complete.
   - (C) if the comma after man should be omitted.
   - (D) if is seated should be changed to is sitting.
   - (E) if NO CHANGE is necessary.

5. Like pianists, the study of the violin requires hours of daily practice.
   (A) if pianists should be changed to piano.
   (B) if pianists should be changed to that of the piano.
   (C) if requires should be changed to require.
   (D) if daily should be omitted.
   (E) if NO CHANGE is necessary.

6. A number of international students from other countries come to study music at Aspen each summer.
   (A) if international should be omitted.
   (B) if come should be changed to comes.
   (C) if Aspen should not be capitalized.
   (D) if summer should be capitalized.
   (E) if NO CHANGE is necessary.

7. Tinker, Evers, and Chance were famous as fielders, and Evers was the better batter of the trio.
   (A) if the comma after Tinker should be omitted.
   (B) if the comma after fielders should be omitted.
   (C) if better should be changed to best.
   (D) if fielders should be capitalized.
   (E) if NO CHANGE is necessary.

8. Accept for one day in March, Margaret attended every session of the council.
   (A) if Accept should be changed to Except.
   (B) if the comma should be omitted after March.
   (C) if attended should be changed to intended.
   (D) if council should be changed to counsel.
   (E) if NO CHANGE is necessary.

9. Developing rapidly in the favorable environment, the plants of the tropical rain forests grow taller than those in any other area of the continent.
   (A) if Developing rapidly should be changed to Since they develop rapidly.
   (B) if the comma after environment should be omitted.
   (C) if forests should be changed to forest.
   (D) if those should be omitted.
   (E) if NO CHANGE is necessary.

10. If neither of the two candidates for mayor will agree to run a campaign free of mudslinging, who is to set an example for the candidates for other offices.

(A) if will agree should be changed to agree.
(B) if the comma after mudslinging should be omitted.
(C) if up should be inserted after set.
(D) if the period after offices should be changed to a question mark.
(E) if NO CHANGE is necessary.

11. The speakers' long-winded and garrulous lectures seemed to go on forever, and their listeners were unable to conceal their boredom.

(A) if speakers' should be changed to speaker's.
(B) if and garrulous should be omitted.
(C) if the comma after forever should be omitted.
(D) if were should be changed to had been.
(E) if NO CHANGE is necessary.

12. For years, automobile manufacturers have claimed, the air bag would drive the cost of cars beyond the reach of consumers.

(A) if the comma after years should be omitted.
(B) if the comma after claimed should be omitted.
(C) if would drive should be changed to drove.
(D) if consumers should be changed to consumers'.
(E) if NO CHANGE is necessary.

13. Like humans do, lemurs seek out shady spots for an after-lunch siesta in the heat of the day.

(A) if humans should be changed to human beings.
(B) if do should be omitted.
(C) if the comma after do should be omitted.
(D) if seek should be changed to seeks.
(E) if NO CHANGE is necessary.

14. The residents of Belmont are more concerned with traffic and parking problems than with the decline in the academic standards in the schools or with the alleged corruption in the police force.
    (A) if <u>are</u> should be changed to <u>is</u>.
    (B) if <u>than with</u> should be changed to <u>than</u>.
    (C) if <u>or</u> should be changed to <u>nor</u>.
    (D) if <u>alleged</u> should be omitted.
    (E) if NO CHANGE is necessary.

15. The heroine of this novel works as a waitress, a secretary, as a nurse, and an investigator for the Internal Revenue Service.
    (A) if <u>works</u> should be changed to <u>worked</u>.
    (B) if the first <u>as</u> should be omitted.
    (C) if the second <u>as</u> should be omitted.
    (D) if <u>investigator</u> should be capitalized.
    (E) if NO CHANGE is necessary.

TYPE 5

Directions

Which sentence below expresses the thought most effectively?

1. (A) Hoping to understand the doctor's explanation, the student nurses gave her their complete and total attention.
   (B) Being as they hoped to understand the doctor's explanation, the student nurses gave her complete and total attention.
   (C) Hoping to understand the doctor's explanation, the student nurses gave her their complete attention.
   (D) Hoping to understand the explanation, the doctor got complete attention from the student nurses.
   (E) The complete and total attention of the student nurses was given to the doctor who hoped to understand her explanation.

2. (A) Young children learn to speak foreign languages more easily than older children and adults.

(B) Foreign languages are more easily learned by young children than they are learned by older children and by adults.

(C) Learning to speak foreign languages is easier for young children than it is for older children and adults.

(D) Older children and adults have more trouble learning to speak foreign languages than that of young children.

(E) Foreign languages are learned more easily as far as speaking goes by young children than older children or adults.

3. (A) The system is neither fair to lower-income taxpayers nor middle-income recipients of the benefits.

(B) The system is unfair to both lower-income taxpayers and middle-income recipients of the benefits.

(C) The system is unfair both to lower-income taxpayers and middle-income recipients of the benefits.

(D) The system is fair neither to lower-income taxpayers or to middle-income recipients of the benefits.

(E) The system is fair neither to lower-income taxpayers nor middle-income recipients of the benefits.

4. (A) From the thirty-five cents worth of seed that he had planted in May comes a hundred dollars worth of fall flowers.

(B) Thirty-five cents worth of seeds, that were planted in May by him, produces one hundred dollars worth of flowers in the fall.

(C) He gets one hundred dollars worth of fall flowers from thirty-five cents worth of seed having been planted by him in May.

(D) He got one hundred dollars worth of fall flowers from thirty-five cents worth of seeds planted in May.

(E) Planting thirty-five cents worth of seeds in May, and harvesting one hundred dollars worth of flowers in the fall.

5. (A) The city now requires you to separate bottles and cans, and one must also tie newspapers in bundles.
   (B) You are now required by the city to separate bottles and cans, and required to tie newspapers in bundles.
   (C) One is required by the city to tie newspapers in bundles and also to separate cans and bottles now.
   (D) Now the city requires that bottles and cans be separated, and you must tie newspapers in bundles.
   (E) The city now requires bottles and cans to be separated and newspapers to be tied in bundles.

6. (A) Both of the classes are required for admission to the advanced biochemistry course.
   (B) Both classes are required for admission for the advanced biochemistry requisite course.
   (C) Both classes is requisite for admission into the advanced biochemistry course.
   (D) For admission of the advanced biochemistry course, both classes are required.
   (E) To be admitted to the advanced biochemistry course, both classes are required.

7. (A) As a rule, as interest rates are declining, the price of stocks are rising.
   (B) Usually, the price of stocks rises as interest rates declines.
   (C) As a rule, the decline of interest rates are accompanied by the rise in stock prices.
   (D) Normally, stock prices arise as interest rates decline.
   (E) As a rule, stock prices rise as interest rates decline.

8. (A) The bank offered free clocks to encourage both increased savings deposits and to decrease withdrawals.
   (B) The bank offered free clocks to encourage increased savings depositors and to decrease withdrawals.
   (C) To encourage both increased savings deposits and decrease withdrawals, the bank offered free clocks.
   (D) To encourage increased savings deposits and decreased withdrawals, the bank offered free clocks.
   (E) The bank offered free clocks both to encourage increased savings deposits and decrease withdrawals.

9. (A) After half an hour of sprints, the rowers complained about themselves being pressed too hard.
   (B) The rowers complained about themselves being pressed too hard after a half hour of sprints.
   (C) After half an hour of sprints, the rowers complained about their being pressed too hard.
   (D) The rowers complained about themselves as pressed too hard, after half an hour of sprints.
   (E) The rowers complained about themselves and pressed too hard after half an hour of sprints.

10. (A) The delegates are willing to talk about compromise but not to do anything to bring that about.
    (B) The delegates are willing to talk about compromise but not to do anything to bring it about.
    (C) The delegates are willing to talk about compromise but doing nothing to bring it about.
    (D) The delegates are willing to talk about compromise but doing nothing to bring that about.
    (E) The delegates are willing to talk about compromise and doing nothing about it.

11. (A) The students have no interest in fiction rather than the thrillers or romances.
    (B) The students have no interest in fiction which were not thrillers or romances.
    (C) The students have no interest in fiction other than thrillers or romances.
    (D) The students have no interest for fiction other than the thrillers or romances.
    (E) The students have no interest for fiction except thrillers or romances.

12. (A) When living in New York, his rent alone consumed half his salary.
    (B) When in New York, his rent alone consumed half of his salary.
    (C) When living in New York, half of his salary was spent on rent alone.
    (D) When living in New York, he spent half of his salary on rent alone.
    (E) When he lived in New York, he spends half of his salary on rent alone.

13. (A) The number of tennis players far exceeds those of golfers.
    (B) The number of tennis players far exceeds golfers.
    (C) The number of tennis players far exceeds that of golfers.
    (D) The number of tennis players is more than golfers, by far.
    (E) The number of tennis players is far in excess of golfers.

14. (A) She is as fast, if not faster, than any runner in the city.
    (B) She is as fast as, if not faster than, any other runner in the city.
    (C) She is as fast, if not faster than any other runner in the city.
    (D) She is as fast as, if not faster, any runner in the city.
    (E) She is as fast as, if not faster than, any runner in the city.

15. (A) Skilled in market analysis, Edmond Harbin is an advisor to three mutual funds.
    (B) Because he is skilled in market analysis, Edmond Harbin is an advisor in three mutual funds.
    (C) A skilled man in the analysis of the market, Edmond Harbin is an advisor of three mutual funds.
    (D) As a man who is skilled in market analysis, Edmond Harbin is an advisor to three mutual funds.
    (E) As an advisor to three mutual funds, Edmond Harbin is a man who is skilled in market analysis.

TYPE 6

Directions

In each of the following, select the best answer from the four suggested.

1. The stadium is not wholly _____.
   (A) sold out; but the game will still be televised.
   (B) sold out, however, the game will still be televised.
   (C) sold out however the game will still be televised.
   (D) sold out; the game will still be televised, however.

2. Born in Switzerland and reared in England, she _____.
   (A) both speaks French and English fluently.
   (B) fluently speaks both French and English.
   (C) speaks English and French both fluently.
   (D) both fluently speaks French and English.

3. Finally deciphered in 1972, _____.
   (A) linguists have been struggling to explain the language for years.
   (B) linguists for years have struggled to explain the language.
   (C) the language was explained by linguists after years of struggle.
   (D) after years of struggle, linguists have explained the language.

4. He showed no interest in reading novels _____.
   (A) which was not science fiction.
   (B) rather than science fiction.
   (C) other than science fiction.
   (D) which were other than science fiction.

5. _____, musical comedy composers are often classically trained musicians.
   (A) Like Gershwin and Rodgers
   (B) As Gershwin and Rodgers
   (C) Like *Show Boat* and *South Pacific*
   (D) As in *Show Boat* and *South Pacific*

6. Though the company is as large _____ any other in the city, it pays no state or local taxes.
   (A) , if not larger than
   (B) as, if not larger than,
   (C) as if not larger than
   (D) or larger than

7. _____, an event that may happen six months from now, the laws will protect the sea birds of the peninsula.
   (A) If and when it was enacted
   (B) If it may be adopted
   (C) When and if it is adopted
   (D) If and when they are enacted

8. The danger is not that the forest habitat will disappear, _____.
   (A) but that chemical pollution will make it uninhabitable.
   (B) but it is that chemical pollution may make it uninhabitable.
   (C) but uninhabitability due to chemical pollutants.
   (D) but pollution making it uninhabitable.

9. Your responsibilities will be to keep the files in order, to order office supplies, _____.
   (A) answer the phone, and make coffee.
   (B) answer the phone and to make coffee.
   (C) to answer the phone, and make coffee.
   (D) to answer the phone, and to make coffee.

10. The danger of tuberculosis in the tropics far exceeds _____.
   (A) malaria and yellow fever.
   (B) that of malaria and yellow fever.
   (C) those of malaria and yellow fever.
   (D) malaria and yellow fevers.

TYPE 7

Directions

In the following items, three of the four sentences illustrate a similar type of error. Choose the correct sentence.

1. (A) A solar eclipse of the sun, if total and complete, will plunge the earth into darkness.
   (B) The principal purpose of the elections is chiefly to make certain that each and every citizen has a chance to express a preference.
   (C) Frequently, the population of zebra often declines in the dry season.
   (D) The number of seeds that germinate depends on the moisture in the soil and the temperature of the air.

2. (A) Both George Eliot's novels and the poems of Tennyson are more popular now than they were twenty years ago.
   (B) It is not the cost but it is the inconvenience of air travel that bothers me.
   (C) He will neither eat a sensible diet nor exercise regularly, despite his doctor's warnings.
   (D) Either she forgot to set her alarm clock last night or a freeway accident has made her late.

3. (A) Sherlock Holmes was acclaimed for his ability to use logic and reduction in solving crimes.
   (B) The bicycles can be put together or dissembled using only a single wrench in less than three minutes.
   (C) The air raid shelter was filled with necessary items like flour and sugar, but it had no source of heat and light.
   (D) We cannot have real justice until we have a retribution of the material goods of this country.

4. (A) Failing to find the seat number on her ticket, she sat in the first vacant space she could find.
   (B) Hoping to put on weight before the physical exam, high calorie foods like peanuts and candy made up most of his diet.
   (C) Disagreeing sharply with both his teacher and the other students in the class, his original reading of the story was never taken seriously.
   (D) Despite arriving at the ticket office two hours before sales began, the concert was sold out before I reached the box office.

5. (A) My aunt, as well as her four children, are planning to vacation in Florida this winter.
   (B) His records in the high jump, not one of which has yet been broken, are expected to last for years.
   (C) There is a robin, two blue jays, and two orioles perched in the branches of that tree.
   (D) In addition to the golf balls and tennis rackets, a stout canoe paddle are also on the shopping list.

6. (A) I am hoping to see him yesterday, but I arrived too late.
   (B) The house has been sold three times, but its price has increased each year.
   (C) I will have seen this film three times, but she saw it more often than I.
   (D) He had been waiting at the station for more than an hour yesterday when his train finally arrives.

7. (A) "I really expect to win some money this time," he said hopefully.
   (B) The house is painted a faded yellow color, with green shutters that bang noisy in the wind.
   (C) Reading quick, she finished the book in one day and began the sequel immediately.
   (D) Unlike trout, catfish can very easily survive in muddy and turbidly waters.

8. (A) It is as far, if not farther, as a man can walk in a day from Weston to Easton.

   (B) The government has usually, and in the future will continue to, encouraged the electorate to study the ballot propositions carefully.

   (C) The music of Schoenberg is radically different from Schubert.

   (D) People who file their taxes early can, and often do, receive their refunds before other taxpayers have even begun to prepare their returns.

9. (A) He had forgotten to sign his score card, and this made him ineligible to continue in the tournament.

   (B) Forgetting to sign his score care, he was ineligible to continue to play in the tournament.

   (C) He forgot to sign his score card, which caused him to be ineligible to continue playing in the tournament.

   (D) He had forgotten to sign his score card, and that caused his ineligibility for the rest of the tournament.

10. (A) The lecturer from New Orleans who teaches at Tulane and Loyola, have flown on to Tampa.

    (B) The center, as well as the taller of the two guards, are in foul trouble and are on the bench.

    (C) The team, but not the band or the rooting section, is flying to El Paso three days before the game.

    (D) Neither of the coaches from New York whose teams lost in the semifinals are planning to attend the awards ceremony.

11. (A) They danced like professionals giving an exhibition, seeming to be unaware of and uninterested in each other.

    (B) At her suggestion, lunching at a coffee shop where both of them ate large servings of delicious French bread and unsalted butter.

    (C) Cries, bells, hammerings, roars of buses, muttering engines, whistles and wind—the sounds of the city surrounding me like a mantle.

    (D) The tool used generations ago by Japanese peasants to harvest rice by twisting it around stalks.

12. (A) The article describes a four-year-old Romanian girl who American adoptive parents are bringing to Chicago.

(B) Whom do you suppose is the real author of this puzzling book?

(C) I cannot convince myself that any judge is wise enough to be trusted with the power to tell others who they can read.

(D) Many law enforcement officers on whom the responsibility for enforcing the law falls are uncertain about its justification.

13. (A) The park provides a habitat for small herds of ibex and chamois, a conservatory for alpine plants, and, in the winter, an ideal location for cross-country skiing.

(B) Before we can move in, we will have to paint the kitchen, carpet the hall, and the windows will have to be replaced.

(C) The Colorado River flows through Colorado, Arizona, and the state of Nevada.

(D) The work is varied: cake baking, cake decorating, to make bread, rolls, and pies, and to make salads.

14. (A) There aren't hardly any microorganisms that can live in water heated to such high temperatures.

(B) He will not allow no one to use his lawnmower.

(C) She can barely walk to the grocery store without becoming tired.

(D) There is scarcely no gasoline on sale at a price below a dollar a gallon.

15. (A) Like Shakespeare wrote, reputation is worth more than jewels.

(B) Because of his love for outdoor life, he had always wanted to live in Montana, like his grandparents had.

(C) As the forecasters warned, the heavy showers made the streets like rivers.

(D) As Hemingway, Fitzgerald wrote an unsuccessful comic novel before his first big success.

TYPE 8

Directions

In this section, you are to rewrite sentences in your head. You will be told how to begin the new sentence. Keep in mind that your new sentence should have the same meaning and contain essentially the same information as the sentence given you.

1. That some of the species of South American monkeys engage in infanticide is among the surprising revelations in Jane Harrison's study.

   Rewrite, beginning with <u>Jane Harrison's study</u> . . . The next words will be

   (A) surprises us by revealing
   (B) surprising reveals
   (C) surprisingly reveals
   (D) contains the surprising revelation

2. The Raiders are now in second place in the Western division because they lost two games in a row.

   Rewrite, beginning with <u>Having lost two games in a row,</u> . . . The next words will be

   (A) the Western division
   (B) the Raiders
   (C) second place
   (D) now the Western division

3. Visits to my Aunt Priscilla and my mother-in-law are the chief pleasures of my trips to Chicago.

   Rewrite, beginning with <u>While visiting Chicago,</u> . . . The next words will be

   (A) my Aunt Priscilla
   (B) my chief pleasure
   (C) I chiefly enjoy
   (D) my trip's

GRAMMAR AND USAGE PRACTICE TEST 211

4. Had you left for the station half an hour earlier, you would not have missed the train.

   Rewrite, beginning with **If you** . . . The next words will be

   (A) would have left
   (B) would of left
   (C) would leave
   (D) had left

5. The fisherman must choose between accepting a smaller catch of tuna and violating the laws to protect the dolphin.

   Rewrite, beginning with **Either to accept a smaller catch of tuna**
   . . . The next words will be

   (A) or violating
   (B) or to violate
   (C) or protecting
   (D) or the violation

6. According to the magazine, the Grand Duke, his Duchess, and their three children are staying at the Hotel Negresco in Nice.

   Rewrite, beginning with **The Grand Duke, as well as his Duchess and the three children,** . . . The next words will be

   (A) are, according to the magazine, staying
   (B) are staying, according to this magazine
   (C) is staying
   (D) are at

7. Scientific tests have shown that some animals that eat only green leaves are wholly free of colon cancers.

   Rewrite, beginning with **Eating only green leaves,** . . . The next words will be

   (A) some animals
   (B) animals
   (C) has been shown
   (D) in scientific tests

8. The novels of Jarbin, like those of Verdan, depend upon a series of increasingly unlikely encounters among characters.

   Rewrite, beginning with <u>Like Verdan,</u> . . . The next words will be

   (A) the novels of Jarbin
   (B) Jarbin's novels
   (C) the characters in
   (D) Jarbin writes

9. The advertisement calls for a person with ability in selling, buying, and bookkeeping.

   Rewrite, beginning with <u>A person with the ability to sell, buy, and</u> . . . The next words will be

   (A) keep books
   (B) to keep books
   (C) bookkeeping
   (D) ability in bookkeeping

10. When it is impossible to find a parking space in downtown Arlington, one can always depend on the lot at the railroad station.

    Rewrite, beginning with <u>When you cannot find a parking space in downtown Arlington,</u> . . . The next words will be

    (A) one can
    (B) one always
    (C) you depend
    (D) you can

11. The restaurant is popular because its food is delicious, its prices are low, and its views are spectacular.

    Rewrite, beginning with <u>Its delicious food,</u> . . . The next words will be

    (A) its prices which are low
    (B) low prices
    (C) that it has low prices
    (D) that its prices are low

12. I finished the exam in the required time with almost no difficulty.

    Rewrite, beginning with <u>With hardly</u> . . . The next words will be

    (A) any difficulty
    (B) almost any difficulty
    (C) no difficulty
    (D) no amount of difficulty

13. For more than two hundred years, the role of Orpheus has been sung by both male and female singers.

    Rewrite, beginning with <u>Male and female singers</u> . . . The next words will be

    (A) sing
    (B) sang
    (C) have sung
    (D) had sung

14. Knowing the risk of investing in junk bonds, the broker, nevertheless, urged his clients to buy the uninsured securities.

    Rewrite, beginning with <u>Despite</u> . . . The next words will be

    (A) the fact that he knew about
    (B) his knowing about
    (C) that he knew about
    (D) his having knowledge about

15. The cake will rise properly if the eggs are beaten for four full minutes.

    Rewrite, beginning with <u>By beating the eggs for four full minutes,</u> . . . The next words will be

    (A) the rising
    (B) the cake
    (C) you will insure
    (D) the cake's

TYPE 9

Directions

Choose the numbered sequence in the most logical paragraph order. Even though you might prefer a sequence not listed, you must select one of these four answers.

1. (1) A tray of pebbles filled with water set beneath the plant will supply some of the necessary moisture.
   (2) The lipstick plant can be grown in a well-heated American home.
   (3) But it must have an atmosphere that is more humid than that of our centrally heated houses.
   (4) The plant will thrive if the temperature remains between 65 and 75 degrees.

   (A) 1, 3, 4, 2
   (B) 2, 1, 3, 4
   (C) 2, 3, 1, 4
   (D) 2, 1, 4, 3

2. (1) The Society for the Prevention of Cruelty to Animals, however, had said there was nothing illegal about killing a rat, provided the death was quick and painless.
   (2) A Vancouver performance artist who was about to squash a rat between two canvases was thwarted by animal-rights activists.
   (3) Earlier, they had tried to have the event declared illegal.
   (4) The disappearance of concrete blocks intended to be used to squish the rat led to the cancellation of the performances.

   (A) 1, 2, 4, 3
   (B) 2, 3, 1, 4
   (C) 2, 4, 3, 1
   (D) 4, 3, 2, 1

3. (1) In the robin, she sees only a source of dread.
(2) In the skies and flowers, she finds a beauty that is unendurable.
(3) She cites the most common events of the season: the robins' return, the blue skies, the flowers.
(4) Emily Dickinson's poem is about a woman who is so unhappy that her misery is intensified by its contrast with the joy of spring in the natural world.

   (A) 1, 2, 3, 4
   (B) 3, 1, 2, 4
   (C) 4, 1, 2, 3
   (D) 4, 3, 1, 2

4. (1) Hollis Martins has recently moved from Seattle to Oceanside.
(2) He is accompanied by his wife, Janice, and their three children.
(3) She is a former resident of Oceanside and is delighted to be back in the town where she grew up.
(4) Her children will attend the same elementary school that she attended twenty years ago.

   (A) 1, 2, 3, 4
   (B) 1, 3, 4, 2
   (C) 1, 3, 2, 4
   (D) 1, 4, 3, 2

5. (1) The plant's flowering is determined by the amount of light it receives each day.
(2) As the days grow shorter in the fall, it will shed its leaves and burst into blossom.
(3) In the longer days of spring and summer, it will produce large, glossy leaves.
(4) One of the most striking of the flowering species is the so-called flamingo's wing.

   (A) 1, 2, 3, 4
   (B) 3, 4, 1, 2
   (C) 4, 1, 2, 3
   (D) 4, 3, 2, 1

6. (1) But his opposition to the separation, he argues, is based upon its harmful effect on the county's school budget.
   (2) Supervisors Craig and Ferguson support the drive to separate Ox Valley from the city and to incorporate a new township.
   (3) He is in charge of the city assessor's department and the size of his budget would shrink if the size of the city decreases.
   (4) Supervisor Daniels, on the other hand, strongly opposes the action.

   (A) 1, 2, 3, 4
   (B) 2, 3, 4, 1
   (C) 2, 4, 3, 1
   (D) 4, 3, 1, 2

7. (1) Before he began his weight-loss program, James Zedrik was one hundred and twenty pounds overweight.
   (2) At the completion of the three year program, he weighed just below the average weight of men his age, height, and frame.
   (3) In his first six months, he ate chiefly liquid foods and followed a carefully monitored program of exercise.
   (4) Gradually, he increased his intake of solid foods and at the same time exercised more strenuously.

   (A) 1, 2, 3, 4
   (B) 1, 3, 4, 2
   (C) 1, 2, 4, 3
   (D) 2, 1, 3, 4

8. (1) On the horizon, you can see the small outlines of the cargo ships on their way to Japan.
   (2) The sands of the beach are nearly white, and the palms reach almost to the water.
   (3) The shallows are clear and cool, filled with small fish and other marine life.
   (4) Further out, the waves break gently on the coral reef.

   (A) 1, 2, 3, 4
   (B) 2, 1, 4, 3
   (C) 2, 4, 1, 3
   (D) 2, 3, 4, 1

9. (1) His decision to send ships to patrol the coast of Columbia in search of drug runners now presents a dilemma.

(2) If he does not withdraw the ships, relations with Columbia will deteriorate.

(3) If he withdraws the ships, people at home will see him as backing down on a promise.

(4) The president is eager to win the good opinion of both the Latin Americans and his North American countrymen.

(A) 2, 3, 4, 1
(B) 2, 4, 3, 1
(C) 4, 1, 2, 3
(D) 4, 2, 3, 1

10. (1) Travelers to Hawaii these days can choose among three distinctly different kinds of environment.

(2) Those with less ambition can rest in the sun at one of the islands' many spalike resorts.

(3) Geology buffs with strong legs can clamber up the sides of active volcanoes.

(4) Finally, those who snorkel will find unsurpassed clear, blue waters and marine life.

(A) 1, 3, 2, 4
(B) 1, 4, 3, 2
(C) 2, 4, 3, 1
(D) 2, 3, 1, 4

TYPE 10

Directions

Each of the following items presents a paragraph in which a sentence is missing. Read each paragraph and then choose, from the four sentences that follow it, the one that is most suitable as the missing sentence.

1. Norton Air Force Base is one of the military bases that will be closed in the near future. The Lockheed Corporation has proposed establishing a commercial aircraft maintenance center at Norton. If successful, the move would demonstrate the potential benefits in converting other bases. _____ _____.

   (A) Lockheed will begin its operation in a large Norton hanger complex.
   (B) Lockheed already operates maintenance centers in South Carolina and Arizona.
   (C) Four of the bays in the Norton hangar were built during World War II.
   (D) As airlines increase their dependence upon outside maintenance, more bases throughout the country could be converted.

2. At the end of Puccini's opera *Tosca,* the heroine leaps to her death from the walls of a prison. One story has it that the heroine in a provincial production landed upon a trampoline and was hurled back into full view of the audience. But many opera historians insist the story is apocryphal. _____ _____.

   (A) It seems too good to be true.
   (B) Exactly where did this take place?
   (C) An elephant in a production of *Aida* is said to have stepped upon the toe of the leading soprano.
   (D) There are many stories of accidents on the stage.

3. The revelation of the club's empty treasury leaves the members with three possible actions, none of them attractive. They can sell the land, though today's real estate market is depressed. _____. Or they can hope to find a bank willing to lend them money and pay the high interest rates banks are now charging.

(A) They can make large profits by investing in bonds.

(B) The loss of the money in the treasury is unexplained.

(C) They can rent the land, though renters are scarce and rents are low.

(D) They can wait patiently until interest rates decline.

4. _____. A new drug to reverse hair loss is a good example. More than eighty percent of the men participating in a recent trial found their hair loss ceased, and new hair grew in places that had been bare. But this hair did not match in color or texture the hair on the other parts of their heads.

(A) Science may be winning the battle against baldness.

(B) Many drugs are only partially successful.

(C) Each year brings new drugs to combat baldness.

(D) Each year brings remarkable advances in pharmacology.

5. _____. A good speaker or writer must know the facts on both sides of the issue he is addressing. And he must understand his audience. Finally, he must speak or write directly and correctly.

(A) Are speaking and writing similar?

(B) Do speaking and writing require the same skills?

(C) Will a good speaker be a good writer?

(D) What makes a good speaker or writer?

6. The members of the first triumvirate were Julius Caesar, Pompey, and Crassus. Crassus was wealthy. Pompey had extensive military experience. And Caesar was immensely popular. He was also a great writer, orator, and administrator. _____
_____.
   (A) Few people knew that he suffered from epilepsy.
   (B) He would eventually be responsible for Pompey's downfall.
   (C) Of the three, Crassus has the least interest for historians.
   (D) He would rise to power upon the shoulders of the other two.

7. Television news cameras covered the arrival of the flag-draped coffins from Panama. President Bush's cheerful news conference, which took place at the same time, was shown on the same split screen. The president was furious and charged the networks with attempting to make him look frivolous. _____
   _____. They know that if they appear to be deliberately attempting to embarrass a president, they will suffer the consequences of strengthening the perception that network television is cynical and unpatriotic.
   (A) The split-screen pictures appeared on all three major networks.
   (B) The pictures did have that effect, as they were shown on all three networks.
   (C) But the networks probably did not split the screen to make the president look foolish.
   (D) In the past, the president has hinted that he is dissatisfied with his treatment by the television networks.

8. _____. First-born children, studies show, are more likely to fear the prospect of injury or accident than children with older brothers or sisters. Though some fears, like the fear of the dark, decrease or disappear as we grow older, others, like the fear of performing in public, are likely to increase. The fear of fires is more common in adults than in children.
   (A) Childhood is the time of fear.
   (B) Childhood is not the only time of fear.
   (C) Some children are more fearful than others.
   (D) Children should never be laughed at because they are afraid.

9. By paying $105 a month for the next five years, Florida parents of a six-year-old son or daughter can guarantee that child four years of tuition at any college or university. Predictions of college costs in excess of $150,000 by the year 2007 are encouraging many parents to participate in state-sponsored plans like the one in Florida. _____. Ten states now have laws that guarantee a pay-now, tuition-later plan. And many upper-middle-class parents have greater peace of mind.

(A) But who will make up the difference if this money is invested unwisely?

(B) Still, many futurists predict tuitions will be even higher.

(C) So far, Michigan, Florida, and Wyoming have implemented the plan.

(D) If there is not enough money, will the states make up the difference?

10. _____. It is mistaken or misleading in its account of Jane Austen's relationship with the family. It gravely misinterprets five of the six major novels. It gets one or two dates wrong, and the proofreading is careless. The jacket design is unattractive.

(A) For a book published by a reputable academic publisher, this biography contains a large number of both major and minor faults.

(B) For some years, we have been waiting for a first-rate new biography of Jane Austen, and this book is the answer.

(C) The book is marred by a few trivial errors.

(D) The University Press has recently published a critical biography of Jane Austen.

ANSWER KEY FOR GRAMMAR AND USAGE PRACTICE TEST

Type 1	Type 3	Type 5	Type 7	Type 9
1. D	1. A	1. C	1. D	1. C
2. B	2. C	2. A	2. C	2. B
3. B	3. C	3. B	3. C	3. D
4. E	4. A	4. D	4. A	4. A
5. E	5. A	5. E	5. B	5. C
6. B	6. B	6. A	6. B	6. C
7. B	7. A	7. E	7. A	7. B
8. C	8. C	8. D	8. D	8. D
9. E	9. A	9. C	9. B	9. C
10. A	10. A	10. B	10. C	10. A
11. B	11. D	11. C	11. A	
12. C	12. A	12. D	12. D	Type 10
13. D	13. B	13. C	13. A	1. D
14. C	14. C	14. B	14. C	2. A
15. A	15. B	15. A	15. C	3. C
				4. B
Type 2	Type 4	Type 6	Type 8	5. D
1. A	1. B	1. D	1. C	6. D
2. D	2. C	2. B	2. B	7. C
3. B	3. A	3. C	3. C	8. B
4. E	4. C	4. C	4. D	9. C
5. C	5. B	5. A	5. B	10. A
6. E	6. A	6. B	6. C	
7. D	7. C	7. D	7. A	
8. C	8. A	8. A	8. D	
9. C	9. E	9. D	9. A	
10. C	10. D	10. B	10. D	
11. D	11. B		11. B	
12. C	12. B		12. A	
13. C	13. B		13. C	
14. E	14. E		14. B	
15. E	15. C		15. C	

SPELLING, PUNCTUATION, AND VOCABULARY
PRACTICE TEST

ANSWER SHEET FOR SPELLING, PUNCTUATION, AND VOCABULARY
PRACTICE TEST
(Remove This Sheet and Use It to Mark Your Answers)

SPELLING
TYPE 1

1 Ⓐ Ⓑ Ⓒ
2 Ⓐ Ⓑ Ⓒ
3 Ⓐ Ⓑ Ⓒ
4 Ⓐ Ⓑ Ⓒ
5 Ⓐ Ⓑ Ⓒ

6 Ⓐ Ⓑ Ⓒ
7 Ⓐ Ⓑ Ⓒ
8 Ⓐ Ⓑ Ⓒ
9 Ⓐ Ⓑ Ⓒ
10 Ⓐ Ⓑ Ⓒ

SPELLING
TYPE 2

1 Ⓐ Ⓑ Ⓒ
2 Ⓐ Ⓑ Ⓒ
3 Ⓐ Ⓑ Ⓒ
4 Ⓐ Ⓑ Ⓒ
5 Ⓐ Ⓑ Ⓒ

6 Ⓐ Ⓑ Ⓒ
7 Ⓐ Ⓑ Ⓒ
8 Ⓐ Ⓑ Ⓒ
9 Ⓐ Ⓑ Ⓒ
10 Ⓐ Ⓑ Ⓒ

PUNCTUATION
TYPE 1

1 Ⓐ Ⓑ
2 Ⓐ Ⓑ
3 Ⓐ Ⓑ
4 Ⓐ Ⓑ
5 Ⓐ Ⓑ

6 Ⓐ Ⓑ
7 Ⓐ Ⓑ
8 Ⓐ Ⓑ
9 Ⓐ Ⓑ
10 Ⓐ Ⓑ

11 Ⓐ Ⓑ
12 Ⓐ Ⓑ
13 Ⓐ Ⓑ
14 Ⓐ Ⓑ
15 Ⓐ Ⓑ

PUNCTUATION
TYPE 2

1 Ⓐ Ⓑ Ⓒ Ⓓ Ⓔ
2 Ⓐ Ⓑ Ⓒ Ⓓ Ⓔ
3 Ⓐ Ⓑ Ⓒ Ⓓ Ⓔ
4 Ⓐ Ⓑ Ⓒ Ⓓ Ⓔ
5 Ⓐ Ⓑ Ⓒ Ⓓ Ⓔ

6 Ⓐ Ⓑ Ⓒ Ⓓ Ⓔ
7 Ⓐ Ⓑ Ⓒ Ⓓ Ⓔ
8 Ⓐ Ⓑ Ⓒ Ⓓ Ⓔ
9 Ⓐ Ⓑ Ⓒ Ⓓ Ⓔ
10 Ⓐ Ⓑ Ⓒ Ⓓ Ⓔ

11 Ⓐ Ⓑ Ⓒ Ⓓ Ⓔ
12 Ⓐ Ⓑ Ⓒ Ⓓ Ⓔ
13 Ⓐ Ⓑ Ⓒ Ⓓ Ⓔ
14 Ⓐ Ⓑ Ⓒ Ⓓ Ⓔ
15 Ⓐ Ⓑ Ⓒ Ⓓ Ⓔ

VOCABULARY
TYPE 1

1 Ⓐ Ⓑ Ⓒ Ⓓ Ⓔ
2 Ⓐ Ⓑ Ⓒ Ⓓ Ⓔ
3 Ⓐ Ⓑ Ⓒ Ⓓ Ⓔ
4 Ⓐ Ⓑ Ⓒ Ⓓ Ⓔ
5 Ⓐ Ⓑ Ⓒ Ⓓ Ⓔ

6 Ⓐ Ⓑ Ⓒ Ⓓ Ⓔ
7 Ⓐ Ⓑ Ⓒ Ⓓ Ⓔ
8 Ⓐ Ⓑ Ⓒ Ⓓ Ⓔ
9 Ⓐ Ⓑ Ⓒ Ⓓ Ⓔ
10 Ⓐ Ⓑ Ⓒ Ⓓ Ⓔ

11 Ⓐ Ⓑ Ⓒ Ⓓ Ⓔ
12 Ⓐ Ⓑ Ⓒ Ⓓ Ⓔ
13 Ⓐ Ⓑ Ⓒ Ⓓ Ⓔ
14 Ⓐ Ⓑ Ⓒ Ⓓ Ⓔ
15 Ⓐ Ⓑ Ⓒ Ⓓ Ⓔ

VOCABULARY
TYPE 2

1 Ⓐ Ⓑ Ⓒ
2 Ⓐ Ⓑ Ⓒ
3 Ⓐ Ⓑ Ⓒ
4 Ⓐ Ⓑ Ⓒ
5 Ⓐ Ⓑ Ⓒ

6 Ⓐ Ⓑ Ⓒ
7 Ⓐ Ⓑ Ⓒ
8 Ⓐ Ⓑ Ⓒ
9 Ⓐ Ⓑ Ⓒ
10 Ⓐ Ⓑ Ⓒ

SPELLING TYPE 1

Directions

Choose the correct spelling for the word parts combined below.

1. rely + able =
   (A) relyable
   (B) reliable
   (C) relible

2. hope + ing =
   (A) hopeing
   (B) hopping
   (C) hoping

3. reckless + ness =
   (A) recklessness
   (B) recklesness
   (C) recklesnes

4. hate + full =
   (A) hateful
   (B) hatfull
   (C) hatefull

5. dense + ity =
   (A) denseity
   (B) density
   (C) denssity

6. illegible + ly =
   (A) illegably
   (B) illegibly
   (C) illegiblely

7. labor + tory =
   (A) labratory
   (B) labrotory
   (C) laboratory

8. notice + able =
   - (A) noticeable
   - (B) noticable
   - (C) noticible

9. lively + ness =
   - (A) liveliness
   - (B) livelyness
   - (C) livlyness

10. reveal + ing =
   - (A) revealling
   - (B) revealing
   - (C) revealeing

SPELLING TYPE 2

Directions

Choose the correct spelling.

1. (A) tomorrow
   - (B) tommorow
   - (C) tommorrow

2. (A) liesurely
   - (B) leisurly
   - (C) leisurely

3. (A) enviroment
   - (B) environment
   - (C) envirinment

4. (A) adress
   - (B) address
   - (C) addres

5. (A) recieved
   - (B) receeved
   - (C) received

6. (A) amatuer
   (B) amateur
   (C) amature

7. (A) mocassin
   (B) moccasin
   (C) moccassin

8. (A) priviledged
   (B) priveleged
   (C) privileged

9. (A) foreigner
   (B) foriegner
   (C) forreigner

10. (A) seperate
    (B) sepparate
    (C) separate

PUNCTUATION TYPE 1

Directions

Choose the correct word to fill in the blank.

1. Show possession: The _____ ring is on the counter.
   (A) woman's
   (B) womans'

2. Show possession: My three _____ cars are in the drive-way.
   (A) uncle's
   (B) uncles'

3. The fault, I _____ was his.
   (A) believe,
   (B) believe

4. I _____ the fault is his.
   (A) believe,
   (B) believe

5. The players are as follows _____ Jones, Inman, and Brooks.
   (A) Smith,
   (B) : Smith,

6. The players are _____ Jones, Inman, and Brooks.
   (A) Smith,
   (B) : Smith,

7. The film contains an accurate _____ of the events before the accident.
   (A) re-creation
   (B) recreation

8. The vote indicates the need for _____
   (A) re-form.
   (B) reform.

9. She asked what the score _____
   (A) was?
   (B) was.

10. "What's the _____ she asked.
    (A) score,"
    (B) score?"

11. I don't care how much it _____ I'm not going to pay.
    (A) costs,
    (B) costs;

12. The game was sold _____ so I couldn't go.
    (A) out,
    (B) out;

13. Buy a dozen eggs at the _____ and fill the car with gas.
    (A) market,
    (B) market;

14. She said to me, _____ I borrow your pen?"
    (A) May
    (B) "May

15. "May I borrow your _____ she asked.
    (A) pen,"
    (B) pen?"

PUNCTUATION TYPE 2

Directions

Decide what mark or marks of punctuation should be placed in the underlined space.

I. The real question is who, if anyone____will pay for the
                                        1
    upkeep____
            2

    (A) (,)   (D) (;)
    (B) (.)   (E) (—)
    (C) (?)

II. The illnesses of men____are no more likely to be fatal
                            3
    than those of women____
                         4

    (A) no punctuation   (D) (.)
    (B) (')   (E) (!)
    (C) (,)

III. You will need warm clothes____heavy socks, and stout
                                 5
    shoes____you will also need a good flashlight.
          6

    (A) no punctuation   (D) (:)
    (B) (,)   (E) (;)
    (C) (.)

232   GRAMMAR AND USAGE

IV. "The problem," he said, "is the high cost of borrowing___
                                                          7

  (A) no punctuation   (D) (")
  (B) (.)   (E) (.")
  (C) (".)

  V. The movie doesn't work___it fails to engage the interest of
                            8
     its audiences___
                  9

  (A) no punctuation   (D) (;)
  (B) (.)   (E) (,)
  (C) ('.)

 VI. How is it possible to advocate greater rights for South African
     blacks___and at the same time to support right-wing
            10
     legislators in this country___
                               11

  (A) no punctuation   (D) (.)
  (B) (;)   (E) (?)
  (C) (:)

VII. It is the woman___whom I used to see every summer in
                   12
     Cleveland___who recently remarried, not her sister.
               13

  (A) no punctuation   (D) (;)
  (B) (,)   (E) (—)
  (C) (.)

VIII. He wished to take classes in biology, chemistry___physics, or
                                                      14
      math___but none of these classes was offered at night.
           15

  (A) no punctuation   (D) (;)
  (B) (,)   (E) (:)
  (C) (—)

VOCABULARY TYPE 1

Directions

Which word best fills the blank in the sentence below?

1. Unable to stay interested in a subject for any length of time, he _____ in a new one every three or four weeks.
   - (A) meddles
   - (B) persists
   - (C) dabbles
   - (D) hustles
   - (E) tries

2. I sent flowers and a message of _____ to the funeral home.
   - (A) clemency
   - (B) condolence
   - (C) leniency
   - (D) compassion
   - (E) competence

3. Because of his _____ in high school, he was not admitted to the university.
   - (A) indigence
   - (B) privation
   - (C) temperance
   - (D) palsy
   - (E) apathy

4. His exclusive interest in _____ ideas makes him a weak student of religion.
   - (A) heretical
   - (B) sectarian
   - (C) evangelical
   - (D) secular
   - (E) pious

5. To _____ the monotony of the long trip, the children played word games.
   (A) rebate
   (B) relieve
   (C) assure
   (D) revile
   (E) shorten

6. Because of my vacation plans in August, I asked to _____ my serving on jury duty until September.
   (A) defer
   (B) avoid
   (C) deter
   (D) exchange
   (E) eliminate

7. By choosing her words with great skill, she was able to _____his guilt without ever accusing him of a crime.
   (A) introduce
   (B) indict
   (C) infiltrate
   (D) announce
   (E) insinuate

8. His _____ goal is the vice presidency, to be followed in four years by the presidency, the capstone of his career.
   (A) final
   (B) primary
   (C) personalized
   (D) penultimate
   (E) terminal

9. The film presents the unlikely love affair of a sophisticated and elegant woman and a _____ man.
   (A) gauche
   (B) civilized
   (C) cultivated
   (D) honest
   (E) artful

10. Though he appeared to have recovered from his injuries, one day after leaving the hospital he _____.
    (A) rejuvenated
    (B) reinvigorated
    (C) departed
    (D) relapsed
    (E) rallied

11. The number of similar or identical sentences in the second essay makes it clear that it must be a _____ from the first.
    (A) copy
    (B) forgery
    (C) plagiarism
    (D) imitation
    (E) deviation

12. Publications such as magazines are called _____ because they appear at regular intervals.
    (A) serials
    (B) rotations
    (C) chronological
    (D) periodicals
    (E) spasmodic

13. His refusal to give me a written warranty made me _____ about the condition of the car.
    (A) sensitive
    (B) suspicious
    (C) suspenseful
    (D) susceptible
    (E) supportive

14. As the number and size of the rain forests _____, the danger from the greenhouse effect is greater.
    (A) diminish
    (B) deteriorate
    (C) subside
    (D) shorten
    (E) weaken

15. The editorial _____ higher taxes and proposes that the additional income they provide be used to reduce the national debt.
    (A) discloses
    (B) decries
    (C) foments
    (D) accommodates
    (E) advocates

VOCABULARY TYPE 2

Directions

Choose the word division that shows the meaningful parts of the word.

1. polyunsaturated
    (A) poly/unsaturated
    (B) poly/un/saturated
    (C) polyun/satu/rated

2. introduction
    (A) in/tro/duction
    (B) intro/duction
    (C) introduc/tion

3. window dresser
    (A) win/dow/dresser
    (B) win/dow/dress/er
    (C) window/dress/er

4. retrospective
    (A) retros/pective
    (B) retrospect/ive
    (C) retro/spect/ive

5. leafhopper
    (A) leaf/hopp/er
    (B) leafhopp/er
    (C) leaf/ho/pper

6. international
   (A) inter/nation/al
   (B) intern/ation/al
   (C) in/ter/nat/ional

7. supernatural
   (A) supern/atural
   (B) super/nat/ural
   (C) super/natur/al

8. xenophobia
   (A) xe/noph/obia
   (B) xenoph/obia
   (C) xeno/phobia

9. hopelessly
   (A) hope/less/ly
   (B) hop/eless/ly
   (C) hopeless/ly

10. individual
    (A) indi/vidual
    (B) in/dividual
    (C) in/di/vidual

ANSWER KEY FOR SPELLING, PUNCTUATION, AND
VOCABULARY PRACTICE TEST

Spelling Type 1	Punctuation Type 1	Vocabulary Type 1
1. B	1. A	1. C
2. C	2. B	2. B
3. A	3. A	3. E
4. A	4. B	4. D
5. B	5. B	5. B
6. B	6. A	6. A
7. C	7. A	7. E
8. A	8. B	8. D
9. A	9. B	9. A
10. B	10. B	10. D
	11. B	11. C
Spelling Type 2	12. A	12. D
1. A	13. A	13. B
2. C	14. B	14. A
3. B	15. B	15. E
4. B		
5. C	**Punctuation Type 2**	**Vocabulary Type 2**
6. B	1. A	1. B
7. B	2. B	2. B
8. C	3. A	3. C
9. A	4. D	4. C
10. C	5. B	5. A
	6. E	6. A
	7. E	7. C
	8. D	8. C
	9. B	9. A
	10. A	10. B
	11. E	
	12. A	
	13. A	
	14. B	
	15. B	

ANSWERS AND COMPLETE EXPLANATIONS FOR GRAMMAR AND USAGE PRACTICE TEST

TYPE 1

1. (D) The verb should be *would have suspected.*

2. (B) The correct form is *who,* subject of the clause *who made the better showing in the televised debate.*

3. (B) The verb should be the singular *was prepared* to agree with the singular subject *None.*

4. (E) There are no errors in this sentence.

5. (E) There are no errors in this sentence.

6. (B) The phrase should be made parallel with the others in the series: *that he is good looking.*

7. (B) *Smart* and *intelligent* mean the same thing. One of the terms should be deleted.

8. (C) In an indirect question, the pronoun should precede the verb: *he can.*

9. (E) The sentence is correct as given.

10. (A) *Anyone* should be two words: *Any one.*

11. (B) The verb should be the singular *remembers* to agree with the singular *None.* The plural is correctly used in *who have* to agree with the plural *survivors.*

12. (C) The idiom is *other than,* and the phrase should read *than that.*

13. (D) The comparative *lower* should be used with a comparison of only two incomes, those of husband and wife.

14. (C) With the correlatives *not . . . but,* the structure after *but* should be parallel to *to please,* an infinitive.

15. (A) The comparison in the prepositional phrase is to a paint-

er, not his painting. The following phrase should begin with *Graham.*

TYPE 2

1. (A) *That your horse won* is a noun clause, a proper subject of the verb *is.* In choice (C), the gerund requires a possessive. There is an agreement error in choice (E).

2. (D) The antecedent of *that* is the plural *tickets,* but the subject of the sentence is the singular *one.* The verbs should be *were reserved* and *has.*

3. (B) With *neither . . . nor,* the subject of the verb is the singular *butter.* Since calories can be counted, *less* should be *fewer.*

4. (E) The first four answers have parallelism errors with the correlatives *both . . . and.* By eliminating the correlatives, choice (E) avoids the errors and is more concise.

5. (C) The singular subject (*one*) requires a singular verb (*has promised*). The pronoun should be *whoever,* subject of the clause *whoever wins the primary.*

6. (E) Though there are two adjectives, the subject of the sentence is the singular *nature,* so the main verb must be *relegates.* Since *fiction* is singular, the correct pronoun is the singular *it.* Both choice (D) and choice (E) avoid the agreement errors, but choice (D) is wordier and uses *which* and a nonrestrictive clause where a restrictive clause with *that* should be used (or the prepositional phrase).

7. (D) Choice (A) is wordy (*annually* means *each year*) and misuses the idiom *descend on.* But choices (B) and (C) make *lured* a dangling participle. The idiom (*descended into*) in choice (E) is wrong in this context.

8. (C) In choices (A) and (B), the two parts of the comparison (*Switzerland* and *mountains*) are not parallel. Choice (E) makes no grammatical sense. Choices (C) and (D) are grammatically correct, but choice (D) is wordy.

9. (C) With the verb *knocked,* the adverb *loudly,* not the adjective *loud,* should be used. To maintain a logical sequence of verb

tenses, the two past tenses (*stopped, ran*) should be followed by a third past tense (*knocked*).

10. (C) The subject of the first clause is *whoever*, but in the clause *whomever the wind reaches*, *wind* is the subject and *whomever* is the object. The adjective should be *fewest* not *least*.

11. (D) The problem here is parallelism. The most concise version of the sentence will use three nouns, *eagerness, willingness*, and *optimism*. Choice (E), though parallel, is wordier than choice (D).

12. (C) Choices (A), (B), and (E) are all sentence fragments and dependent clauses. In choice (D), the plural verb is an agreement error.

13. (C) Since the introductory phrase uses the singular *his knowledge*, the subject must be singular. Since *his* is the possessive case of *he*, the subject must also be a human, a *nurseryman*, not *science*.

14. (E) The error in choices (A), (B), (C), and (D) is the same, an ambiguous pronoun (*which* or *this*).

15. (E) There are parallelism errors with the correlatives *both . . . and* in choices (A) and (B). Choice (C), though grammatically correct, changes the meaning of the original sentence slightly. Choice (D) awkwardly separates the adjective *deceptive* from the words it modifies.

TYPE 3

Passage 1

1. (A) No change is needed.

2. (C) With two independent clauses, the semicolon is correct.

3. (C) The series in apposition should be introduced by a comma.

4. (A) Though choice (B) is not wrong, it uses one word more. The apostrophe here follows the *s*, as *delegations* is plural.

5. (A) In choices (C) and (D), some meaning is lost by the omission of *stark*. Choice (A) uses the correct idiom.

6. (B) With *funds,* the verb must be plural. *There* is correct; *they're* means *they are,* and *their* is a possessive form of *they.*

7. (A) The phrase *fewer and fewer* is correct and concise.

8. (C) It is easy to coin a verb by adding *-ize* to an adjective or noun (*privatize*) and to coin a noun by adding *-ation* (*privatization*), but usually a clearer and often shorter way of saying the same thing already exists. The diction of *privatization option* is pretentious. The phrase *private financing* is clear and shorter.

Passage 2

9. (A) Either *everyone* or *everybody* can be used, but both are singular so the verb must be *has.*

10. (A) The phrase *In fact* should be retained at the beginning of the sentence, since the sentence is correcting the mistaken belief referred to in the first sentence. The phrase *As a matter of fact* is not wrong, but it takes fives words to say what *In fact* says in two.

11. (D) *A number* is plural and calls for the plural *require.*

12. (A) The comma at the end of the clause is necessary in this case to set off the parenthetical phrase that follows. While this phrase need not be considered parenthetical, you can be sure that it is treated as such because of the comma after *happen* (which may not be changed because it is not underlined), which must be paired with a preceding comma to be correct.

13. (B) The phrase that ends the sentence can stand as an appositive. The other versions are needlessly wordy.

14. (C) The subject of the sentence is the singular *insomniac.* Only in choice (C) are the pronouns and the verb in agreement with their antecedent.

15. (B) Paragraph 2 begins with a reference to *another type* of insomnia, but paragraph 1 has not identified one. Paragraph 2 logically follows only paragraph 3, which does describe types of insomnia.

TYPE 4

1. (B) The clause *used only at Mead's Supermarket* is restrictive (*only*) and should not be set off by commas.

2. (C) Rockabye Records, the name of the store, is singular, so the verb should be the singular *is*.

3. (A) *Listen* should be *listened* to be consistent with the past tense in *drove*.

4. (C) The relative clause, *who is seated* . . . , is restrictive, and so there should not be a comma between *man* and *who*.

5. (B) The object of *Like* must parallel *the study of the violin*.

6. (A) Since it simply repeats the meaning of *from other countries*, the word *international* should be omitted.

7. (C) The superlative *best* should be used with a comparison of more than two.

8. (A) The proper form here is the preposition *except; accept* is a verb.

9. (E) The sentence is correct as it is written.

10. (D) The sentence is a question and should be punctuated with a question mark.

11. (B) Since *garrulous* means the same as *long-winded*, the word should be omitted.

12. (B) The comma after *claimed* interferes with the logical movement of the sentence.

13. (B) The initial phrase should be *like humans*, a preposition and its object.

14. (E) The sentence is correctly written.

15. (C) To maintain the parallelism in the series, the second *as* should be omitted.

TYPE 5

1. (C) In choice (D), the modifier is misplaced. In (A), (B), and (E), *total* and *complete* mean the same thing.

2. (A) Avoiding the passive voice, choice (A) is the most concise version.

3. (B) The errors are chiefly those of parallelism with the correlatives *both . . . and* and *neither . . . nor*.

4. (D) Most of the errors are of verb tense. Choice (E) is a sentence fragment.

5. (E) The best version uses an active verb and avoids the change of pronouns.

6. (A) The faulty sentences have errors of preposition idiom, agreement, or a dangling modifier.

7. (E) Choices (B) and (C) have agreement errors, and (D) includes an error in diction (*arise*).

8. (D) Choice (B) has a failure of parallels (*depositors* and *withdrawals*), and the other versions have errors with the *both . . . and* correlatives.

9. (C) Choice (C) correctly uses the possessive *their* before the gerund *being pressed*.

10. (B) Choice (B) has the correct parallelism (*to talk/to do*) and the correct pronoun (*it*).

11. (C) Choice (C) uses the correct idioms *interest in* and *other than*.

12. (D) The opening phrase will dangle if it is not followed by its understood subject *he*.

13. (C) The correct pronoun is *that*, a singular to agree with the singular *number*.

14. (B) The sentence requires the *as* after *fast*, the *than* after *faster*, and the *other* after *any*.

15. (A) Choice (A) is the most concise version, and its prepositions are idiomatic.

TYPE 6

1. (D) Two complete sentences without a conjunction are joined by a semicolon.

2. (B) The parallel nouns *French* and *English* follow the correlatives *both* and *and*.

3. (C) To prevent an opening dangling modifier, the main clause must begin with what *was deciphered*, that is, *language*.

4. (C) The correct idiom here is *other than*.

5. (A) The opening phrase refers to *composers*, not to *compositions*. The version with the preposition (*like*) and two nouns is correct.

6. (B) The phrase must include both *as* and *than*, with *if not larger than* set off by commas.

7. (D) The pronoun in the opening phrase refers ahead to the plural *laws*, so only the plural *they* is correct.

8. (A) The parallel structure here is *not that* followed by a subject and verb and *but that* followed by a subject and verb.

9. (D) To preserve parallelism in the series, use the infinitive four times.

10. (B) The pronoun after *exceeds* refers to the singular *danger*.

TYPE 7

1. (D) Each of the other sentences uses repetitive words: *total/ complete, principal/chief, each/every, frequently/often*.

2. (C) The other three sentences have errors of parallelism with correlatives: *both ... and, not ... but*, and *either ... or*.

3. (C) There are diction (word choice) errors in the use of *reduction, dissembled*, and *retribution*.

4. (A) The repeated errors are dangling modifiers, two participles and a gerund, at the beginning of each sentence.

5. (B) The error here is subject-verb agreement.

6. (B) Three of the four sentences have errors of tense in one of the verbs.

7. (A) The errors are due to confusion between adjectives and adverbs: *noisy, quick,* and *turbidly.*

8. (D) Each of the first three sentences omits a necessary word: *than, encourage,* and *that of.*

9. (B) The other versions of the sentence use a pronoun (*this, which, that*) with no specific antecedent.

10. (C) The errors are of subject-verb agreement. The subjects are all singular.

11. (A) Three of the choices are sentence fragments. They have no main verbs.

12. (D) The error is in case with *who* or *whom.*

13. (A) The repeated error is the parallelism failures in a series.

14. (C) The double negatives (*aren't/hardly, not/no one, scarcely/no*) are the errors here.

15. (C) The problems here are with the use of *like* and *as.*

TYPE 8

1. (C) The most concise revision would change *surprising* to the adverb *surprisingly,* modifying *reveals.*

2. (B) The modifier that now begins the sentence will dangle unless it is followed by its understood subject, *the Raiders.*

3. (C) Again, to avoid the dangling modifier, you must begin with its understood subject, *I.*

4. (D) The correct verb form in the *if* clause is *had left.*

5. (B) With the correlatives *either . . . or,* the phrases that follow must be parallel: *to accept . . . to violate.*

6. (C) The subject of the revised sentence is the singular *Duke,* so the correct verb is the singular *is staying.*

7. (A) Beginning with *some animals* prevents the dangling participle.

8. (D) The main clause must begin with the name of the writer who is *like Verdan.*

9. (A) To maintain the parallelism in the series, the needed verb is the infinitive form without the *to,* which had been dropped in the second of the three parts.

10. (D) The pronoun must be *you* to parallel the pronoun in the opening clause.

11. (B) The revised series will read *delicious food, low prices,* and *spectacular views.*

12. (A) Since *hardly* is a negative, you must avoid using a second negative in the phrase.

13. (C) The proper tense of the verb is the present perfect, now in the plural.

14. (B) Using the gerund is the most concise way of revising here.

15. (C) The opening phrase will dangle if it is not followed by the understood subject (*you*) who beats the eggs.

TYPE 9

1. (C) Sentences 3 and 4 using *it* and *the plant* must follow sentence 2, which identifies the *lipstick plant.* Sentence 1 logically follows sentence 3, with its allusion to humidity.

2. (B) The pronoun *they* in sentence 3 must follow sentence 2. Sentence 1 follows logically after sentence 3, and sentence 4 concludes the paragraph.

3. (D) Sentence 4 must come first, since it identifies the *she* of sentences 1, 2, and 3. The details of sentences 1 and 2 refer back to sentence 3, so sentence 3 must follow sentence 4.

4. (A) The pronoun of sentence 2 (*he*) must refer to sentence 1, and the pronoun of sentence 3 (*she*) must refer to sentence 2.

5. (C) Sentences 4 and 1 must come first to identify the plant. The order of sentences 2 and 3 can be reversed, but they must follow sentences 4 and 1.

6. (C) Sentence 4's use of *on the other hand* marks it as following sentence 2. The pronouns of sentences 3 and 1 must refer back to sentence 4.

7. (B) The order of the sentences can be determined by looking carefully at the references to time—*before, first six months,* and *completion.*

8. (D) The paragraph is organized by progressing from the shore to the horizon.

9. (C) Sentences 2 and 3, which explain the dilemma, must follow sentence 1, which says the dilemma exists.

10. (A) Sentence 4 (*finally*) must be last, and sentence 2 (*less ambition*) must follow sentence 3. The logical opening sentence is 1.

TYPE 10

1. (D) This sentence is related to the first sentence and the third sentence of the paragraph, which is about converting closed bases to civilian uses.

2. (A) Choices (C) and (D) shift the focus of the paragraph, while (B) is inconclusive.

3. (C) The missing sentence, according to the first, must be an unattractive choice.

4. (B) The paragraph presents a drug with good and bad effects. Only choice (B) qualifies the success of the discovered drugs.

5. (D) The paragraph lists the requirements of a good speaker or writer, rather than comparing the two.

6. (D) This sentence continues to focus on Caesar but also connects him to the other members of the triumvirate.

7. (C) The sentence must lead logically to the last, which suggests the networks were innocent of malice.

8. (B) Though the second sentence is about childhood fears, the third and fourth are not.

9. (C) The focus of the sentences before and after the blank is on the state-sponsored plans. No criticism of these plans is implied.

10. (A) All of the rest of the paragraph harshly criticizes the book's major and minor faults.

GRAMMAR AND USAGE REVIEW

1. PARTS OF SPEECH, ADJECTIVES AND ADVERBS, LINKING VERBS, COMPARATIVES AND SUPERLATIVES

PARTS OF SPEECH

None of the multiple-choice tests of English grammar will ask a student to explain a dangling participle or to pick out the adjectives and adverbs in a sentence. But to make the best use of this book, you must know the meaning of several of the important grammatical terms, and you must be able to tell a noun from a verb and an adverb from an adjective.

Most of the tests ask you either to find an error in a sentence or to recognize that a sentence is correct. For example, one type of question will ask if the following sentence is correct and, if not, which underlined part has an error.

Freshened by rain that fell during the night, the garden
    A   B
smelled fragrantly and glistened brightly. No error.
     C   D   E

Faced with this question, most students will see that the problem is in the word *fragrantly*. Should it be *fragrantly* or *fragrant?* (In fact, it should be *fragrant*.) When you ask even those who rightly select choice (C) as the error why they picked choice (C) instead of choice (D), the usual answer is *(C) sounds wrong, and (D) sounds right*. Sometimes, we have to depend on the *it-sounds-right/it-sounds-wrong* approach. But most of the time, this method will not work. To perform well on tests of standard written English, you must be able to see what grammatical question the test is really asking. In the example, the real issue is not which sounds better, *smells fragrant* or *smells fragrantly,* but whether we use an adverb or an adjective with the verb *smells*. And so we have to begin at the beginning—with a review of the parts of speech on which questions will be based.

252 GRAMMAR AND USAGE

Noun: a word used as a person, a place, a thing.
Examples: *woman, boy, hope, Boston, car, noun.*

Pronoun: a word used as a substitute for a noun.
Examples: *I, you, he, she, it, me, him, her, we, they, who, whom, which, what, this, that, one, none, someone, somebody, myself, anything, nothing.*

Verb: a word used to assert action or state of being.
Examples: *kill, eat, is, are, remain, think, study, become.*

Adjective: a word used to modify a noun or pronoun. To modify is to describe, to qualify, to limit or restrict in meaning. In the phrase *a large, red barn*, both *large* and *red* are adjectives which modify the noun *barn*.
Examples: *fat, thin, hot, cold, old, new, red.*

Adverb: a word used to modify a verb, an adjective, or another adverb. In the phrase *to eat a very large meal very slowly*, the two *very*'s and *slowly* are adverbs. The first *very* modifies an adjective (*large*), the second modifies an adverb (*slowly*), and *slowly* modifies the verb (*eat*).
Examples: *very, rather, quickly, quite, easily, hopelessly.*

ADJECTIVES AND ADVERBS

A common error in the sentences on the exams is the misuse of an adjective or an adverb. Adjectives modify nouns and pronouns; adverbs modify verbs, adjectives, and other adverbs. Errors occur when an adjective is used to do an adverb's job or an adverb to do an adjective's.

Which of the following sentences have adjective or adverb errors?

1. As the debate progressed, the defenders of tax reform grew more and more excited.
2. As the debate progressed, the defenders of tax reform spoke more and more excited.
3. Asleep awkwardly on his side, the man snored loud enough to shake the bedroom.
4. Lying awkward on his side, the sleeper snored loudly enough to shake the bedroom.

Sentence 1 is correct. Sentences 2, 3, and 4 have adjective/adverb errors. In sentence 2, the adjective *excited* modifies the verb *spoke*, describing how they spoke. But we need an adverb to modify a verb, so the correct word here is *excitedly*. The adjective *excited* is correct in the first sentence because it modifies the noun *defenders*, not the verb *grew*. In sentence 3, the adverb *awkwardly* is properly used to modify the adjective *asleep*, but the adjective *loud* should not be used to modify the verb *snored*. Sentence 4 correctly uses the adverb *loudly* but mistakenly uses the adjective *awkward* to modify the verbal adjective *lying*.

Be careful not to confuse *most* and *almost*. *Most* is an adjective, the superlative of *much* or *many*, as in *most children like ice cream*, but *most* may be used as an adverb to form the superlative of another adjective or adverb as in *most beautiful* or *most quickly*. *Almost* is an adverb meaning *nearly*. You can say *most people* or *most men*, but you must say *almost every person* or *almost all men*. A phrase like *most every person* or *most all men* is incorrect because the adjective *most* cannot modify the adjectives *every* or *all*.

LINKING VERBS

It is easy enough to remember that adjectives modify nouns and adverbs modify adjectives, verbs, and other adverbs. The hard part is deciding what word the adjective or adverb modifies. Why must we say *the defenders grew more and more excited* when we also must say *the defenders spoke more and more excitedly?* We do so because there are a number of verbs, called *linking verbs*, which express a state of being rather than an action. These verbs are followed by an adjective, not an adverb. The most common linking verb is the verb *to be* in all its forms (*am, is, are, was, were,* for example), and many other linking verbs are equivalent in meaning to the verb *to be*. They include the following:

to seem   to become   to remain   to appear

In addition, the verbs *to feel, to taste, to smell, to look* are usually linking verbs and will be followed by an adjective rather than an adverb: *I am sad. She became sad. They remain happy. He appears happy. The cloth feels soft. The food tastes bad. The garden smells sweet.* In each of these sentences, the adjective modifies the noun or pronoun subject of the sentence.

When you see a linking verb in a sentence on an exam, be alert to the possibility of an adverb-for-adjective error. But do not assume that the verbs on this list will never have adverbial modifiers.

The detective looks *carefully* at the footprints.
The butler looks *suspicious.*
The detective looks *suspiciously* at the butler.

As these sentences illustrate, *looks* may or may not be a linking verb. If the verb expresses an action rather than describes a state, and the modifier describes that action, use an adverb.

COMPARATIVES AND SUPERLATIVES

Adjectives and adverbs have three forms: positive (*quick, quickly*), comparative (*quicker, more quickly*), and superlative (*quickest, most quickly*). Many of the comparatives and superlatives are formed by adding *-er* and *-est* to the adjective stem, though some words (*good, better, best; well, better, best*) change altogether, and some simply add *more* or *most* (*eager, more eager, most eager; quickly, more quickly, most quickly*).

When it is clear that only two are compared, use a comparative not a superlative. When the comparison involves more than two, use a superlative.

Compared to Smith, Jones is *richer.*
Of all the oil-producing countries, Saudi Arabia is the *richest.*
Of the two finalists, Smith hits *harder.*
Of the eight boxers, Jones hits *hardest.*
Of the eight boxers, Jones hits *harder* than Smith, but
Williams hits *hardest* of all.

EXERCISE 1: PARTS OF SPEECH, ADJECTIVES AND ADVERBS, LINKING VERBS, COMPARATIVES AND SUPERLATIVES

Choose the correct form in each of the following sentences. Answers are on page 322.

1. (Most, Almost) every person in the stadium was wearing an orange cap.

2. After $2,500 worth of cosmetic surgery, she appears quite (different, differently) from the woman we had known.

3. The ship appeared (sudden, suddenly) out of the fog.

4. Of all the players in the tournament, Smith has the (better, best) volley.

5. Of the two finalists, Jones has the (better, best) serve.

6. The pie tasted so (bad, badly) that he left the piece uneaten.

7. Dickens has a (noticeable, noticeably) more inventive imagination than Gaskell.

8. I feel (sad, sadly) about his losing so much money on the lottery.

9. It is impossible to take his claims (serious, seriously).

10. The forest smells most (aromatic, aromatically) when the wind is from the south.

11. I don't believe him (most, almost) any time he talks about money.

12. If you look very (careful, carefully), the scratches on the car are (clear, clearly) visible.

13. The eland is the (larger, largest) of all of the antelopes but not the (slower, slowest).

14. Early in the century, the supply of bison (sure, surely) seemed (inexhaustible, inexhaustibly).

15. From a distance, the hill appears to rise (steep, steeply), but it does not look (steep, steeply) from here.

2. CASE

SUBJECT AND OBJECT ERRORS

Nouns and pronouns in English may be used as *subjects* (The *garden* is large. *I* am tired.), as *objects* (David weeded the *garden*. David hit *him*.), and as *possessors* (*David*'s garden is large. *His* arm is broken.). Nouns and pronouns, then, have a subjective case, an objective case, and a possessive case.

Since the form of a noun in the subjective case is no different from the form of the same noun in the objective case (The *bat* hit the *ball*. The *ball* hit the *bat*.), errors of case are not a problem with nouns. But several pronouns have different forms as subjects and objects.

Subject	Object
I	me
he	him
she	her
we	us
they	them
who	whom
whoever	whomever

Where are the errors of case (confusions of the subjective and objective form of the pronoun) in the following sentences?

1. I am going to the play with her.
2. Me and her are going to the games.
3. The committee gave prizes to my brother, my sister, and I.
4. For we Americans, July fourth is a special day.
5. Mary invited my cousin, her sister, a friend from New York, and I to the party.

Sentence 1 is correct, but there are case errors in sentences 2, 3, 4, and 5. In sentence 2, *me* and *her,* the subjects of the sentence, should be *I* and *she* (or better, *She* and *I*). In sentence 3, *I* should be *me,* the object of the preposition *to,* and in sentence 4, the *we* should be *us,* the object of the preposition *for*. In sentence 5, *I* should be *me,* the object of the verb *invited*. It would be easy to spot the error if the sentences simply said *The committee gave prizes to I* or *Mary invited I,* but when the sentence contains elements that separate the verb or the preposition from the pronoun object, it becomes harder to see the error at once. The question writers know this fact and exploit it in all exams. When you see a compound subject or object (that is, two or more subjects or objects joined by *and*), look carefully at the case of pronouns. Imagine how the sentence would read with just the pronoun (*Mary invited I?*).

PRONOUNS IN APPOSITION

An *appositive* is a word or phrase or clause in apposition—that is, placed next to another so that the second explains the first.

Margaret, my sister, and my oldest brother, Hugh, are in New York.

In this sentence, *sister* is in apposition to *Margaret* and *Hugh* is in apposition to *brother.* A pronoun in apposition is in the same case as the noun or pronoun to which it is in apposition. Thus in a sentence like *The outfielders, Jack, Joe, and I, are ready to play,* the *I,* which is in apposition to the subject, *outfielders,* is subjective. But in a sentence like *The class elected three representatives, Jack, Joe, and me,* the objective *me* is correct because it is in apposition to *representatives,* which is the object of the verb *elected.*

WHO AND WHOM

The demons of case are *who* and *whom.* Your test may not ask you to choose between them at all, but it may do so more than once. If you understand how to deal with *who* and *whom,* questions about the case of other pronouns should give you no trouble. The problem is always the same: Is the pronoun a subject or an object? Is it *I, he, she, who* or *me, him, her, whom?*

Use *who* for a subject, *whom* for an object:

Who is going to the store? (subject of sentence)
Whom are you going with? (object of preposition *with*)
Whom did they choose? (object of verb *choose; they* is the subject of the sentence)

If you have trouble with sentences that are questions, it may help to rephrase the sentence as a statement:

> You are going with whom.
> They did choose whom.

And it may also help if you substitute *I/me* or *he/him* for *who/whom*.

> *He* is going to the store.
> Are you going with *him?*
> Did they choose *him?*

Before going on to nastier examples of *who* and *whom*, we need to define three more terms: *clause, independent clause,* and *dependent clause.* A *clause* is a group of related words containing a verb and its subject. An *independent clause* can stand by itself as a sentence. A *dependent clause,* though it has a subject and a verb, cannot stand by itself as a complete sentence.

> I spoke. (one independent clause with a subject and a verb)

> I spoke and she listened. (two independent clauses—*I spoke/she listened* would be complete sentences)

> I spoke while she listened. (one independent clause—*I spoke*—and one dependent clause—*while she listened*—which, though it has a subject and a verb, is not a complete sentence)

> The girl who is dressed in red is rich. (one independent clause— *The girl is rich*—and one dependent clause—*who is dressed in red*)

The easier questions with *who* and *whom* occur in sentences with only one clause. In sentences with more than one clause, the case of the pronoun (*who* or *whom*) is determined by its use in its own clause. Before you can decide between *who* and *whom*, you must be able to isolate the clause in which the pronoun appears.

1. He will give the book to whoever wants it.
2. He will give the book to whomever Jane chooses.
3. He will give the prize to whoever deserves it.
4. He will give the prize to whomever he likes.

In sentence 1, there are two clauses: *He will give the book to* and *whoever wants it.* The whole second clause (*whoever wants it*) not the pronoun *whoever* is the object of the preposition. In this second clause, *whoever* is the subject, *wants* is the verb, and *it* is the object. If you find this sort of sentence difficult, isolate the clause and substitute *he/him* for *who/whom* or *whoever/whomever*. Here *he wants it* should be easy to recognize as preferable to *him wants it.*

In sentence 2, there are again two clauses: *He will give the book to* and *whomever Jane chooses.* Again the whole clause is the object of the preposition, but the subject of the second clause is *Jane,* the verb, *chooses,* and *whomever,* the object of the verb *chooses.* (Jane chooses *him,* not Jane chooses *he.*) Sentences 3 and 4 follow the same principles. In sentence 3, *whoever* is the subject of the second clause; in sentence 4, *he* is the subject and *whomever* is the object of *likes.*

Remember that *whom* by itself will be the object of a preposition like *to.* (*To whom* did he give the book?), but in this sentence there is only *one* clause.

There is one more complication. You will sometimes find sentences in which a parenthetical expression occurs with the *who/whom* clause. Phrases like *I think, we know, they believe, he supposes, they say, one imagines* are, in fact, independent clauses and do not affect the case of *who/whom* in a separate clause.

1. He is a man who I think should be in prison.
2. He is a man, one assumes, who is sick.
3. Her husband is a man whom I think she has misunderstood.
4. He is a student whom we know the teachers dislike.
5. They will pay a large fee to whoever they decide is most qualified.

All of these sentences have three, not two, clauses. When deciding on the case of *who* or *whom,* we must pay no attention to the parenthetical phrases *I think, one assumes,* and *we know.* The *who/whom* clauses are *who should be in prison, who is sick, whom she has misunderstood,* and *whom the teachers dislike.* In the first two, *who* is the subject. In sentences 3 and 4, *whom* is the object of the verbs *has misunderstood* and *dislike.* There are two traps in sentence 5, the preposition *to* and the phrase *they decide,* but the clause is *whoever is most qualified.* The whole clause is the object of the preposition *to* and *they decide* is a separate clause. Therefore, it must be *whoever* (*he* is most qualified) because *whoever* is the subject of the clause.

POSSESSIVE ERRORS

The third case of English nouns and pronouns is the possessive, which is used, logically enough, to show possession: *my, your, his, her, its, our, their, whose.* Remember that the possessive form of the pronoun *it* is *its* without an apostrophe. With the apostrophe, *it's* is a contraction and means *it is.* Remember, too, that *their* is the possessive form of the pronoun *they,* while *there* is an adverb meaning *in that place.*

As a rule, use the possessive case before a gerund, that is, a verb used as a noun. Gerunds are formed by adding *-ing* to verb stems: *going, eating, writing, borrowing.* Like nouns, they are used as both subjects and objects.

1. I don't like my brother's borrowing so much money.
2. I don't mind his eating so much ice cream.
3. I don't approve of his driving with such worn-out tires.
4. I recommend his seeing a doctor.

In these sentences, *borrowing, eating, driving,* and *seeing* are gerunds, preceded by possessive forms. If the first sentence had said *brother* rather than *brother's,* it would seem to say *I don't like my brother* rather than *I don't like his borrowing so much.* Similarly, if sentence 2, 3, or 4 had used *him* instead of *his,* the meaning of the sentences would be changed. If an exam question offers you a choice between a possessive and an objective pronoun before a gerund, look carefully at what the sentence is saying. It is likely that the possessive is the better choice.

EXERCISE 2: CASE

Choose the correct form in each of the following sentences. The answers are on page 323.

Part A

1. The study suggests that (we, us) New Englanders are not practical.

2. Everybody at the table chose steak except Tom and (I, me).

3. I don't mind (him, his) using the car.

4. It was (I, me) who telephoned the fire department.

5. Why does he object to (us, our) standing here?

6. It is difficult to imagine how such an invention will affect you and (I, me).

7. Let's you and (I, me) invest together in this project.

8. I'm going to complain about (him, his) talking so loudly.

9. The Secret Service is worried about the (president, president's) riding in an open car.

10. They will award the trophy to one of the finalists, either Jack or (I, me).

Part B

1. The woman (who, whom) was recently elected to the board of directors has been with the company for some years.

2. The accountant (who, whom) we understand did not wish to be interviewed has been asked to appear at the trial.

3. (Who, Whom) do you suppose will buy this car?

4. (Who, Whom) do you suppose the company will choose?

5. Let me speak to (whoever, whomever) is waiting for the general.

6. Let me speak to (whoever, whomever) the general hopes to convince to join his campaign.

7. (Whoever, Whomever) I think deserves the prize always seems to lose.

8. They will give the job to (whoever, whomever) they decide is most likely to support their position.

9. They will give the job to (whoever, whomever) they decide they can agree with about prices.

10. Do you really care about (who, whom) you dance with?

3. AGREEMENT

An agreement error is the faulty combination of a singular and a plural. Agreement errors occur between subjects and verbs and between pronouns and their *antecedents* (the word, phrase, or clause to which a pronoun refers).

All the grammar exams test agreement frequently, and on some tests as many as one-fourth of the questions test for errors of agreement.

SUBJECT AND VERB AGREEMENT

Use a singular verb with a singular subject and a plural verb with a plural subject. The key to seeing errors of subject-verb agreement is identifying the subject correctly. Often, the sentences will try to mislead you by separating the subject and verb.

1. The *sound is* beautiful. (singular subject/singular verb)

2. The *number seems* to increase. (singular subject/singular verb)

3. The *sound* of birds singing and crickets chirping all about the sunlit lakes and woods *is* beautiful. (singular subject/singular verb)

4. The *number* of boats pulling waterskiers on the lakes *seems* to increase every summer. (singular subject/singular verb)

Sentences 1 and 2 here are easy, but in sentences 3 and 4, the plurals that come between the singular subjects and the verbs may make the reader forget that the verbs must be singular to agree with the singular subjects.

In sentences where there are two or more subjects joined by *and,* use a plural verb. Do not confuse compound subjects (two subjects joined by *and*) with prepositional or parenthetical phrases introduced by such words or phrases as *with, as well as, in addition to, along with, in the company of, not to mention,* and the like. A singular subject, followed by a phrase of this sort, still takes a singular verb.

1. The actress and the director *are* in the dressing room.

2. The chairman of Mobil, as well as the president of Texaco and the vice president of Gulf, *is* attending the meeting.
3. The fullback, accompanied by two ends, two guards, and the 340-pound tackle, *is* leaving the field.
4. The conductor, with his 125-piece orchestra, two small brass bands, and the Mormon Tabernacle Choir, *is* ready to begin the concert.

In the first example, there are two subjects (*actress* and *director*) joined by *and,* so the verb is plural. But in the second, third, and fourth sentences, the subject is singular (*chairman, fullback, conductor*), and all the plurals that intervene between the subject and the verb do not change the rule that the verb must be singular to agree with the singular subject.

Two singular subjects joined by *and* (a compound subject) must have a plural verb, but two singular subjects joined by *or, nor, either* . . . *or, neither* . . . *nor* take singular verbs.

1. Mary *and* Jill *are* in the play.
2. Mary *or* Jill *is* in the play.
3. *Neither* Mary *nor* Jill *is* in the play.

In sentences with *either* . . . *or, neither* . . . *nor,* if one subject is singular and one is plural, the verb agrees with the subject nearer the verb.

1. Neither the hunter nor the *rangers are* in sight.
2. Neither the rangers nor the *hunter is* in sight.
3. Either the dog or the *cats are* in the yard.
4. Either the cats or the *dog is* in the yard.

In sentences 1 and 3, the subjects nearer the verb are the plurals *rangers* and *cats,* so the verb is plural. In sentences 2 and 4, the singular subject is nearer the verb, and the verb is singular.

When the following words are used as subjects, use a singular verb: *anyone, anybody, anything, someone, something, everyone, everybody, everything, no one, nobody, nothing, either, neither, each, another, many a.*

1. *Everyone* in the class of six hundred students *is* going on the field trip.
2. *Everybody* in the four western states *is* concerned about the election.
3. *Either* of the answers *is* correct.
4. *Neither* of the teams *has* won a game.
5. *Each* of the contestants *has* won a prize.
6. *Many a* man *has* gone astray.

Notice that many of these sentences begin with the singular subject which is followed by a prepositional phrase with plurals. The exam sentences will often use this structure, hoping that the plurals in the prepositional phrase will distract you from the real point—that the subject is singular. The sentences on the exam may be much longer than these examples so that the verb is even farther away from the singular subject.

Everybody in the crowded shopping center, in the food stores, and in the specialty shops, as well as those who filled the department stores down the street, *was* looking for bargains.

When the subject is *none,* and the meaning is *not one* or *no one else,* use a singular verb. In some instances, the rest of the sentence will make it clear that the plural is more appropriate, but it is more likely that a sentence on the exam which uses *none* as the subject is testing your ability to see that *none* is usually singular.

1. None of the players *is* ready.
2. None of the twenty-two starting players on the two teams *is* ready.
3. None *is* so foolish as a man who will not listen to advice.
4. None *are* so foolish as men who will not listen to advice.

In the first three examples, *none* means *no one* and the verb is singular. In sentence 4, the plural *men* makes it clear that *none* must also be a plural.

Collective nouns like *jury, team, orchestra, crowd, family, Yale*— that is, nouns in which a singular form denotes a collection of individuals—usually take a singular verb. If the collection is thought of as a whole (The jury is deliberating), the verb is singular. If the sentence makes it clear that the members are thought of as acting separately, the verb is plural (My family have settled in five different states).

Watch carefully for agreement errors in sentences with the phrases *the number* or *a number* as subjects. *The number* is singular, but it is likely to be followed by a prepositional phrase with plurals. So long as *the number* is the subject, use a singular verb.

1. *The number* of bugs in my gardens and lawns *is* enormous.
2. *The number* of tests in my classes this semester *is* larger than last year's.
3. *The number* of people killed every year in highway accidents, drownings, and airplane crashes *has* increased every year since 1942.

A *number* can take either a singular or plural. Use a plural when *a number* means *many*.

1. *A number* of tests *are* given in this class.
2. *A number* of bugs *are* crawling on my roses.
3. *A number* of theories to account for the high incidence of lung disease *have* been discussed in the study.
4. *A number* that many people consider to be unlucky *is* thirteen.

In the first three examples, *a number* means *many* and the verbs are plural. In sentence 4, *a number* refers to one number (thirteen), and the verb is singular.

Be wary of nouns based on Latin and Greek that form their plurals with *a* at the end. *Criteria* is a plural (one criterion, two criteria) as are *data* (one datum), *phenomena* (one phenomenon), and *media* (one medium).

1. The media *are* guilty of sensationalism.
2. The criteria for admission *are* listed in the catalog.

The tests will frequently include agreement errors in sentences in which the verb precedes the subject, often by using an opening of *There is* or *There are*.

1. There *are* hidden away in a lonely house out on the heath a brother and sister living alone.
2. There *is* in London and New York newspapers a self-satisfaction that is not found in the papers of smaller cities.

Both of these sentences are correct, though it would be easy to miss the agreement error if the first had used *is* and the second, *are*. Do not let the singular nouns in the prepositional phrases in the first sentence or the plurals in the second distract you from finding the subjects of the verbs—the compound subject *brother and sister* in the first and the singular *self-satisfaction* in the second. The test writer's technique here is like that in those sentences that pile up plurals between a singular subject at the beginning of the sentence and the verb at the end. But in this case, the verb comes first.

PRONOUN AGREEMENT

Since personal pronouns have distinctive singular and plural forms (*he/they, his/their, him/them*), pronoun agreement errors are as common as noun-verb agreement errors. The number (that is, singular or plural) of a pronoun is determined by its *antecedent* (the word, phrase, or clause to which it refers), and pronouns must agree in number with their antecedents. Most of the rules that apply to the agreement of nouns and verbs also apply to the agreement of pronouns and their antecedents.

1. The *workers* finished *their* job on time.
2. The *group* of workers finished *its* job on time.
3. The *men* earn *their* money.
4. The *man* earns *his* money.
5. The *men* who earn *their* money are tired.

In sentence 1 here, the plural *their* agrees with the plural *workers*. In sentence 2, the singular *its* agrees with the singular subject, the collective noun *group*. In sentences 3 and 4, the antecedents are *men* and *man*, so the pronouns are *their* and *his*. In sentence 5, the antecedent to the pronoun *their* is *who*. To determine whether *who* is singular or plural, we must look at its antecedent. In this sentence, it is the plural *men*.

In the subject-verb agreement questions, so long as you know whether the subject is singular or plural, you should have no trouble. In pronoun agreement questions, you must know what word is the antecedent of the pronoun and whether that word is singular or plural. As the following sentences will demonstrate, these questions are more difficult.

1. Rosen is the only one of the five American musicians *who have entered* the competition *who is* likely to win a medal.
2. The leader of the senators *who are* gathered to discuss the tax on oil is the only one *who represents* an oil-producing state.

In the first sentence, the antecedent of the first *who* is the plural *musicians*. Therefore, *who* is plural and the correct verb is *have*. But the antecedent of the second *who* is *one* (and the antecedent of *one* is *Rosen*), and so the verb in this clause must be the singular *is*. In the second sentence, the antecedent of the first *who* is the plural *senators* (thus, *are*) while the antecedent of the second *who* is the singular *one* (thus, *represents* not *represent*).

Use a singular pronoun when the antecedent is *anyone, anybody, anything, someone, somebody, something, everyone, everybody, everything, no one, nobody, either, neither, each, another, one, person, man, woman, kind, sort.*

1. *None* of the girls in the class finished *her* assignment on time.
2. *Everybody* on the men's team has *his* weaknesses.
3. *Neither* of the women paid *her* bills.
4. *Each* of the boys ate *his* ice cream.
5. *One* of the twenty men in the upper balcony dropped *his* program into the orchestra.

When two or more antecedents are joined by *or* or *nor*, the pronoun should agree with the nearer antecedent.

1. Neither the mother nor the *daughters* brought *their* cars.
2. Neither the daughters nor the *mother* brought *her* car.

EXERCISE 3: AGREEMENT

Choose the correct form in each of the following sentences. Answers are on page 324.

1. None of the candidates who (is, are) campaigning in New Hampshire (is, are) willing to speak to that organization.

2. Either the general or the sergeant-at-arms (is, are) responsible for greeting the new Greek minister.

3. None of the applicants who (has, have) failed to submit photographs (is, are) likely to be called for an interview.

4. Mr. Lombardi, as well as his wife and three children, (was, were) found before midnight.

5. The newly discovered evidence, together with the confirming testimony of three eyewitnesses, (make, makes) his conviction certain.

6. The criteria for admission to Yale Law School in New Haven (includes, include) a score of above 600 on the test.

7. Precise and symmetrical, the basalt columns of the Devil's Postpile in the Sierras (looks, look) as if (it, they) had been sculpted in an artist's studio.

8. Neither the teacher nor the student (is, are) in the classroom.

9. Mr. and Mrs. Smith, in addition to their four children, (is, are) vacationing in Orlando.

10. Jack is one of eight quarter-milers who (has, have) reached the final heat.

11. The number of penguins that (is, are) killed by DDT (increases, increase) each year.

12. Either I or Mary Jane (is, are) going to Detroit.

13. Everyone in the theater, filled with more than six hundred people, (was, were) bored.

14. Neither Sally nor the twins (has, have) finished (her, their) practice teaching.

15. Neither the twins nor Sally (has, have) finished (her, their) practice teaching.

16. Neither she nor I (was, were) dancing, for we felt tired.

17. The president, no less than all the other members of the first family, (enjoy, enjoys) bowling.

18. The number of books about corruption in the government written by participants in the Watergate affair (seem, seems) to grow larger every month.

19. A number of the books about Watergate (has, have) been translated into Russian.

20. The data used in determining your federal tax (is, are) to be submitted with your letter of appeal.

REVIEW EXERCISE: SECTIONS 1, 2, and 3

Some of the following sentences may be correct. Others contain problems covered in Sections 1, 2, and 3 of the Grammar and Usage Review. There is not more than one error in any sentence.

If there is an error, it will be underlined and lettered. Find the one underlined part that must be changed to make the sentence correct. Choose (E) if the sentence contains no error. Answers are on page 325.

1. No one but the president, secretary, and me was at the
           A   B   C

   meeting, and we voted unanimously to spend all of the money
                                     D

   in the treasury. No error.
                  E

2. Many a young man of twenty-five or thirty have dreamed of
                                        A

   retiring at fifty, but few, when they reach that age, find
                                    B

   that the sum they had thought could support them is adequate.
                 C   D

   No error.
    E

3. Having lived for two years near both the highway and the
         A   B

   airport, I am used to the noises of cars and planes, which no
                                               C

   longer disturb my sleep. No error.
            D   E

4. The book's public-relations prose, its long-windedness, and
               A   B

   its tendency uncritically to list ideas ultimately makes it
                   C   D

   a wholly useless study that should never have been published.
   No error.
    E

5. It is depressing to realize that in a country as rich as this,
                           A   B

   thousands of people live out their life without ever having
                            C   D

   enough to eat. No error.
             E

6. My family includes several serious and responsible members,
            A

   my sister and I, for example, but even we have had next to no
        B   C   D

   influence on public life. No error.
                   E

7. The result of all the tests, according to the surgeon, was not
                         A   B

   likely to alarm either her husband or her. No error.
         C   D   E

8. Some smaller players will tackle only whoever comes near them,
                             A   B

   while others will tackle whoever they can catch. No error.
            C   D   E

9. Though the first question on the test seemed simple, there were
                               A   B

   simply too many questions for me to finish on time. No error.
    C   D   E

10. There are several runners on the team <u>who</u> are <u>faster</u> in the
                                          A   B

shorter races than the runners of the opposing team, but in
  C

the field events, they are <u>best</u>. <u>No error</u>.
                           D   E

4. VERBS

When you look up a verb in the dictionary, you will find an entry like the following:

    eat, v.t. (ate, eaten, eating)
    chop, v.t. (chopped, chopping)
    be, v.i. (was or were, been, being)
    go, v.i. (went, gone, going)
    run, v.i.,t. (ran, run, running)

The *v.* indicates that the word is a verb, and the *t.* or *i.* that it is transitive (that is, takes an object) or intransitive (that is, does not take an object). Some verbs, like *run,* can be either intransitive (I run faster than David) or transitive (I run a factory in Kansas City).

The present infinitive of the verb is formed by adding the preposition *to* to the form given first (*to eat, to chop, to be, to go, to run*), and most verbs (though *not* the verb *to be*) form their present tenses from the infinitive (*I eat, I chop, I go, I run*). The second form of the verb, given in the parentheses, is the past tense (*ate, chopped*), and the third is past participle (*eaten, chopped*), the form which is combined with an auxiliary to form the perfect tenses (*I have eaten, I have chopped, I will have gone*). The *-ing* form is the present participle.

VERB TENSES

To deal more fully with verb errors, we will need to review and define some additional terms. Each verb has *number, person, voice,* and *tense. Number* is simply singular or plural. The three *persons* of a verb are first (*I, we*), second (*you*), and third (*he, she, it, they*). Active (I hit the ball) and passive (The ball was hit by me) are the *voices* of verbs. If the subject of a verb performs the action of the verb, the verb is *active,* while if the subject receives the action, the verb is *passive*. The *tenses* of a verb are the forms that show *the time* of its action or state of being. Most of the verb errors that appear on the exams are errors of agreement or errors of tense.

The following chart gives the tenses of the verbs *to be* and *to chop*.

PRESENT TENSE: ACTION OR STATE OF BEING IN THE PRESENT

	Singular	*Plural*
first person	I am/I chop	we are/we chop
second person	you are/you chop	you are/you chop
third person	he, she, it is/he, she, it chops	they are/they chop

PAST TENSE: ACTION OR STATE OF BEING IN THE PAST

	Singular	*Plural*
first person	I was/I chopped	we were/we chopped
second person	you were/you chopped	you were/you chopped
third person	he, she, it was/he, she, it chopped	they were/they chopped

FUTURE TENSE: ACTION OR STATE OF BEING IN THE FUTURE

	Singular	*Plural*
first person	I will be/I will chop	we will be/we will chop
second person	you will be/you will chop	you will be/you will chop
third person	he, she, it will be/he, she, it will chop	they will be/they will chop

PRESENT PERFECT TENSE: ACTION IN PAST TIME IN RELATION TO PRESENT TIME

	Singular	Plural
first person	I have been/I have chopped	we have been/we have chopped
second person	you have been/you have chopped	you have been/you have chopped
third person	he, she, it has been/he, she, it has chopped	they have been/they have chopped

PAST PERFECT TENSE: ACTION IN PAST TIME IN RELATION TO ANOTHER PAST TIME

	Singular	Plural
first person	I had been/I had chopped	we had been/we had chopped
second person	you had been/you had chopped	you had been/you had chopped
third person	he, she, it had been/he, she, it had chopped	they had been/they had chopped

FUTURE PERFECT TENSE: ACTION IN A FUTURE TIME IN RELATION TO ANOTHER TIME EVEN FURTHER IN THE FUTURE

	Singular	Plural
first person	I will have been/I will have chopped	we will have been/we will have chopped
second person	you will have been/you will have chopped	you will have been/you will have chopped
third person	he, she, it will have been/he, she, it will have chopped	they will have been/they will have chopped

There should be no trouble with the present, past, and future tenses, but some examples of the perfect tenses may be helpful. Remember that the *present perfect* tense is used to describe action in *past* time in relation to the present. An example of a *past* tense is *I chopped wood last week.* An example of a *present perfect* tense is *I have chopped wood every Tuesday for three years.* That is, the wood chopping is an action begun in the past and continuing to the present. An example of a *past perfect* tense is *I had chopped wood every Tuesday until I bought a chain saw.* That is, the woodchopping was an action in the past that preceded another past action, buying a chain saw. In this sentence, *had chopped* is a *past perfect tense,* and *bought* is a *past* tense. An example of the future perfect tense is *By 1995, I will have chopped enough wood to heat six houses.* That is, the woodchopping will continue into the future but will be past in 1995.

Almost all verb tense errors on the exams occur in sentences with two verbs. Always look carefully at the tenses of the verbs in a sentence. Does the time scheme make sense? Is it consistent and logical? Since tense reflects the time of the actions, there can be no single rule about what tenses should be used. Meaning, in this case, the time scheme of the action, will determine tense. Sometimes the meaning will require a change of tense. For example,

Yesterday, I ate breakfast at seven o'clock, and tomorrow I will eat at nine.

We have both a past (*ate*) and a future (*will eat*) in this sentence, but other words which explain the time scheme (*yesterday, tomorrow*) make it clear that both a past and a future tense are necessary. On the other hand, consider this example.

In the seventeenth century, the performances at public theatres took place in the afternoon, and the actors dress in splendid costumes.

In this sentence, the change from the past (*took*) to the present (*dress*) makes no sense. Both verbs refer to past actions (*in the sixteenth century*); both should be in the past tense (*took, dressed*).

To spot errors in verb tense, you must look carefully at the verbs and the other words in the sentence that establish the time scheme. Adverbs like *then, subsequently, before, yesterday,* and *tomorrow,* and prepositional phrases like *in the dark ages* and *in the future,* work with the verbs to make the time of the actions clear.

The following are sentences very much like those used on examinations to test verb tenses. Which of the italicized verbs are incorrect?

1. The winds blew sand in the bathers' faces, so they gathered up their towels and *will leave* the beach quickly.
2. The new variety of plum was developed by Burbank who *begun* to work with fruits after the Civil War.
3. In the year 2010, I *am* fifty years old.
4. I *had spoke* with her briefly many times before, but today's conversation was the first in which she *spoke* frankly about her political ambitions.

All but one of the italicized verbs are incorrect. In the first sentence, the shift to the future tense (*will leave*) makes no sense after the two other verbs in the past tense. The verb should be *left*. In the second sentence, the past tense, *began,* or better, the past perfect, *had begun,* is necessary. The *am* of the third sentence should be *will be,* a future tense. In the fourth sentence, *had spoke* incorrectly tries to form the past perfect tense using the past tense (*spoke*) instead of the past participle *spoken*. The second *spoke* is a correct use of the past tense.

Participles, the form of the verb used as an adjective, have only two tenses, present (*going, chopping, eating*) and past (*having gone, having chopped, having eaten*), but tense errors are possible. Be sure that sentences with a participle have a coherent time sequence. A sentence like *Eating my lunch, I took the car to the gas station* makes sense if you eat and drive at the same time. If your meaning is *after lunch,* you must write *Having eaten my lunch, I took the car to the gas station.*

We expect a simple sentence that begins in the past tense to continue to refer to action in the past.

1. Greek sailors in the first century *thought* that their ships *traveled* faster with light ballast and small sails.
2. Egyptian astronomers *believed* that the sun *rose* when the jackal *howled*.

In both of these sentences, all the verbs are, rightly, in the past tense. But there is one kind of sentence which occasionally appears on advanced grammar exams which works differently.

1. Greek sailors in the first century *discovered* that the prevailing winds in the Ionian Sea *blow* from east to west.
2. A handful of ancient astronomers *realized* that the earth *revolves* about the sun and the moon *circles* the earth.

In these sentences, though the main verbs are in the past tense (*discovered, realized*), the verbs in the subordinate clauses are in the present tense (*blow, revolves, circles*). Because the action or state the clauses describe continues to be true (the earth still revolves around the sun) the present tense is correct. Logical meaning is the key to tense. Sentences like these will occur infrequently and are likely to appear in the sentence correction form of question.

SUBJUNCTIVES

In dependent clauses expressing a condition that is untrue or contrary to fact (*if I were sick, if he had arrived five minutes earlier*) the verb is said to be subjunctive, and its forms are different from those of the verbs in statements of fact. The following are examples of subjunctive forms of the verb.

If I *were* sick . . .
If I *arrive* on time . . .   (present tense)

If I *had been* sick . . .
If I *had arrived* on time . . .   (past tense)

If he *were* here . . .
If he *arrives* on time . . .   (present tense)

If he *had been* here . . .
If he *had arrived* on time . . .   (past tense)

For the exams, what you must remember about subjunctive verbs is that *would have* should never be used in the *if* clause. The question will probably be like one of the following:

1. If Holmes would have arrived a few minutes sooner, the murderer would not have escaped.
   (A) would have arrived   (D) arrives
   (B) did arrive   (E) would arrive
   (C) had arrived

2. If the economic situation would have improved in the
                                   A
   first three months of this fiscal year, the banks would
                                                        B
   not have had to foreclose on so many mortgages. No error.
        C   D   E

In question 1, choice (C) is the correct answer. The contrary-to-fact clause (*if*) requires a past subjunctive form. In question 2, the error is choice (A). (Never use *would have* in the *if* clause.) The correct form of the verb in this clause is *had improved*.

LIE/LAY, RISE/RAISE, SIT/SET

Lie is an intransitive verb (that is, it takes no object) meaning *to rest* or *to recline*. *Lay* is a transitive verb (it must have an object) meaning *to put* or *to place*. The confusion between the two verbs probably arose because the past tense of the verb *to lie* (to recline) is the same as the present tense of the verb *to lay* (to place).

Yesterday I *lay* in bed till noon.
intransitive verb—past tense—no object

I *lay* the paper on the table.
transitive verb—present tense—object (paper)

	Present Tense	Past Tense	Past Participle	Present Participle
to rest, to recline *intransitive*	lie	lay	lain	lying
to place, to put *transitive*	lay	laid	laid	laying

1. I like *laying* my head in a pile of sand when I am *lying* on the beach.
2. I *laid* the book on the table and *lay* down on the couch.
3. I have *laid* the book on the table.
4. I have *lain* in bed all morning.

Like *lie, rise* and *sit* are intransitive verbs. Like *lay, raise* and *set* are transitive verbs.

	Present Tense	Past Tense	Past Participle	Present Participle
to go up, to ascend *intransitive*	rise	rose	risen	rising
to lift *transitive*	raise	raised	raised	raising
to be seated *intransitive*	sit	sat	sat	sitting
to put *transitive*	set	set	set	setting

1. I *raise* the window shade and watch the sun *rise*.
2. I *raised* the shade after the sun had *risen*.
3. The sun *rose* before I had *raised* the shade.
4. *Raising* the shade, I watched the sun *rising*.

EXERCISE 4: VERBS

Choose the correct verb form in the following sentences. Answers are on page 325.

1. If you (had, would have) eaten fewer potato chips, you would not be ill now.

2. In 1620, Philips discovered that a candle lighted at only one end (lasts, lasted) longer than one lighted at both ends.

3. I (waited, have waited) for her on the platform.

4. I (have waited, had waited) for her for two hours when she arrived at noon.

5. He (will go, will have gone) to the city tomorrow.

6. If I (were, was) thinner, I would buy a new wardrobe.

7. The thief climbed up the trellis, opened the window, and (steps, stepped) quietly into the room.

8. The letters (lying, laying) on the table have been (lying, laying) there for a week.

9. I (lay, laid) my briefcase on the table and (lay, laid) down on the couch.

10. In this car, the windows (rise, raise) at the press of a button.

11. (Sitting, Setting) the flowers on the table, she noticed the cat (setting, sitting) on the chair nearby.

12. At nine o'clock, a grill (rises, raises) to prevent any entry into the vault.

13. When I reach retirement age in 1995, I (will be, will have been) sixty years old.

14. When I reach retirement age in 1995, I (will work, will have worked) for the post office for thirty years.

15. If you (had been, were) more careful, you would not have dented the fender of the car.

16. If you (had been, were) more careful, you would make fewer mistakes.

5. MISPLACED PARTS, DANGLING MODIFIERS

MISPLACED PARTS

The grammatical errors discussed in parts 1, 2, and 3 are likely to be tested in a question which asks you to identify an error in a single sentence. The first part of this section discusses misplaced parts of the sentence. Since a misplaced part is often awkward but not, strictly speaking, a grammatical error, the questions testing for misplaced parts usually present five versions of the same sentence and ask you to select the sentence that is not only grammatically correct but also clear and exact, free from awkwardness and ambiguity. This form of question may also, of course, be used to test for the kinds of error already discussed.

A well written sentence will be clear and concise. Given a choice between two sentences which say all that must be said and are error free, choose the shorter version. This is *not* to say that any shorter sentence is the right answer. Sometimes a shorter sentence will have a grammatical error, omit part of the original thought, or change the meaning. Here is a sample question.

Fifteen women have formally protested their being overlooked for promotion.
(A) their being overlooked for promotion.
(B) themselves being overlooked for promotion.
(C) their overlooking for promotion.
(D) overlooking themselves for promotion.
(E) themselves as overlooked for promotion.

Answer (C) is the shortest of the five choices here, but it is the wrong answer. It changes the meaning by leaving out *being*. The right answer is choice (A), for a reason you already know—the possessive (*their*) before the gerund (*being overlooked*). The shorter version, then, is not always the best answer, but the right answer will be as short as it can be without sacrificing grammatical correctness and clarity of content.

The basic rule for dealing with misplaced parts of the sentence is *Keep related parts together*. Avoid any unnecessary separation of closely related parts of the sentence. Avoid odd or unnatural word order. Keep modifiers as near as possible to the words they modify. Be especially careful with the adverbs *only, just, almost, nearly, even, hardly, and merely.* Their placement can be crucial to the meaning of a sentence. Look closely at the following two sentences.

1. I almost walked to the park.
2. I walked almost to the park.

There may, at first, appear to be no difference between sentence 1 and sentence 2. But in sentence 1, *almost* clearly modifies *walked.* In sentence 2, it modifies the phrase *to the park.* The meaning of sentence 1 is either *I almost walked (rather than rode, or hopped, or ran)* or *I almost walked (but then decided not to).* The meaning of sentence 2 is *I did walk (but not quite as far as the park).*

Place modifying words, phrases, and clauses in positions that make clear what they modify.

1. I bought a jacket in a Westwood shop *made of leather.*
1. I bought a jacket *made of leather* in a Westwood shop.

2. The soprano had dreamed of singing at the Met *for many years.*
2. *For many years,* the soprano had dreamed of singing at the Met.

3. The committee decided *after the next meeting* to hold a dance.
3. The committee decided to hold a dance *after the next meeting.*

4. The ice cream cone I licked *rapidly* melted.
4. The ice cream cone I licked melted *rapidly.*
4. The ice cream cone I *rapidly* licked melted.

In the first version of sentences 1, 2, and 3, the placement of the italicized phrases makes the meaning of the sentence unclear, but the revisions place the phrases closer to the words they modify. In the first version of sentence 4, the adverb *rapidly* may modify either *licked* or *melted,* but it is not clear which meaning is intended. The two revised versions are clear, with two different meanings.

The normal word order in an English clause or sentence is subject-verb-object: *The dog bit the boy.* Although there are bound to be times when another word order is necessary, keep in mind that the clearest sentences will move from subject to verb to object and keep the three elements as close as possible. One type of question presents the problem of lack of sentence clarity when there are several modifiers of the same word. Normally we want to keep the subject close to the verb, but if the subject has modifiers we also must keep these modifiers close to the subject. The following is a typical question of this sort. Which is the best version of the underlined portion of the sentence?

The tuba player, unlike the drummer, whose arms and hands must be strong, relying upon the power of his lungs, is likely to have an unusually well developed chest.

(A) The tuba player, unlike the drummer, whose arms and hands must be strong, relying upon the power of his lungs, is likely

(B) Unlike the drummer, whose arms and hands must be strong, and relying upon the power of his lungs, the tuba player is likely

(C) Relying upon the power of his lungs unlike the drummer, whose arms and hands must be strong, the tuba player is likely

(D) Because of relying upon the power of his lungs, unlike the drummer, whose arms and hands must be strong, the tuba player is likely

(E) Unlike the drummer, whose arms and hands must be strong, the tuba player, relying upon the power of his lungs, is likely

The subject here is *player* and the verb is *is*. There are two units modifying the subject (*player*): *unlike the drummer, whose arms and hands must be strong* and *relying on the power of his lungs*. How can we place both of these elements close to the subject and at the same time avoid separating the subject from the verb? The best we can do is to put the subject between the two modifiers. By putting the longer of the two modifiers at the beginning, we reduce the length of the separation of subject and verb. The best choice, then, is (E).

DANGLING MODIFIERS

Dangling modifiers are phrases that have nothing to modify. They most frequently occur at the beginning of a sentence and are usually verbals: participles (verbal adjectives), gerunds (verbal nouns), and infinitives.

Participles

A participle is a verb used as an adjective. The present participle ends in *-ing* (*eating, seeing, writing,* for example), while the past participle is that form of the verb used to form the perfect tense (*eaten, seen, written,* for example). Whenever you see a sentence that begins with a participle, check to be sure that the participle logically modifies the subject that immediately follows the comma that sets off the participial phrase. In the following sentences, the first version begins with a dangling participle. The revised versions correct the sentence to eliminate the error.

1. *Waiting* for the bus, the sun came out.
   While we were waiting for the bus, the sun came out.

2. *Fishing* for trout, our canoe overturned.
   While we were fishing for trout, we overturned our canoe.
   Fishing for trout, we overturned our canoe.

3. *Having finished* chapter one, chapter two seemed easy.
   After I had finished chapter one, chapter two seemed easy.
   Having finished chapter one, I found chapter two easy.

4. *Having had* no soup, the salad was welcome.
   Because I had no soup, the salad was welcome.
   Having had no soup, I found the salad welcome.

Sentences 1 and 2 use present participles; sentences 3 and 4 use past participles. The second of the two revisions of these sentences illustrates that a sentence can begin with a participle that does not dangle, and the exams will probably contain sentences that begin with a participle used correctly. But you may be sure that they will also contain sentences with dangling participles to test your ability to recognize this error.

Gerunds

Gerunds, verbal nouns, look like participles, but they are used as nouns rather than adjectives. In the sentence *Waiting for the bus is very boring, waiting* is a *gerund,* used as a *noun* and the subject of the sentence. But in the sentence *Waiting for the bus, I became bored, waiting* is a *participle,* used as an *adjective* and modifying the subject, *I.* The following sentences contain dangling gerunds, corrected in the revision that follows.

1. By changing the oil regularly, your car will run better.
   By changing the oil regularly, you can make your car run better.

2. By working very hard, better grades will result.
   By working very hard, you will get better grades.

3. After sneezing, my handkerchief was useful.
   After sneezing, I found my handkerchief useful.
   After I sneezed, my handkerchief was useful.

Infinitives

An *infinitive* is the simple, uninflected form of a verb, usually written with the preposition *to; to go* is an infinitive, while *goes* or *going* are inflected forms, that is, with additional sounds (*es, ing*) added to the infinitive. Dangling infinitives show up much less frequently on the exams than dangling participles or gerunds, but the principle of the error is the same. As with dangling participles and gerunds, you can correct a sentence with a dangling infinitive by making sure that the subject of the sentence that follows the comma is what the infinitive really modifies. The first version of the following sentences contains a dangling infinitive, corrected in the revisions.

1. To play the violin well, constant practicing is necessary.
   To play the violin well, you must practice constantly.

2. To make cookies, sugar and flour are needed.
   To make cookies, you need sugar and flour.

Prepositional Phrases and Elliptical Clauses

An *ellipsis* is the omission of a word or words. An *elliptical clause* or *phrase* is one in which the subject and verb are implied, but omitted. For example, in the sentence *When in New York, I stay at the Plaza,* the implied subject and verb of *When in New York* are *I am,* but they have been omitted. It is acceptable to use an ellipsis like this, but if the implied subject does not follow, the phrase will dangle.

1. Though rich and beautiful, her marriage was a failure.
2. While on guard duty, her rifle was lost.
3. When a very young child growing up in Brooklyn, his father sent him to summer camp in New Hampshire.
4. On the ship's observation deck, three gray whales were sighted.

The first three of these sentences begin with dangling elliptical clauses. Adding *she was* in the first and second clause and *he was* in the third, that is, filling in the ellipsis, will correct the sentences. The fourth sentence illustrates that even a prepositional phrase may dangle. An observer, not the three whales, is much more likely to be on this ship's observation deck. Dangling modifiers are, like this one, often not only incorrect but ridiculous too. Whenever you see a sentence that begins with a participle, gerund, elliptical phrase, or infinitive, look very carefully to see whether or not the phrase dangles. And remember that some will be correct.

EXERCISE 5: MISPLACED PARTS, DANGLING MODIFIERS

All of the following sentences contain misplaced parts or dangling modifiers. Rewrite each sentence to eliminate the errors. Answers are on page 327.

1. After making a par despite a very bad drive, the crowd cheered loudly for Nancy Lopez.
2. Having failed to read the book carefully, his remarks in class were either imperceptive or irrelevant.
3. By keeping your eye on the ball and not on your partner, the overhead may become your most consistent shot.
4. Hoping to win a place on the team, her free-skating performance must be first-rate.
5. To do well in this exam, both stamina and concentration are absolutely essential.

6. For months we had anticipated seeing Elton John's performance, and to get the best possible view of the stage, our seats were on the center aisle in the front row.

7. When only eight years old, he sent his son to boarding school in Arizona.

8. Though only five feet four, his quickness of reflex and the uncanny accuracy of his volley have made him the best doubles player on the team.

9. At temperatures below 250 degrees, you should stir the boiling syrup very briskly.

10. I have never, if I remember correctly, been in Venice in October.

11. By applying the insecticide carefully, damage to the environment can be avoided.

12. I just have enough money to pay my telephone bill.

6. PARALLELISM

Errors of parallelism will occur when two or more linked ideas are expressed in different grammatical structures. In a sentence like *I am interested in* <u>*nuclear physics,*</u> <u>*to play tennis, and*</u> <u>*going to the theatre,*</u> each of the three elements of the series is in a different grammatical form: a noun, an infinitive, and a gerund phrase. To make the series parallel, one would use any *one* of the forms three times.

I am interested in nuclear physics, tennis, and theatre.
(three nouns)

I am interested in studying nuclear physics, playing tennis, and going to the theatre.
(three gerunds)

I like to study nuclear physics, to play tennis, and to go to the theatre.
(three infinitives)

To find errors of parallelism, look first to be sure there are two or more ideas, words, or phrases that are similar; then check to see that the coordinate ideas are expressed by the same part of speech, verb form, or clause or phrase structure. The first version of the following sentences is *not* parallel. The revisions that follow each sentence correct the parallelism errors.

1. I admire *his cheerfulness* and *that he perseveres.*
   I admire *his cheerfulness* and *his perseverance.*

2. *To dance* and *singing* were his favorite pastimes.
   Dancing and *singing* were his favorite pastimes.
   To dance and *to sing* were his favorite pastimes.

3. *Her cleverness* and *that she looks innocent* helped her escape.
   Her cleverness and *innocent appearance* helped her to escape.

4. *To ship* a package by air freight is more expensive than *if you send* it by parcel post.
   To ship a package by air freight is more expensive than *to send* it by parcel post.

The following are common parallelism errors in the examinations. In the examples, the first version is in error; the revision or revisions correct the sentence.

Unnecessary Shifts in Verb Tenses

1. She *bought* her ticket at the box office and *sits* in the first row.
   She *bought* her ticket at the box office and *sat* in the first row.

2. Every day he *runs* five kilometers and *swam* half a mile.
   Every day he *runs* five kilometers and *swims* half a mile.
   Every day he *ran* five kilometers and *swam* half a mile.

Unnecessary Shifts from an Active to a Passive Verb

1. John *plays* tennis well, but ping-pong *is played* even better by him.
   John *plays* tennis well, but he *plays* ping-pong even better.

2. The editor *wrote* his article in thirty minutes, and it *was typed* by him in five.

The editor *wrote* his article in thirty minutes and *typed* it in five.

Unnecessary Shifts in Person

We divide personal pronouns into three classes: the first person (singular, *I;* plural, *we*), the second person (*you*), and the third person (singular, *he, she, it, one;* plural, *they*). Though it is possible that a sentence will refer to more than one person (*I* went to Florida, and *she* went to Georgia), in sentences where the change of person is not part of the meaning, the pronouns should be consistent. The first version of each of the following sentences is incorrect.

1. *One* should drive slowly and *you* should keep your eyes on the road.

One should drive slowly and keep *one's* eyes on the road.

You should drive slowly and keep *your* eyes on the road.

2. To win at poker, *a player* must know the odds and *you* must observe your opponents carefully.

To win at poker, *you* must know the odds and observe your opponents carefully.

To win at poker, *a player* must know the odds and observe *his or her* opponents carefully.

Parallelism errors are likely to occur in a list or series. In the following examples, the second version of the sentences corrects the parallelism errors.

1. The game has three steps: *getting* your pieces to the center, *capturing* your opponent's pieces, and you must *end* with a throw of double six.

The game has three steps: *getting* your pieces to the center, *capturing* your opponent's pieces, and *ending* with a throw of double six.

2. I talked on, trying to be *charming, gracious,* and *to keep* the conversation going.

I talked on, trying *to be* gracious and charming and *to keep* the conversation going.

The second example begins with a series of two adjectives (*charming, gracious*), but the expected third adjective is an infinitive. The revised version eliminates the series and makes the two infinitives (*to be, to keep*) parallel.

Sentences incorporating a series set up expectations of parallel structures. In a series of three or more, the first two elements will establish a pattern. Assume a series is to include three parts: *mow the grass, weed the garden,* and *empty the trash.* One can say: (1) *I want you to mow the lawn, weed the garden, and empty the trash* or (2) *I want you to mow the lawn, to weed the garden, and to empty the trash.* In (1), the series begins with the infinitive using *to,* and the *to* is understood in the next two parts. The series is *mow, weed, empty.* In (2), the *to* is used with all three verbs. But if the sentence read *I want you to mow the lawn, weed the garden, and to empty the trash,* the parallelism would be lost.

Do not expect every element in parallel structures to be identical all the time. It is proper, for example, to say *I want you to wash the kitchen and the bathroom, go to the store, and cash a check at the bank.* The parallel elements here are *to wash,* (*to*) *go,* and (*to*) *cash,* but other elements within the series are different.

One sure sign of a sentence that must have parallel grammatical constructions is the use of *correlatives.* Correlatives are coordinating conjunctions used in pairs to express similarity or equality in thought. Whenever any of the following correlatives are used, they should be followed by similar grammatical constructions. Memorize this list, and whenever you see these words in a sentence on the exam, you can be very sure that parallelism is one of the problems in the question.

both . . . and	first . . . second
not only . . . but also	not merely . . . but
not only . . . but	not so much . . . as
not . . . but	as much . . . as
either . . . or	more . . . than
neither . . . nor	less . . . than

In a sentence with *both . . . and,* look first to see exactly what the grammar is immediately after the *both;* then make sure the same structure follows the *and.*

In the following examples, the first version illustrates an error, corrected in the revision or revisions.

1. The opera is *both* a complex work *and* original.

   The opera is *both* complex *and* original.
   both, adjective, *and*, adjective

   The opera is *both* a complex *and* an original work
   both, article, adjective, *and*, article adjective

2. He *not only* is selfish *but also* deceitful.

   He is *not only* selfish *but also* deceitful
   not only, adjective, *but also*, adjective

   He *not only* is selfish *but also* is deceitful.
   not only, verb, adjective, *but also*, verb, adjective

3. The book is *not only* about pigs *but also* flowers.

   The book is *not only* about pigs *but also* about flowers.
   not only, preposition, noun, *but also*, preposition, noun

4. The letter is *either* for you *or* your husband.

   The letter is for *either* you *or* your husband.
   either, pronoun, *or*, pronoun, noun

   The letter is *either* for you *or* for your husband.
   either, preposition, pronoun, *or*, preposition, pronoun, noun

Note that in the fourth sentence the corrected versions are not identical (for *you*/for *your husband*). The parallel must be in structure, but one part may contain additional words. It is correct to write *The letter is either for you or for your handsome first husband,* since both *either* and *or* are followed by prepositional phrases beginning with *for.*

EXERCISE 6: PARALLELISM

If there is an error in the following sentences, choose the underlined lettered part in which the error occurs. Some of the sentences will contain no errors. Answers are on page 328.

1. Because I grew up in Switzerland, I read and speak both French
       A   B   C   D
    and German. No error.
                 E

2. It is not his reckless spending of my money but that he spends
     A   B
    it on other women that has led me to file for divorce. No error.
    C   D   E

3. Educational reform is now being brought about by students who
                                A
    are more concerned with the value of their education than
                                      B
    getting a piece of paper with B.A. written on it. No error.
          C   D   E

4. A person's aptitude for foreign languages is important to
           A   B
    State Department examiners, but, on this exam, it is your
                                              C
    ability to read French that will make the difference. No error.
                             D   E

5. Law school not only enables one to practice law, but also
                        A   B
    teaches you to think more clearly. No error.
      B   C   D   E

6. I want you not only to paint and sand the screens but also
              A   B   C
    to put them in the cellar. No error.
     D   E

7. What one expects to get out of a long term investment should be
         A   B   C
    considered carefully before you see your broker. No error.
                  D   E

8. Come to the next class meeting prepared to take notes, to
     A   B
    speak briefly, and with some questions to ask. No error.
         C   D   E

9. Her grace and charm, <u>her ability to see</u> both sides of a
                              A
   question, and <u>her willingness</u> to accept criticism <u>are</u>
                        B   C
   qualities <u>that</u> I especially admire. <u>No error.</u>
             D   E

10. We <u>must look</u> <u>closely</u> <u>both at the data</u> in this year's report
            A   B   C
    and the results of last <u>year's</u> analysis. <u>No error.</u>
                            D   E

11. The process of natural selection <u>requires that</u> animals be able
                                     A
    to adapt <u>to changing climates</u>, to discover new foods,
             B
    <u>and defend themselves</u> against <u>their</u> enemies. <u>No error.</u>
            C   D   E

12. The new employee <u>soon</u> <u>proved himself</u> <u>to be</u> not only capable
                     A   B   C
    but also <u>a man who could be trusted.</u> <u>No error.</u>
             D   E

13. <u>As soon as</u> school <u>ended,</u> he jumped into his car, drove to the
       A   B
    pool, <u>changes</u> his clothes, and <u>swam</u> twenty laps. <u>No error.</u>
          C   D   E

14. To complete your application, <u>you</u> must fill out three forms,
                                   A
    <u>pay</u> the enrollment fee, <u>submit</u> a recent photograph, and
    B   C
    <u>enclose</u> a copy of your high-school transcript. <u>No error.</u>
    D   E

15. I must remember <u>to buy soap and a toothbrush,</u>
                    A
    <u>to have the car washed,</u> <u>to order my Christmas cards and gift</u>
             B   C
    subscriptions, and <u>cash a check</u> before the bank closes.
         C   D
    <u>No error.</u>
        E

REVIEW EXERCISE: SECTIONS 4, 5, and 6

Some of the following sentences may be correct. Others contain problems covered in Sections 4, 5, and 6 of the Grammar and Usage Review. There is not more than one error in any sentence.

If there is an error, it will be underlined and lettered. Find the one underlined part that must be changed to make the sentence correct. Choose (E) if the sentence contains no error. Answers are on page 329.

1. <u>Laying aside</u> his guns, the western hero seems <u>to lose</u> his
      A   B
   distinguishing feature, and <u>he became</u> <u>like anyone else.</u>
                             C   D
   <u>No error.</u>
     E

2. Timur's campaigns <u>were initiated</u> less from geopolitical
                             A
   considerations <u>than the need</u> to provide plunder for his army,
                   B
   which <u>resembled</u> a vast mobile city <u>existing only for</u> conquest
         C   D
   and pillage. <u>No error.</u>
             E

3. In calling <u>*Vanity Fair* a "novel without a hero,"</u> Thackeray
                      A
   <u>suggests</u> that none of his characters, <u>not even Amelia or</u>
     B   C
   Dobbin, <u>is</u> completely admirable. <u>No error.</u>
     C   D   E

4. The psychosomatic origin of migraine headaches <u>has been</u>
                                         A
   <u>suspected</u> for years, but <u>it was not</u> until 1970 that doctors
     A   B
   <u>realized</u> that a patient's thinking about pain <u>is</u> likely to prolong
     C   D
   an attack. <u>No error.</u>
            E

5. The fog of myth and superstition <u>was dispelled</u> not by professors

                                        A

<u>but men like</u> Prince Henry the Navigator and his captains

     B

<u>who went out</u> to explore the globe <u>and to chart</u> the known world.

     C   D

<u>No error.</u>

  E

6. <u>Raising the window shade slowly,</u> the bright sunshine <u>poured</u>

              A   B

into the room and <u>illuminated</u> the broken crystal <u>lying</u> on the

                    C   D

floor. <u>No error.</u>

        E

7. <u>Having narrowly missed colliding with another car</u> while trying

                    A

to change lanes on the freeway, all three of my passengers

told <u>me</u> that I <u>was</u> a terrible driver. <u>No error.</u>

     B   C   D   E

8. The Prince was <u>embarrassed but not injured</u>

                      A

when a demonstrator broke through the <u>cordon</u> of security

                                    B

guards <u>and splashes</u> red paint on <u>his</u> white suit. <u>No error.</u>

         C   D   E

9. After beginning at the bottom <u>as a stockboy,</u> <u>he</u> <u>rose</u> to the

                                 A   B   C

presidency of the store <u>in only eight years.</u> <u>No error.</u>

                     D   E

10. You must be very careful <u>to read the instructions</u> on the test

                                A

booklet, <u>to mark the correct space</u> on your answer sheet, and

                    B

<u>stop writing</u> as soon as the proctor <u>announces</u> the end of the

   C   D

exam. <u>No error.</u>

       E

7. AMBIGUOUS PRONOUNS

In conversation and in informal writing, we often use pronouns that have no single word as their antecedent. *This* happens all the time, for example, the *this* that begins this sentence. It refers to the general idea of the preceding sentence but not to a specific noun. In the exams, you should regard a pronoun that does not have a specific noun or word used as a noun as its antecedent as an error. This sort of error is more likely to occur in the kind of question which gives you choice of revisions. The correct answer will either get rid of the ambiguous pronoun or supply a specific antecedent. Which is the best version of the following sentence?

1. The sun was shining brightly, *which* pleased me.
2. The sun was shining brightly, and *this* pleased me.
3. The sun was shining brightly, and *that* pleased me.
4. Because the sun was shining brightly, *this* pleased me.
5. There was bright sunshine, and *this* pleased me.

The fifth is the best version, for the pronoun *this* has a specific antecedent (*sunshine*). In the first four sentences, none of the pronouns has a specific antecedent. A revision like *That the sun was shining brightly pleased me* would also be correct, since this version simply removes the ambiguous pronoun. The four wrong answers demonstrate that you cannot correct an ambiguous pronoun by substituting another pronoun. The ambiguity will remain until you revise to supply a specific antecedent or to get rid of the pronoun altogether.

You must also be careful with sentences with a pronoun and a choice of antecedents. In a sentence like *Mark told Luke that he owed him five dollars,* we cannot know for certain who owes money to whom. A sentence with an ambiguity of this sort may appear in a question asking you to select an underlined error.

For many years, the American consumer preferred a cola to a
                                         A   B

lemon, orange, or grapefruit flavored drink; recent surveys show a surprising rise in the consumption of it. No error.
C   D   E

The error here is choice (D), the ambiguous pronoun *it* which may refer to any one of four flavors.

EXERCISE 7: AMBIGUOUS PRONOUNS

All of the following sentences contain ambiguous pronouns. Identify the ambiguous pronoun and revise the sentence to eliminate the error. Answers are on page 330.

1. I came in fifteen minutes late, which made the whole chemistry class incomprehensible to me.

2. I want to go to law school because this is the best way to prepare myself for a career in politics.

3. I wrote checks for my phone bill, the gas bill, and my union dues, and this made my account overdrawn.

4. He ate a salad, a pizza, an order of chili, and a large wedge of apple pie in only seven minutes, and, needless to say, this gave him indigestion.

5. I bought a radio and a record player at the second-hand store, but when I plugged it in, it would not work.

6. Both Dave and Vince were scheduled to work Saturday morning, but because his car wouldn't start, he didn't appear until noon.

7. I am told that I think clearly and write well, and these are important in historical studies.

8. Marine iguanas have armored skin, strong claws, and sharp teeth, and this makes them seem ferocious, though they are harmless vegetarians.

8. OTHER ERRORS OF GRAMMAR

Chances are that seventy-five percent of the grammar errors on the exam you take will be errors of case, agreement, verb tense, parallelism, or misplaced parts, and most of these errors will appear more than once. The errors discussed in this section occur regularly, though usually only once or twice in each exam.

SENTENCE FRAGMENTS

A complete sentence must be an independent clause. Do not assume that a subject and a verb automatically make a complete sentence. *I go,* though it is only two words long, is a complete sentence, while *When he had finished eating his dinner, had pushed back his chair, placed his napkin by his empty wine glass, and risen from the table* is not. It is a dependent clause, a sentence fragment. All of the following are sentence fragments.

1. Hoping to be elected on either the first or second ballot.
2. Because the jurors had very carefully examined the evidence presented in the twenty-two days of testimony.
3. The runners from six South American countries, together with the volleyball teams from Canada, Cuba, and the United States.

To complete sentence one, we must add a subject and verb either in an independent clause following this dependent clause or by changing *Hoping* to *He hoped, She hoped, Carol hoped,* or something of the kind. The *Because* at the beginning of the second sentence marks it as a dependent clause. The third sentence has no main verb.

DOUBLE NEGATIVES

It's hard to miss the double negative in a sentence like *I don't want no peas.* The errors are much less obvious with other negative adverbs such as *hardly, but, scarcely, seldom, rarely,* and the like. When you see these words in a sentence, be on the lookout for a double negative like the following.

1. I spent ten dollars on gasoline, and now I don't have hardly any money.
   (Correct to: *I have hardly any money*)

2. In the twilight, a batter can't hardly see a fastball.
   (Correct to: *can hardly see*)

3. I don't have but a dollar, and that will not scarcely pay my check.
   (Correct to: *I have but . . . will scarcely pay*)

OMISSION OF NECESSARY WORDS

Good writing is concise. Given a choice on the exam between two grammatically correct sentences whose meaning is the same, you should choose the shorter version. But be sure there are no necessary words missing. When we read carelessly, sentences like these (which are *not* correct) appear to be complete.

1. People who read rapidly can easily and often have overlooked important details.
2. He always has and, I'm afraid, always will eat like a pig.

Both of these sentences need two main verbs and try to do the work with one. The verbs *have overlooked* and *will eat* are complete, but we cannot say *can overlooked* or *has eat*. We must write *can easily overlook and often have overlooked* and *always has eaten and . . . always will eat*. In a sentence like *He always does and always will eat like a pig,* we need not repeat the verb *eat,* but when the auxiliary verbs require different forms of the verb, the sentence must include both forms.

Watch very carefully for a missing preposition in sentences with two adjectives joined by a conjunction and followed by prepositions, phrases like *bored by and hostile to, fearful of and concerned about.* There are prepositions missing in the following sentences.

1. He doesn't like watching football games, but he is impressed and enthusiastic about some of the cheerleaders.
2. I am uninterested and bored by shopping for clothes.

We cannot say *impressed about* or *uninterested by.* So we must say *impressed by and enthusiastic about* and *uninterested in and bored by.*

Be especially wary with comparisons. Be certain that the two elements that are compared are equivalent. You cannot say *The man's time in the hundred meters was much faster than the woman* because the two elements being compared are different—*time* versus *woman.* The sentence must read *The man's time in the hundred meters was much faster than that of the woman* or *The man's time in the hundred meters was much faster than the woman's.*

What words must be added to correct the following sentences?

1. He is, sensibly, more interested in getting a good job than a rich wife.
2. The amount of vitamin C in eight ounces of tomato juice is much greater than eight ounces of milk.
3. There are far fewer single parents in Maine, Vermont, and New Hampshire than Massachusetts or Connecticut.

Sentence 1 needs a phrase like *than in getting a rich wife.*
Sentence 2 should end with *than that in eight ounces of milk.*
Sentence 3 should read *than in Massachusetts or Connecticut.*

You must often include *any* or *any other* after comparisons using *than* or the phrase *different from.* Your exam is likely to ask you to choose among the five versions of a sentence like this.

The poetry of Keats is <u>different from any English poet.</u>
(A) different from any English poet.
(B) different than any English poet.
(C) different from that of any English poet.
(D) different from that of any other English poet.
(E) different from any English poet's.

There are several problems here. To begin with, the preferred English idiom is *different from* rather than *different than.* And both choices (A) and (B) have missing words, since, as they stand, they make a comparison between *poetry* and a *poet.* The right answer must add *that of* or make *poet* possessive. The difference between choices (C) and (D) is the addition of *other* in choice (D). The *other* is necessary, since Keats was also a poet. For this reason, choice (D) is the correct answer. Choice (E) would also need to add *other* to be correct.

The difference between *any* and *any other* is a difference in meaning. Had the sentence been about a Latin poet, say Virgil, it might read *The poetry of Virgil is different from that of any English poet* without the *other.* If I say *Evans is faster than any other runner at Yale, and Jones is faster than any runner at Yale,* I am also telling you that Evans is a runner at Yale and Jones is not. Any sentence appearing on the exam will make its meaning clear; chances are the right answer will include the phrase *that of any other.*

Another favorite form of question testing the same error is a sentence with a *like* . . . or *unlike* . . . at the beginning or end.

1. Like Shelley, Byron's poetry is sensuous.
2. Like New York, Chicago's traffic is snarled on Friday afternoons.
3. The market in Boston never closes, like New York.
4. Her bank account is never overdrawn, unlike her husband.

In all of these sentences, the two compared elements are not parallel. The first sentence compares *Byron's poetry* with *Shelley,* not with *Shelley's poetry,* and the second compares *New York* and the *traffic* in Chicago. Any of the following revisions will correct the first sentence.

Like Shelley, Byron wrote sensuous poetry.
(*Shelley = Byron*)

Like Shelley's, Byron's poetry is sensuous.
(*Shelley's poetry = Byron's poetry*)

Like that of Shelley, Byron's poetry is sensuous.
(*Shelley's poetry = Byron's poetry*)

Similarly, the fourth sentence, which compares a *bank account* to a *husband,* must be revised. Either of the following is correct.

Her bank account is never overdrawn, unlike her husband's.
Her bank account is never overdrawn, unlike that of her husband.

DIRECT AND INDIRECT QUESTIONS

Direct questions are followed by question marks. Indirect questions are questions within a sentence that is not a question.

Direct: Did you hear my new record?
Indirect: I asked if you heard my new record.

Direct: The premier asked, "How can we save Venice?"
Indirect: The question is how we can save Venice.

In direct questions, the verb usually precedes the subject. In indirect questions, the subject should precede the verb. Thus, in a sentence like *I wonder how I can afford to buy a new car,* where the question is indirect, the subject (*I*) comes before the verb (*can afford*). In a direct question, *How can I afford a new car?*, the verb (*can*) precedes the subject.

LIKE AND AS

Like is a preposition, that is, a word used to connect a noun or pronoun to another element of the sentence. We speak of the noun or pronoun as the object of the preposition and phrases such as *like me* or *like New York* as prepositional phrases. *Like* should be followed by a noun (*like the wind*) or a pronoun (*like her*). It should not be used in place of the conjunction *as* to introduce a clause with a subject and verb or an implied verb. All of the following are correct.

1. As you said, he is overweight, like me.
2. Like zinnias, marigolds are easy to grow.
3. Marigolds are easy to grow, as zinnias are.
4. He is as fast as I. (The verb *am* is understood.)
5. He is fast, like me.
6. As I said, peaches taste good, as summer fruits should.

WHO, WHICH, AND THAT—RESTRICTIVE AND NONRESTRICTIVE CLAUSES

Given a choice among *who, which,* or *that,* use *who* when the antecedent is a single human being (*the man who, John Smith, who*) or a group thought of as individuals (*the lawmakers who, the players who, the jurors who*). Use *that* or *which* for a group thought of as a group (*the senate that; the team, which; the jury that*).

Conservative grammarians distinguish between *which* and *that,* using *that* in defining or restrictive clauses and *which* in nondefining or nonrestrictive clauses. A restrictive clause identifies or defines the noun it modifies, while a nonrestrictive clause merely describes or adds information.

1. The novel *that he wrote in 1860* was not published until 1900. (restrictive clause)

302 GRAMMAR AND USAGE

2. The novel *The Guardian, which he wrote in 1860,* was not
published until 1900.
(nonrestrictive clause)

3. The musicians *who missed two rehearsals* played badly.
(restrictive clause)

4. The musicians, *who rehearse every day,* are on stage.
(nonrestrictive clause)

The pronoun *who* can introduce either a restrictive or a nonrestrictive
clause. If the clause is nonrestrictive, it should be set off by commas.
Though it is extremely unlikely that a test will ask you to discriminate
between the use of *that* and *which,* the point may appear in a sentence
with a second and more obvious sort of error. But you should be alert
to the possibility of a question that asks you to decide about the use of
commas with a *who* clause. Sentences with a human antecedent
wrongly using *which* or *that* instead of *who* are common.

EXERCISE 8: OTHER ERRORS OF GRAMMAR

Answers are on page 330.

Part A

Identify the sentence fragments in the following.

1. Representing the farm belt attitude toward price subsidies, the
delegations from Kansas, Nebraska, and Iowa, as well as food
processors from Texas, Louisiana, and Georgia.

2. So David wept.

3. The Colt Company, a leader in the industry, and celebrated for
introducing the first energy-efficient nine-room house at a cost
under sixty thousand dollars.

4. Is he?

5. When glaciers ground extensive tracts of the granite to a highly
polished finish.

Part B

All of the following sentences contain errors described in Section 8. Identify the error and correct the sentence.

1. The price of meat has gone up steeply in the past six months, according to an unofficial government survey, but there is some consolation for yogurt eaters; yogurt prices haven't risen hardly at all.

2. While calculating their income tax returns, people can and often have made mistakes.

3. During the Renaissance, Venice was wealthier and more important than any city in the world.

4. I wonder how can we finish both the painting and the window-washing in a single day.

5. People have and probably will say for many years to come that Mead's *Coming of Age in Samoa* should be required reading for anyone interested in anthropology.

6. I invested my money in the bank, which pays a higher rate of interest than any other in the city.

7. What Congress decides today will determine the kind of world people must live in the future.

8. The Orsinis hoped to establish their influence throughout Tuscany like the Borgias did in Rome.

9. The embassy claimed that the rights of Soviet Jewish citizens are no different from any Russians.

10. If you use two tablespoons of soy sauce, you will not need scarcely any salt.

11. Scientists argue that water plants can be as effective, if not more effective than chemicals in water purification.

12. The question is when can we afford to take the time to finish the report.

13. He never has and never will be able to play left field as well as Williams.

14. He bought the turkey at Jack's Ranch Market that offered a special price on poultry.

15. Despite their inventive plots and catchy melodies, the musical plays of Sondheim are less popular and less frequently recorded than Cole Porter.

16. As Spain, France was eager to send its navigators to Africa and America.

17. Her trills are as good or better than those of any other soprano.

18. The predators follow the herds of zebra who migrate more than fifteen hundred miles each year.

19. Like the senator explained, what transpired in Chicago in the 1930s now happens all over the country.

20. I am puzzled about how can he afford to make the payments on his cars and a boat while his income is so small.

9. ERRORS OF DICTION, IDIOM, AND STYLE

DICTION

The cause of a diction error, the choice of the wrong word, is not knowing exactly what each word means. Obviously, the more words you know, the fewer diction errors you will make. But the usage sections of the exams are not intended to test the range of your vocabulary, and the words that are misused are rarely obscure or difficult. They are much more likely to be words we all know—or think we know—but confuse with words that look or sound similar. A list of words that are easily mixed up can go on for pages. You should be aware of the following examples, but don't try to memorize the list. Just be sure when you are taking a test to read *each word* carefully.

allude (refer to)—elude (escape from)
allusion (reference)—illusion (false or misleading appearance)
invoke (ask solemnly for)—evoke (summon)
afflict (cause suffering to)—inflict (impose)
aggravate (intensify)—irritate (annoy)

anxious (apprehensive)—eager (ardent)
fortuitous (accidental)—fortunate (lucky)
detain (confine, delay)—retain (keep, hire)
precede (go before)—proceed (advance, continue)
there (in that place)—their (belonging to them)—they're (they are)
its (of it)—it's (it is)

Fewer/Less, Many/Much, Number/Amount

Use *fewer* (not *less*), *many* (not *much*), and *number* (not *amount*) with items that can be counted or numbered.

fewer gallons, many gallons, the number of gallons

Use *less, much,* and *amount* with items that cannot be counted or numbered.

less gasoline, much gasoline, the amount of gasoline

Between/Among

Use *among* with three or more persons or things. When there are only two, use *between.*

The estate was divided between his wife and his daughter.
The vote was split among the three candidates.

Affect/Effect

Affect is a verb meaning *to influence.* As a verb, *effect* means *to bring about,* but as a noun *effect* means a *result* or an *influence.*

1. The *effect* (result) of his decision was to *effect* (bring about) a change in the voting laws that has *affected* (influenced) every candidate for office.

2. Her decision will not *affect* single taxpayers, but it will have some *effect* on married couples.

In the second sentence, both *affect* and *effect* mean *influence,* but *affect* is a verb and *effect* a noun.

IDIOM

This Grammar and Usage Review began by saying that you must not choose your answers by the *it-sounds-right/it-sounds-wrong* principles, but unless you have memorized every idiom in the English language—and no one has—there is nothing to rely on in choosing between idioms except the it-sounds-right principle. Should I say *agree with, agree to,* or *agree upon?* Depending upon the sentence, any one of the three may be right.

I *agree with* your opinion
The plaintiff *agreed to* pay damage of one hundred dollars.
The committees have *agreed upon* a compromise.

Idioms are the usual way in which educated people put words together to express thought. Careful speakers or writers say *different from,* not *different than,* and *other than,* not *other from.* Most of the idiom problems arise from the use of prepositions. Since prepositions are so often insignificant words (*to, from, of, by*), it is easy to miss an obvious idiom error if you read carelessly.

There are no rules for idiom, and as the example of *agree* illustrates, idiom will often depend upon meaning. Some tests will occasionally use an idiom uncertainty to distract you from a real error. Which is the better of these two sentences?

1. The issue is *how can we make our streets free of crime.*
2. The issue is *how we can make our streets free from crime.*

Is it *free from* or *free of?* Neither sounds wrong, and, in fact, either is acceptable. The sentence is really testing word order with an indirect question, and sentence 2 (*we can*) is the better sentence.

One choice the exams often ask you to make is between a three-word phrase made up of a noun or adjective followed by a preposition and a gerund (a word ending in *-ing*) or a similar phrase with the same noun or adjective followed by an infinitive (the preposition *to* and the verb): *hope of going* or *hope to go; ability in running* or *ability to run; afraid of jumping* or *afraid to jump.* You must, finally, depend upon your ear and the context, but if neither version sounds clearly right or wrong, choose the infinitive. It is the better percentage play.

Apes have demonstrated some *ability for reasoning deductively.*
Apes have demonstrated some *ability to reason deductively.*

There are some established English idioms which appear regularly on standardized examinations. The *correct* idioms are given *first.*

different from not *different than*
die of not *die from*
try to not *try and*
except for not *excepting for*
in regard to not *in regards to*
plan to not *plan on*
prior to not *prior than*
type of not *type of a*

STYLE

To this point, we have been concerned with errors of grammar, usage, diction, and idiom. With errors of this sort, you can point to a problematical single word or phrase and identify an error. In some questions, you will be asked to choose between several versions of a sentence, none of which contains a specific error of grammar or usage. One of the answers will be better than the others for reasons of style, that is, because it conveys meaning with superior precision, conciseness, clarity, or grace.

Between an awkward sentence that is grammatically correct and a smoother sentence with a grammatical error, you must always prefer the correct version. But when neither of the two sentences has an error, you must base your decision on style. *Verbosity,* or unnecessary wordiness, is the most tested stylistic weakness. In sentence correction questions, you will often be able to eliminate three of the five sentences for grammar or usage errors and have to decide between two grammatically correct sentences, one of which is less verbose.

<u>After the shipment of bananas had been unloaded, a tarantula's nest was discovered by the foreman</u> in the hold of the ship.

(A) After the shipment of bananas had been unloaded, a tarantula's nest was discovered by the foreman
(B) After unloading the shipment of bananas, a tarantula's nest was discovered by the foreman
(C) Having unloaded the shipment of bananas, a tarantula's nest was discovered by the foreman
(D) After the shipment of bananas had been unloaded, the foreman discovered a tarantula's nest
(E) After the shipment of bananas had been unloaded, the foreman discovers a tarantula's nest

Choices (B), (C), and (E) cannot be right—choices (B) and (C) because of the dangling gerund and dangling participle, choice (E) because of the improper verb tenses (a past perfect and a present). Both choices (A) and (D) are grammatical, but because it uses the passive voice, choice (A) is wordier than choice (D). Given a choice like this, prefer the sentence in the active voice. It is impossible to write the same sentence using a passive verb without using at least two more words than the active voice requires.

I hit the ball. (four words, active)
The ball was hit by me. (six words, passive)

You should note also the ambiguity in choice (A) in that you are not sure if the *foreman,* the *nest,* or both are in the *hold* of the ship.

In our eagerness to be expressive, we sometimes waste words by saying the same thing twice.

1. His prose is *clear* and *lucid.*
2. The *annual* celebration *takes place every year.*
3. Her argument was *trivial,* and *it had no importance.*

There are many phrases which take two or more words to say what one word can say equally well. *Due to the fact that* takes five words to say what *because* says in one. A verbose sentence will use a phrase like *his being of a generous nature* using six words where a phrase like *his generous nature* would say the same thing in three and *his generosity* in two. The following are examples of verbose phrases and formulas with a concise alternative.

VERBOSE	CONCISE
due to the fact that	because
owing to the fact that	because
inasmuch as	because
which was when	when
for the purpose of + gerund for the purpose of eating	to + verb to eat
in order to + verb in order to fly	to + verb to fly
so they can + verb so they can appreciate	to + verb to appreciate
not + negative adjective not useless	positive adjective useful
each and every	every
he is a man who	he is
. . . is a . . . that soccer is a game that	is soccer is
the truth is that the truth is that I am tired	often omit altogether I am tired
the fact is that the fact is that you were late	often omit altogether you were late
it is it is money that talks	often omit altogether money talks
there are there are some flowers that are poisonous	often omit altogether some flowers are poisonous
in a situation where	where
in a condition where	where

EXERCISE 9: ERRORS OF DICTION, IDIOM, AND STYLE

Answers are on page 332.

Part A

All of the following sentences contain an error of diction or idiom. Identify the error and correct the sentence.

1. Led by the oldest graduate present, with classes more or less in chronological order, the alumni parade winds it's way from Weld Hall to the Ford Theatre, where the annual meeting is held.

2. Governor Smith's way of running the state is noticeably different than Governor Eliot's.

3. There are fewer cars on the road, less accidents, and a lower death rate since the gasoline shortage.

4. Since his speeches usually have considerable affect on the Senate, the president will speak tonight.

5. The squabbles between the four original New England states delayed the calling of a convention.

6. I will plan on attending the meeting if I am not delayed.

7. Inflicted with poor eyesight and hearing as a result of her indigent childhood, she nevertheless rose to be the top money winner in women's badminton.

8. By calling her client's widowed mother, the lawyer hoped to effect the jury, but the strategem had no effect.

Part B

All of the following sentences are verbose. Cross out all the unnecessary words without changing the meaning of the sentences.

1. Though trailing thirty-one to ten, the team showed great resiliency and an ability to bounce back; when the fourth quarter ended, the score was thirty-one to thirty.

2. She is so compulsive about avoiding noise that she refuses to begin to do her homework until there is total and complete silence in the dorm.

3. When I look back in retrospect on all that has happened, it is clear that I made the right decision.

4. At the present moment in history, there are now over two thousand unregistered handguns in Alpine County alone.

5. Raised in a well-to-do and affluent suburb of New York, she was unable to adjust to the lack of physical comforts in rural Saskatchewan.

6. Unless the president presents a workable and practicable program to conserve and keep energy from being wasted, none of the New England states is likely to support him.

7. The true facts of the case made it clear that he was obviously a victim of a hideous injustice.

8. The subtle distinctions and nice discriminations of her philosophical essays are too fine for any but the most learned and erudite to understand, even with several rereadings.

9. Many dramatists and playwrights, Congreve among them, wrote about the elegance and corruption of the Restoration society.

10. The photography of the mountainous hill regions where the peasants live is beautiful; unfortunately, the film opened when the potential audience to whom it might have appealed had sated its appetite for travelogues.

REVIEW EXERCISE: SECTIONS 7, 8, and 9

If there is an error of grammar, diction, or verbosity in the following sentences, choose the underlined and lettered part in which the error occurs. Some of the sentences will contain no errors. Answers are on page 333.

1. Gordon's novel, written <u>with an eye to</u> conservative readers,
                                    A
   has <u>less scenes</u> of action and more with moral lessons <u>than</u>
            B   C
   <u>any other work</u> published this year. <u>No error.</u>
            D   E

2. An independent clause <u>can stand alone</u> <u>as a sentence;</u>
   $\qquad\qquad\qquad\quad$ A $\qquad\qquad$ B

   a dependent clause <u>occupies</u> a subordinate position and
   $\qquad\qquad\qquad$ C

   cannot <u>by itself</u> be a complete sentence. <u>No error.</u>
   $\qquad\quad$ D $\qquad\qquad\qquad\qquad\qquad\qquad$ E

3. Though his lawyer <u>argued his case</u> cogently, concisely, and
   $\qquad\qquad\qquad\qquad$ A

   <u>forcefully,</u> Jones <u>was still</u> found guilty <u>and sentenced to</u>
   $\quad$ B $\qquad\qquad\qquad$ C $\qquad\qquad\qquad$ D

   three years in jail. <u>No error.</u>
   $\qquad\qquad\qquad\qquad$ E

4. Since the mountains <u>i</u>n California are higher <u>than New York,</u>
   $\qquad\qquad\qquad\qquad\qquad\qquad\qquad\qquad\quad$ A

   I and my cousins <u>who like to ski</u> <u>will prefer</u> <u>to spend</u> the
   $\qquad\qquad\qquad$ B $\qquad\qquad\quad$ C $\qquad$ D

   winter on the west coast. <u>No error.</u>
   $\qquad\qquad\qquad\qquad\qquad$ E

5. The courtly lover of Provence worshipped both <u>the Virgin</u> and
   $\qquad\qquad\qquad\qquad\qquad\qquad\qquad\qquad\quad$ A

   an earthly lady and <u>paid his</u> tribute <u>to her</u> in <u>ornate</u> lyric
   $\qquad\qquad\qquad$ B $\qquad\qquad\quad$ C $\qquad$ D

   poems. <u>No error.</u>
   $\qquad\quad$ E

6. Although he <u>took</u> careful notes, <u>studied</u> in the library every
   $\qquad\qquad$ A $\qquad\qquad\qquad$ B

   night, and <u>wrote</u> two extra papers, this industry <u>did not effect</u>
   $\qquad\qquad$ C $\qquad\qquad\qquad\qquad\qquad\qquad\qquad$ D

   his grade in the class. <u>No error.</u>
   $\qquad\qquad\qquad\qquad$ E

7. <u>Like</u> a large room, the American continent once offered
   $\quad$ A

   <u>an exhilarating spatial freedom,</u> impressing western settlers
   $\qquad\qquad\qquad$ B

   <u>first with</u> its sublime beauty and afterwards with
   $\qquad$ C

   <u>its opportunities for exploitation.</u> <u>No error.</u>
   $\qquad\qquad\qquad$ D $\qquad\qquad\qquad$ E

8. When the Queen entered, the <u>musicians which were</u>
                                    A
on the stage withdrew quietly, but the actors were <u>too surprised</u>
                                                           B
<u>to be able</u> to <u>know what to do.</u> <u>No error.</u>
     C   D   E

9. I have <u>no interest</u> and <u>no intention</u> to become involved with
              A   B
<u>this foolish debate</u> about priorities <u>in</u> Central America.
          C   D
<u>No error.</u>
     E

10. We will <u>have to start for home</u> much earlier this week, <u>for</u> there
                      A   B
are <u>not but two or three hours</u> of good driving conditions
              C
<u>if we leave</u> after two o'clock. <u>No error.</u>
      D   E

10. PUNCTUATION

This section will certainly not tell you all you ought to know about punctuation to write well. It will describe the kind of punctuation errors that appear most often on the examinations. You are not likely to find sentences that test the use of the dash or the colon or that ask you whether to put the comma inside or outside a parenthesis. But you must know the difference between a comma and a semicolon.

The comma is used to indicate a slight separation of sentence elements. The semicolon indicates a greater degree of separation, and the period marks the end of a sentence. The punctuation errors that will appear most frequently on the exams are the use of a comma where a semicolon is needed and the use of a semicolon where a comma is needed. In compound sentences, that is, sentences with two independent clauses, a semicolon and a comma are *not* interchangeable.

Punctuate the following sentences with either a comma or a semicolon.

1. I had come to China to buy silk and I was not planning to buy anything else.
   I had come to China to buy silk I was not planning to buy anything else.

2. I got my needles from Frankfurt while my threads came from London.
   I got my needles from Frankfurt my threads came from London.

In both examples, the first version needs a comma before the conjunction (*and, while*). In the second version, a semicolon should follow *silk* and *Frankfurt*. The principle is the same in both. With two independent clauses joined by a conjunction, use a comma. With two independent clauses that are not joined by a conjunction, use a semicolon.

Now punctuate the following sentences with either a comma or a semicolon.

1. I looked for a house for sale on the lake hoping to be able to finish my book there.
2. They bundled themselves into the car waved once and drove away.
3. He was not at all interesting a man who talked endlessly about himself and how much money he had.

All three sentences need commas and only commas: after *lake* in sentence 1, after *car* and *once* in sentence 2, and after *interesting* in sentence 3. All of the clauses after the commas are dependent, that is, they cannot stand by themselves as complete sentences. If they were set off by semicolons, they would be sentence fragments.

Here is an example in another form.

The editorials in *Ghost Magazine* are
infuriating to some <u>readers; delightful</u>
1

1. A. NO CHANGE
   B. readers. And
   C. readers,
   D. readers; or

to others. <u>Nevertheless, its</u> circulation
2
has grown more rapidly than that of any
other fantasy magazine.

2. A. NO CHANGE
   B. Nevertheless its
   C. Nevertheless, it's
   D. Nevertheless it's

The correct answers here are 1. (C) and 2. (F). You must use a comma after *readers*. If you use a period or a semicolon, the phrase *delightful to others* is a sentence fragment. In 2, the punctuation is correct. The possessive of the pronoun *it* is *its; it's* is a contraction of *it is*. The comma marks the slight pause after the introductory word *Nevertheless*.

The following is a brief summary of the rules governing commas, semicolons, and colons.

COMMA

Use a comma:

1. in a series of three or more with a single conjunction.

   He bought red, green, and blue neckties.
   I must stop at the bank, have the car washed, and leave my shirts at the laundry.

2. to set off parenthetic expressions.

   The result, I imagine, will be in the paper.
   The check, you will be glad to know, is in the mail.

3. to set off nonrestrictive relative clauses.

   In 1600, when *Hamlet* was first acted, the Globe was London's largest public theatre.
   Montpelier, Concord, and Augusta, which are all small cities, are the capitals of the northern New England states.

4. to separate the two parts of a sentence with two independent clauses joined by a conjunction.

> The film is over, and the audience has left the theatre.
> The mayor is present, but the governor is not here.

5. to set off introductory words, phrases, or clauses.

> Unfortunately, he left his wallet in the car.
> Having looked in the glove compartment, he discovered his wallet was missing.

6. to set off appositives.

> Mr. Smith, the mayor, called the meeting to order.
> The leading batter in the league is John Jones, the first baseman.

Do *not* use a comma to join two independent clauses not joined by a conjunction. Use a period or a semicolon.

> Her novels are always best sellers; they are translated into three languages.
> The boat crossed the lake in fifteen minutes; the canoe took two hours.

Each of these sentences could be written as two sentences with periods at the end. If a conjunction were added, a comma would replace the semicolons.

> Her novels are always best sellers, *and* they are translated into three languages.
> The boat crossed the lake in fifteen minutes, *but* the canoe took two hours.

SEMICOLON

Use a semicolon:

1. to separate two independent clauses in a compound sentence when there is no conjunction between them.

> The hurricane came ashore near Lake Charles; its winds were measured at more than one hundred miles per hour.

The warnings were broadcast early in the day; thus, there was no loss of life.

2. to separate a series when one or more of the elements of the series contains commas.

He bought a red, a green, and a blue tie; three button-down shirts; and a pair of penny loafers.
We will stop in Maumee, Ohio; Erie, Pennsylvania; Albany, New York; and Amherst, Massachusetts.

COLON

Use a colon after an independent clause:

1. to introduce a series.

The following vegetables should be planted in March: radishes, carrots, leeks, turnips, and cabbage.

In this sentence, the clause before the colon is independent. In a sentence like *In March, you should plant radishes, carrots, leeks, turnips, and cabbage* where there is no independent clause before the series, you must *not* use a colon.

2. to join two independent clauses when the second amplifies or interprets the first.

A preliminary step is essential to successful whipped cream: you must chill the bowl and the beaters.

3. to introduce a quotation.

Every English schoolchild knows the opening line of *Twelfth Night:* "If music be the food of love, play on."

OTHER MARKS OF PUNCTUATION

Dash

Use a *dash* to indicate an abrupt break and to set off parenthetical elements already broken up by commas.

I believe—no, I know—he is guilty.

I—er—you—er—forget it!

The general—overdecorated, overconfident, overweight—spoke to the troops on the benefits of self-sacrifice.

The speech—the harangue, I should say—lasted for three hours.

Apostrophe

Use an *apostrophe* to indicate the omission of a letter or letters in a contraction (*I'm, I've, you'd, don't, who's, we're*).

Form the possessive of singular nouns by adding *'s* (*tiger's, cat's, man's*). Form the possessive of plural nouns by adding just the apostrophe (') if the plural ends in *s* (*tigers', cats', dogs'*). Form the possessive of plural nouns that do not end in *s* by adding *'s* (*mice's, men's, children's*).

EXERCISE 10: PUNCTUATION

In the left-hand column, you will find a passage in a "spread-out" format with various words and phrases underlined. In the right-hand column, you will find a set of responses corresponding to each underlined portion. If the underlined portion is correct as it stands, mark the letter indicating "NO CHANGE." If the underlined portion is incorrect, decide which of the choices best corrects it. Consider only underlined portions; assume that the rest of the passage is correct. Answers are on page 333.

Anything it seems is worth
1
fighting about when there's money to be made. How else can we explain the public-relations war being waged between the plastics and paper industries over the best kind of grocery bag to use. If you've been to the
2
supermarket lately, you know what we're talking about.

1. A. NO CHANGE
   B. Anything, it seems is worth
   C. Anything it seems, is worth
   D. Anything, it seems, is worth

2. A. NO CHANGE
   B. bag to use? If
   C. bag to use; if
   D. bag to use! If

Alongside those <u>tried trusty</u>
3

and <u>true brown</u> paper bags that
3

Americans have relied on and treasured since 1883, you'll see a lump of limp, shapeless, non-biodegradable plastic containers that the plastic lobby would try to convince you is the way to go.

Their argument is that plastic bags are more easily <u>portable—</u>
4

<u>at least, for those who go to the</u>
4

<u>store on foot—</u>because they have
4

<u>handles; that</u> they don't leak all
5

over the place when something wet gets loose; and that they can just as easily be used as garbage containers as the paper variety. They are also cheaper for the supermarket, at about 2.6 cents apiece, compared with 4.4 cents for paper bags, and they require less storage space.

The obvious response to this propaganda barrage is that paper bags stand on their <u>own, so to</u>
6

<u>speak, in your trunk, are bio-</u>
6

<u>degradable, make a better waste</u>
6

<u>container can</u> be cut up and used
6

3. A. NO CHANGE
   B. tried, trusty, and true, brown
   C. tried trusty, and true brown
   D. tried, trusty and true brown

4. A. NO CHANGE
   B. portable, at least, for those who go to the store on foot—
   C. portable—at least for those who go to the store on foot—
   D. portable, at least, for those, who go to the store on foot,

5. A. NO CHANGE
   B. handles that
   C. handles, that
   D. handles—that

6. A. NO CHANGE
   B. own so to speak in your trunk, are bio-degradable, make a better waste container, can
   C. own, so to speak, in your trunk; are bio-degradable; make a better waste container; can
   D. own, so to speak, in your trunk, are bio-degradable, make a better waste container, can

to wrap books, packages, or
parcels, or to make Halloween
masks; and—here's the telling
　　　　　　　　7
punch—are actually cheaper
　7
overall because supermarket
checkers can pack them
18 percent faster than
the plastic.

Surveys have been conducted,
　　　　　　　　　　8
of course, and it turns out, not
　　　　　8
too surprisingly, that those who
　8
live alone in city apartments—
typically singles, old people, and
just about anyone who lives in the
middle of Manhattan or
San Francisco—prefer plastic.

The rest of us—suburbanites the
　　　　　　　　　9
pro-plastic folks disparagingly
　　　　　　9
call us—are quite happy with
　9
our brown paper bags, thank you,
and we're still a majority.

7. A. NO CHANGE
   B. masks; and here's the
      telling punch; are
   C. masks, and, heres the
      telling punch, are
   D. masks, and—here's
      the telling punch—
      are

8. A. NO CHANGE
   B. conducted, of course,
      and it turns out not
      too surprisingly
   C. conducted of course,
      and it turns out not
      too surprisingly
   D. conducted of course,
      and it turns out,
      not too surprisingly

9. A. NO CHANGE
   B. us—"suburbanites" the
      pro-plastic folks
      disparagingly call us—
   C. us—"suburbanites,"
      the pro-plastic folks
      disparagingly call us—
   D. us—suburbanites, the
      pro-plastic folks
      disparagingly call us—

REVIEW EXERCISE: SECTIONS 1–10

When you take a grammar exam, you must be able to recognize the kind of error that is being tested for. Certain words or sentence structures should warn you at once of the kind of error likely to occur in the sentence. All of the following words or structures should alert you at once to one or two likely errors. What are these errors? Answers are on page 334.

1. a sentence beginning with a participle

2. a sentence beginning with *Both*

3. a sentence containing a series

4. a sentence beginning with *Either*

5. a sentence containing the word *not*

6. a sentence beginning with a prepositional phrase with *Like*

7. a sentence containing the phrase *a number*

8. a sentence beginning with *Everybody*

9. a sentence containing the word *who*

10. a sentence containing the verb *look*

11. a sentence beginning with the word *One*

12. a sentence beginning with the word *None*

13. a sentence beginning with an elliptical phrase

14. a sentence containing the word *criteria*

15. a sentence containing the word *almost*

16. a sentence containing the word *hardly*

17. a sentence containing a comparison

18. a sentence containing the verb *lie*

19. a sentence beginning with the word *If*

20. a sentence containing the phrase *as well as*

ANSWERS TO THE GRAMMAR AND USAGE REVIEW EXERCISES

EXERCISE 1: PARTS OF SPEECH, ADJECTIVES AND ADVERBS, LINKING VERBS, COMPARATIVES AND SUPERLATIVES

1. *Almost*—an adverb, modifying the adjective *every*.

2. *different*—an adjective, with the linking verb *appeared*.

3. *suddenly*—an adverb, modifying *appeared*. In this sentence *appeared* means *made an appearance* rather than *looked* and is not a linking verb.

4. *best*—the superlative. There are more than two players.

5. *better*—the comparative, with only two compared.

6. *bad*—an adjective, modifying *pie*. *Taste* here is a linking verb.

7. *noticeably*—an adverb, modifying the adverb *more*.

8. *sad*—an adjective, with the linking verb *feel*.

9. *seriously*—an adverb, modifying the verb *take*.

10. *aromatic*—an adjective, with the linking verb *smells*.

11. *almost*—an adverb, modifying the adjective *any*.

12. *carefully*—an adverb. In this sentence *look* means *examine* not *appear* and is not a linking verb.
    clearly—an adverb, modifying the adjective *visible*.

13. *largest*—the superlative. There are many antelopes.
    slowest—the superlative. Again, there are more than two.

14. *surely*—an adverb, modifying the verb *seemed*.
    inexhaustible—an adjective, modifying the noun *supply*. *Seemed* is a linking verb.

15. *steeply*—an adverb, modifying the verb *rise*.
    steep—an adjective, modifying the pronoun *it*, with the linking verb *look*.

322

EXERCISE 2: CASE

Part A

1. *we*—subject of the clause *we are not.*

2. *me*—object of the preposition *except.*

3. *his*—possessive, before the gerund *using.*

4. *I*—subjective case, agreeing with the subject *it.*

5. *our*—possessive, before the gerund *standing.*

6. *me*—object of the verb *affect.*

7. *me*—objective case, in apposition to the objective *us* (*Let's* = *Let us*).

8. *his*—possessive, before the gerund *talking.*

9. *president's*—possessive, before the gerund *riding.*

10. *me*—objective case, in apposition to *finalists,* the object of the preposition.

Part B

1. *who*—subject of the clause *who was elected.*

2. *who*—subject of the clause *who did not wish to be interviewed.* The *we understand* is parenthetical.

3. *Who*—subject of the clause *Who will buy this car.*

4. *Whom*—object of the verb *will choose.* The subject of the clause is *company.*

5. *whoever*—subject of the clause *whoever is waiting for the general.*

6. *whomever*—object of the verb *convince.*

7. *Whoever*—subject of the clause *Whoever deserves the prize.*

8. *whoever*—subject of the clause *whoever is most likely to support their position.*

9. *whomever*—object of the preposition *with.*

10. *whom*—object of the preposition *with.*

EXERCISE 3: AGREEMENT

1. *are, is*—The antecedent of *who* is the plural *candidates;* the subject of *is* is the singular *None.*

2. *is*—the singular *sergeant-at-arms* is the subject of the verb.

3. *have, is*—The antecedent of *who* is the plural *applicants;* the subject of *is* is the singular *None.*

4. *was*—The subject is the singular *Mr. Lombardi.*

5. *makes*—The subject is the singular *evidence.*

6. *include*—The subject is the plural *criteria.*

7. *look, they*—The subject is the plural *columns,* which is also the antecedent of *they.*

8. *is*—The subject is the singular *student.*

9. *are*—The subject is compound, *Mr. and Mrs. Smith.*

10. *have*—The antecedent of *who* is *quarter-milers.*

11. *are, increases*—The antecedent of *that* is the plural *penguins;* the subject of *increases* is the singular *number.*

12. *is*—The subject is the singular *Mary Jane.*

13. *was*—The subject is the singular *Everyone.*

14. *have, their*—The plural *twins* is the subject of *have* and the antecedent of *their.*

15. *has, her*—The singular *Sally* is the subject of *has* and the antecedent of *her.*

16. *was*—The subject is the singular *I.*

17. *enjoys*—The subject is the singular *president.*

18. *seems*—The singular *The number* is the subject.

19. *have*—*A number* here means *many,* so the verb is plural.

20. *are*—The subject *data* is plural.

REVIEW EXERCISE: SECTIONS 1, 2, AND 3

1. (E) The *me* is the object of the preposition *but;* the subject is the singular *No one,* so *was* is also correct.

2. (A) The phrase *many a young man* is singular. The plural would be *many men.*

3. (E) The agreement in this sentence is correct.

4. (D) The subject is plural, a compound subject with *and.*

5. (C) Since *thousands* is plural, *life* should be *lives.*

6. (B) The phrase *my sister and I* is in apposition to *members,* the object of *includes. I* should be *me.*

7. (E) The singular *was* is correct with the singular subject *result. Her* is the object of *alarm.*

8. (D) The subject of the last clause is *they,* the verb is *can catch,* and the object should be *whomever.*

9. (E) The adjective *simple* is correct with the linking verb *seemed.* The adverb *simply* modifies the adverb *too.*

10. (D) With a comparison of two teams, *better* not *best* should be used.

EXERCISE 4: VERBS

1. *had*—Never use *would have* in the *if* clause.

2. *lasts*—Since the discovery is a fact that continues to be true, use the present tense.

3. *waited*—There is nothing in the sentence to suggest a present time to which a present perfect tense is related, so only the past tense makes sense.

4. *had waited*—Here the other verb in the sentence is the past tense *arrived.* Action in past time in relation to another past time is expressed by the past perfect tense.

5. *will go*—The sentence expresses a simple future (*tomorrow*). The future perfect would be used only if the action were related to another time even further in the future.

6. *were*—Since the condition expressed in the *if* clause is untrue (I am not thinner), the present subjunctive should be used. *Was* is the past tense and not a subjunctive.

7. *stepped*—The first two verbs (*climbed, opened*) are in the past tense. There is no reason to change tenses, so the third verb should also be in the past tense.

8. *lying, lying*—The verb here is the intransitive *lie* (to rest). The participal form of *lie* is *lying*.

9. *laid, lay*—The first verb is the transitive verb *lay* (to place) in the past tense. The second verb is the intransitive verb *lie* (to recline) in the past tense. The first verb has an object (*briefcase*); the second has none.

10. *rise*—The intransitive verb *rise* in the present tense is correct here.

11. *Setting, Sitting*—The first verb is the transitive *set* with *flowers* as the object; the second verb, the intransitive *sit,* has no object.

12. *rises*—The intransitive verb *rise* in the present tense is correct here

13. *will be*—The future tense, not the future perfect, is correct here. There is no time even further in the future to which this verb is related.

14. *will have worked*—Here the future perfect is correct because the opening clause defines a time which is even further in the future. In sentence 13, 1995 is in the future but not further in the future than the time at which I will be sixty. But in the second sentence, 1995 will come at the end of the period of thirty years' work.

15. *had been*—The verb in the first clause is subjunctive because it describes a contrary-to-fact situation. The past tense of the verb in the second clause requires a subjunctive in the past tense in the first. In the present tense, this sentence would read: *If you were more careful, you would not dent the fender of the car.*

16. *were*—The correct verb here is the present subjunctive.

EXERCISE 5: MISPLACED PARTS, DANGLING MODIFIERS

There are several ways to rewrite these sentences and eliminate the errors. The following are a few of the possible revisions.

1. As it stands now, the participial phrase at the beginning of the sentence dangles and appears to modify the *crowd* rather than *Nancy Lopez*. One can correct the sentence by beginning *After she made a par* . . . or by leaving the participial phrase unchanged and writing *Nancy Lopez was cheered* after the comma.

2. The sentence also beings with a dangling participle. It can be corrected by beginning with *Because he failed* . . . or by writing *he made remarks in class that were* . . . after the comma.

3. Again, the error is a dangling participle. Revise the sentence to begin with *If you keep* . . . or write something like *you may make the overhead* . . . after the comma.

4. A dangling particple once more. The corrected sentence could begin *If she hopes to win* . . . or could say *she must give a first-rate free-skating performance* after the comma.

5. The error here is a dangling infinitive, which makes it appear that *stamina* and *concentration* are taking the exam. Either add a human agent in the first phrase (*For you to do well*) or begin the second with *you must have.* . . .

6. This is a very difficult sentence because the dangling infinitive is not at the beginning of the sentence but in the middle (*to get the best possible view*). As it stands, the *seats* not the ticket holders are getting the best view. By revising the last clause of the sentence to read *we bought seats on the center aisle* . . . , we eliminate the error.

7. The elliptical phrase here dangles, so the sentence suggests that the father is eight years old. To remove the error, we can remove the ellipsis and write *When his son was only eight years old.* . . . If we wish to keep the opening unchanged, we must write *his son was sent* . . . after the comma.

8. Like sentence 7, this sentence opens with a dangling elliptical phrase. The simplest way to correct the error is to write *Though he is only.* . . .

9. Here the prepositional phrase which begins the sentence seems to modify *you.* Beginning the sentence with the *you* clause and putting the prepositional phrase at the end will correct the error.

10. To avoid the unnecessary separation of the parts of the verb, begin the sentence with *If I remember correctly.* . . .

11. The opening elliptical phrase dangles. Write *By applying the insecticide carefully, you can avoid damage to the environment.*

12. The *just* is misplaced. Write *I have just enough* . . . so that *just* is next to the word it modfies.

EXERCISE 6: PARALLELISM

1. (E) The parallelism here is correct.

2. (B) With the correlatives *not . . . but,* the words after *but* should be parallel to those after *not: not his reckless spending . . . but his spending.*

3. (C) The phrase *more concerned with* should have a parallel after *than: than with getting.*

4. (A) Since the pronoun *your* is used later in the sentence (and cannot be changed, since it is not underlined) the first phrase in the sentence should read *Your aptitude.*

5. (C) Since the pronoun *one* is used earlier in the sentence, *you* should be *one.*

6. (E) The parallelism here is correct.

7. (A) Since the pronoun *you* is used at the end of the sentence, *one* should be *you.*

8. (D) The series of infinitives (*to take, to speak*) should be completed with another infinitive (*to ask some questions*).

9. (E) The series in this sentence maintains parallelism.

10. (C) With the correlatives *both . . . and,* the structure following should be parallel. The correct version is *at both the data.*

11. (C) To maintain the series of infinitives, the sentence should read *and to defend.*

12. (D) With the correlatives *not only . . . but also,* the sentence should read *not only capable but also trustworthy.*

13. (C) The past tense should be used in all the verbs—*ended, jumped, drove, changed, and swam.*

14. (E) The parallelism here is correct.

15. (D) The final verb in this series should be an infinitive (*to cash*) to be parallel with the others.

REVIEW EXERCISE: SECTIONS 4, 5, AND 6

1. (C) Since the main verb in the first part of the sentence is in the present tense (*seems*), there is no reason to shift to a past tense.

2. (B) With *less from* followed by *than,* the *from* should be repeated.

3. (E) The sentence is correct as given.

4. (E) The present tense of *is* is correct, since the subject is a medical fact that continues to be true.

5. (B) With the correlatives *not . . . but,* the *but* should be followed by the preposition *by* to be parallel.

6. (A) *Raising* is the right verb (not *rising*), but the phrase is a dangling participle. It looks as if the *sunshine* raised the shade.

7. (A) Another dangling particple. The *I* of the sentence, not the passengers, narrowly missed the collision.

8. (C) The other verbs of the sentence (*was, broke*) are in the past tense, so *splashed* is correct here.

9. (E) The beginning phrase modifies *he* and does not dangle.

10. (C) The series should have three infinitives: *to read, to mark,* and *to stop.*

EXERCISE 7: AMBIGUOUS PRONOUNS

All of the following are *possible* answers, but certainly not the only right response.

1. The *which* has no specific antecedent. To avoid the ambiguous pronoun, one might write *My coming in fifteen minutes late made* . . . or *I came in fifteen minutes late and found.* . . . One cannot correct the error by substituting another pronoun for the ambiguous *which*.

2. The ambiguous pronoun is *this*. The sentence can be corrected by simply omitting the phrase *because this is* and adding a comma after *school*.

3. The ambiguous pronoun is *this*. Effectively revised, the sentence would read *By writing checks for* . . . *I overdrew my account*.

4. The ambiguous pronoun is *this*. It can be eliminated by concluding the sentence with *and, needless to say, had indigestion*.

5. The antecedent of *it* could be either the radio or the record player. The simple solution is to say *when I plugged the radio* (or *the record player*) *in, it would not work*.

6. The antecedent of *his* and *he* is unclear. As in sentence 5, the solution is to use the noun (*Dave* or *Vince*) in place of *he*.

7. The *these* is ambiguous. One solution is to write *these abilities*.

8. The *this* is ambiguous. One could write *this appearance makes them seem ferocious* or *and they appear ferocious, though*. . . .

EXERCISE 8: OTHER ERRORS OF GRAMMAR

Part A

1. A fragment. There is no main verb, only a participle.

2. A complete sentence. *David* (subject) *wept* (verb).

3. A fragment. There is no verb.

4. A complete sentence. *Is* (verb) *he* (subject).

5. A fragment. The clause is dependent.

Part B

1. Double negative—*haven't risen hardly*.

2. Omission of necessary word—*can make*.

3. Omission of necessary word—Since Venice is a city, *any other city*.

4. Word order in indirect question—*how we can*.

5. Omission of necessary word—*have said*.

6. *Which* for *that*—The clause is restrictive, *bank that* (with no comma).

7. Omission of necessary word—*must live in in the future*.

8. *Like* for *as*—The clause has a subject and verb—*as the Borgias*.

9. Omission of necessary words—*different from those of any other*.

10. Double negative—*not need scarcely*.

11. Omission of necessary word—*as effective as*.

12. Word order in indirect question—*when we can*.

13. Omission of necessary word—*never has been*.

14. *That* for *which*—The clause is nonrestrictive—*Jack's Ranch Market, which*.

15. Omission of necessary words—*than those of Cole Porter*.

16. *As* for *like*—The sentence should begin with a prepositional phrase—*Like Spain*.

17. Omission of necessary word—*as good as*.

18. *Who* for *which*—Zebras are not humans—*Zebra, which migrate*.

19. *Like* for *as*—The clause has a subject and a verb—*As the senator explained*.

20. Word order in indirect question—*how he can afford*.

EXERCISE 9: ERRORS OF DICTION, IDIOM, AND STYLE

Part A

1. *it's*—should be *its*. *It's* means *it is*.
2. *than*—The correct idiom is *different from*.
3. *less*—Since accidents can be numbered, it should be *fewer accidents*.
4. *affect*—*Affect* is a verb; the noun *effect* should be used here.
5. *between*—Since there are four states, use *among*.
6. *plan on attending*—The correct idiom is *plan to attend*.
7. *Inflicted*—The required word here is *Afflicted*.
8. *effect*—The first *effect* should be the verb *affect*. The second *effect* is correct.

Part B

1. *Resiliency* and *ability to bounce back* mean the same thing.
2. One could omit *to do*. *Total* and *complete* mean the same thing.
3. Since *retrospect* means *a looking back*, the prepositional phrase is unnecessary.
4. The phrase *At the present moment in history* is unnecessary with the use of *now*.
5. *Well-to-do* and *affluent* mean the same thing.
6. *Workable* and *practicable* mean the same thing. You also do not need both *conserve* and *keep from being wasted*.
7. Both *true* and *obviously* are unnecessary words here.
8. Either *subtle distinctions* or *nice discriminations* and either *learned* or *erudite* can be eliminated.
9. A *dramatist* is a *playwright*. One or the other is sufficient.
10. With *mountainous, hill* is unnecessary, and *potential* is equivalent to *to whom it might have appealed*.

REVIEW EXERCISE: SECTIONS 7, 8, AND 9

1. (B) *Less* should be *fewer*.

2. (E) The sentence is correct as given.

3. (B) *Forcefully* repeats *cogently*.

4. (A) The sentence should read *than those in New York*.

5. (C) The antecedent of *her* is ambiguous. It could be either *the Virgin* or *an earthly lady*.

6. (D) *Effect* should be *affect*.

7. (E) There is no error in this sentence.

8. (A) Since the musicians are human, the pronoun should be *who*.

9. (A) The sentence should read *no interest in becoming*.

10. (C) The *not* and *but* are both negatives. Eliminate *not*.

EXERCISE 10: PUNCTUATION

1. (D) The phrase *it seems* is parenthetical and should be set off by two commas.

2. (B) The sentence is a question.

3. (B) A series.

4. (C) The dashes set off an interrupting phrase. One could use commas instead of the dashes, but not one comma and one dash as in choice (B). No commas are needed after *least* and *those*.

5. (A) The semicolon here divides the parts of a series.

6. (C) The parenthetical *so to speak* should be set off by commas. The series requires semicolons after *trunk, biodegradable,* and *container* because it contains commas within elements of the series.

7. (A) The dashes set off the interruption. Choice (C) omits the apostrophe in *here's*. The series has been written using semicolons, so the commas are inconsistent in choices (C) and (D).

8. (A) The phrases *of course* and *not too surprisingly* are parenthetical and each requires two commas.

9. (C) The word *suburbanites* should be in quotation marks (quoting the pro-plastic folks) and set off from the subject of the clause by a comma.

REVIEW EXERCISE: SECTIONS 1–10

1. dangling participle.

2. either agreement (the subject will be plural) or parallelism with *both . . . and.*

3. parallelism.

4. either agreement (the verb will agree with the word nearer the verb) or parallelism with *either . . . or.*

5. double negative or parallelism with *not . . . but.*

6. confusion of *like* and *as* or parallelism with the prepositional phrase.

7. agreement—*a number* is singular.

8. agreement—*Everbody* is singular.

9. case of *who/whom*—confusion of *who/that/which.*

10. adverb for adjective—*look* is a linking verb.

11. agreement—*One* is singular—or change of person, the incorrect use of *your* later in the sentence.

12. agreement—*None* is singular.

13. dangling elliptical phrase.

14. agreement—*criteria* is plural.

15. placement of related words.

16. double negative.

17. parallelism—be sure like elements are compared—or omission of necessary words such as *other.*

18. *lie* versus *lay.*

19. tense of subjunctive verbs.

20. agreement—*as well as* is parenthetical and will not make a singular subject plural.